£27-99

Garden History

Garden History

Philosophy and Design
2000 BC–2000 AD

Tom Turner

Spon Press
Taylor & Francis Group

LONDON AND NEW YORK

First published 2005
by Spon Press
2 Park Square, Milton Park, Abingdon, Oxon OX14 4RN

Simultaneously published in the USA and Canada
by Spon Press
270 Madison Ave, New York, NY 10016

Spon Press is an imprint of the Taylor & Francis Group

© 2005 Tom Turner

Typeset in Univers by Florence Production Ltd, Stoodleigh, Devon
Printed and bound in the Great Britain by Butler and Tanner, Frome, Somerset

British Library Cataloguing in Publication Data
A catalogue record for this book is available from the British Library

Library of Congress Cataloging in Publication Data
Turner, Tom.
    Garden History: philosophy and design 2000 BC–2000AD/
    Tom Turner. – 1st ed.
        p. cm.
        Includes bibliographical references and index.
    1. Gardens–History.   2. Gardens–Philosophy–History.
    3. Gardens–Design–History.   I. Title.
    SB451.T87 2004
    712'.09–dc22   2004000896

ISBN 0-415-31748-7 HB
ISBN 0-415-31749-5 PB

Contents

Madrasah–ye Chahar Bagh, Isfahan

Preface

My interest in garden history began with the lectures Frank Clark gave to his last student group at Edinburgh University in 1969.[1] It continued to grow after I moved to Birmingham in 1971. Since I disliked my lodgings, my car – a VW beetle stocked with camping equipment – became a mobile home for weekend trips, which often included visits to gardens.

In 1974 Hal Moggridge asked me to prepare a guidebook for international visitors to Britain, and I drew six garden style diagrams as part of a historical introduction. It is possible that I had seen John Claudius Loudon's diagrams (Figure 8.19) but I do not think so. I was then working in Sylvia Crowe's London office, for Bill Gillespie, and Susan Jellicoe often came for coffee. I asked if she thought my diagrams would be a useful component of the visitors' guide. She looked for a while and said, 'Tom, they're marvellous.' Without this encouragement, the diagrams would surely have been forgotten when the prospective publisher of the guidebook withdrew.

They were resurrected when my wife kindly drew a set of 12 style diagrams for my book, *English Garden Design: History and Styles Since 1650*, which was published in 1986. They were then revised (usually for a lecture to Ted Fawcett's students at the Architectural Association) approximately once every five years. Like the cambium in a tree, the diagrams laid down woody tissue (text) inside and bark (examples) outside. The lecture expanded in a similar fashion: it was supposed to be on Loudon but I soon found it necessary to describe the origins of gardening in Ancient Egypt – 'to set Loudon's views in context'.

Researching the text in libraries was a joy, but not a substitute for following the example – and the itineraries – set by Loudon and later garden history tourists. Robert Holden always said I should travel more, and he was right. The garden visits became a logistical challenge and an adventure. Relating my visits to Susan Jellicoe's photographs, Geoffrey Jellicoe's acute observations and Marie-Luise Gothein's narrative became an absorbing occupation, with Loudon often in my thoughts. His sparkling prose and utter freedom from prejudice were examples I should like to have followed.

In thanking the four for their company, I am aware of how much easier my journeys have been. Loudon's wife relates that:

> He proceeded by Grodno to Wilna, through a country covered with the remains of the French army, horses and men lying dead by the roadside, and bands of wild-looking Cossacks scouring the country. On entering Kosnow three Cossacks attacked his carriage, and endeavoured to carry off the horses, but they were beaten back by the whips of the driver and servants . . . He proceeded to Moscow, where he arrived on the 4th of March, 1814, after having encountered various difficulties on the road. Once, in particular, the horses in his carriage being unable to drag it through a snow-drift, the postilions very coolly un-harnessed them and trotted off, telling him that they would bring fresh horses in the morning, and that he would be in no danger from the wolves, if he would keep the windows of his carriage close, and the leather curtains down.[2]

I have not found records of how Gothein travelled between 1900 and 1914 but she must have used steamers, trains, trams and cabs. Jellicoe used trains and ships before the Second World War and added planes and cars afterwards. Having slept through a rail journey he made, some 70 years later, I laughed to read his advice that 'if taking the early train from Innsbruck to Salzburg one should stay awake to see the wonderful view of Melk'.[3] I used modes of transport similar to the Jellicoes', with the addition of a folding bicycle. Except for the occasional mechanical problem it was, for example, great fun to cycle from my home to a London station and then, four hours later, to bump along the Via Appia Antica from Ciampino Airport into Rome. For a cyclist, the best European capitals are Amsterdam and Copenhagen. The worst is Athens. It has smoother roads than Lisbon and Prague (its nearest rivals for the lowest place in my personal list of European capitals ranked for their friendliness to cyclists) but suffers from greater heat, choking fumes, aggressively undisciplined motorists and dogs which rush you with the apparent hope of transmitting rabies.

The other group of people I wish to thank are the students who have studied the subject with me since 1995 and their programme leader, Kemal Mehdi, who bribed my wife with hellebore splits to persuade her to persuade me to teach the course in garden history (which I had, admittedly, planned). I have leaned a great deal from the students, while always enjoying the classes. I also thank Caroline Mallinder for encouraging the project at the time of its late-mid-life crisis, in 1996, and for bringing it to press in 2004. It has taken 30 years, though the work has often headed in different directions or been laid aside. A further delay resulted from the compilation of a *Garden History Reference Encyclopedia CD* (published by Gardenvisit.com in 2002), which contains the text of Marie-Luise Gothein's *History of Garden Art* (1928 edn), my 1986 book, *English Garden Design*, some 100 other e-Texts and additional examples linked to the diagrams. Readers of this book can use the CD, from which it derives, to follow up points and find additional examples.

I also thank my colleagues Professor Mehrdad Shokoohy, for advice on Chapter 4, and Michael Lancaster for help over many years and his advice on the drawings and jacket design in the weeks before he died.

Readers of this book can use the website (www.gardenvisit.com) and the CD to discover more about the history of garden design and landscape architecture.

Notes

1   Clark, H. F., *The English Landscape Garden*, London: Pleiades Books, 1948. I think Clark hoped to revise this book in the light of Lovejoy, A. O., *The Great Chain of Being: A study of the history of an idea*, Cambridge, Mass: Harvard University Press, 1936, which he kindly lent me.

2   Loudon J. C., *Self Instruction for Young Gardeners*, London: Longman, 1845, p. 23.

3   Jellicoe, G. A., *Gardens of Europe,* London: Blackie & Son, 1937, p. 83.

A garden historian's travelling kit at Mycenae, with the probable site of Homeric gardens in the valley below

Chapter 1

Design philosophy
2000 BC–2000 AD

A garden is 'a piece of ground fenced off from cattle, and appropriated to the use and pleasure of man: it is, or ought to be, cultivated'.[1] Repton's definition has good etymological support: the words garden, yard, *garten, jardin, giardino, hortus*, paradise, *paradiso*, park, *parc, parquet*, court, *hof, kurta*, town, *tun*, and *tuin* all derive from the act of enclosing outdoor space. Thus the Old English word *geard*, meaning 'fence', produced our words 'garden' and 'yard'. In American English an outdoor space attached to a house is known as a yard, if appropriated to use, and as a garden if appropriated to pleasure. Repton's afterthought, that a garden 'is, or ought to be, cultivated' makes one smile at how little changes in the long history of gardens and gardening.

The enclosure of outdoor space began *c*. 10,000 BC. Though it can never be known when or where the first garden was made, one can imagine that it was formed by one of our ancestors who, living in a cave, had put up a barrier to protect the family from marauding beasts and brutes. In time, such barriers would have pushed outwards. Branches could then have been laid from rock to ground and branch to branch, creating fenced enclosures to protect domestic animals, to grow food and to enable the family to relax in the glorious sunshine of a neolithic evening. The first pleasure gardens, surely, were made by women.

Agriculture, settlement and garden-making began in West Asia. This is where the first cities developed. Civilisation then spread eastward, which is beyond the scope of this book, and westward. In the region named 'Europa' by the Greeks, wandering tribes lived in dark forests, cooked in crude pots and made flint tools. Knowledge of architecture and gardens reached Minoan Crete and mainland Greece, whence it spread to Italy, Spain, France, Germany, Holland, Scandinavia, Britain and the Americas. For 4,000 years this path of garden evolution travelled northward and westward, until the shores of California were reached. The eastern and western traditions then began to merge, as did the social, artistic and philosophical structures which govern the development of gardens.

1.1 Garden walls give protection from animals and thus facilitate the growth of plants

1.2 Repton loved to see cattle 'animating' a park (Sheringham Park)

1.3 Fruit and vegetables flourish in a walled garden (Chateau Montriou)

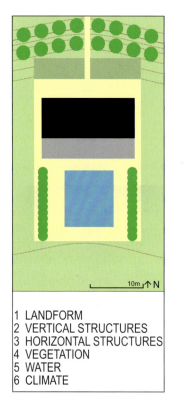

1 LANDFORM
2 VERTICAL STRUCTURES
3 HORIZONTAL STRUCTURES
4 VEGETATION
5 WATER
6 CLIMATE

1.4 Six compositional elements for outdoor design

Garden theory

A theory is 'a system of ideas explaining something', especially one based on general principles. Garden design theory should therefore explain the 'What, Where, Why and How' of making gardens. Questions about 'When and Who'[2] are the subject of subsequent chapters. This chapter reviews:

- Garden objectives (*Why* gardens are made)
- Locations (*Where* to make gardens)
- Garden types (*What* kinds of garden to make)
- Aesthetics (*How* to shape gardens).

Responses to these questions guide composition of the six elements used in making gardens and landscapes, listed below and represented on the plans and diagrams in this book by the colours and symbols shown in brackets:

1 Landform (contours)
2 Water (blue)
3 Vertical structures, e.g. buildings (black)
4 Horizontal structures, e.g. paving (yellow for pedestrians, grey for vehicles)
5 Vegetation (pale green for grass, bright green for ornamental shrubs, dark green for trees, blue green for non-garden vegetation)
6 Climate (indicated by a north point).

Many historic garden designs were inscribed directly onto the ground. Today it is more common to draw on a sheet of paper or a computer screen before using a tape and level to set out the plan on the ground. While architectural styles are best shown in elevation, garden styles are best represented by plans, diagrams and models. To highlight the differences between garden styles, diagrams are best.

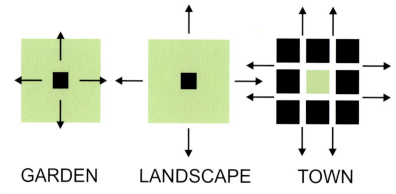

GARDEN   LANDSCAPE   TOWN

1.5 The relationship between garden design, landscape design and urban design

Skill with the six compositional elements is also necessary for the design of towns, making gardens crucibles for town design. Many of the world's best-designed cities have been inspired by garden concepts. The word 'tun', from which 'town' derives, means 'fence' in Old High German. In Old English 'tun' came to be applied to a cluster of buildings in an enclosure. Designing towns and gardens involves the lay-out of enclosed outdoor space. Sixteenth-century Isfahan, seventeenth-century Paris, eighteenth-century London, nineteenth-century Washington, DC and the Garden Cities of the twentieth century were composed like gardens, to their immense benefit. Garden design (Figure 1.5) deals with the internal layout of enclosed space; landscape design concerns relationships between enclosures and their surroundings; urban design considers relationships between the elements that comprise cities. The arts are separate but interrelated.

Design objectives

'Why?' is the first question for design theory. Vitruvius has a pre-eminent position in this discussion because his writings, *c.* 27 BC, constitute the oldest design manual to have survived. He was a Roman and had spent most of his working life in Julius Caesar's army. The full title of his work was *De architecture libri decem* (*The Ten Books on Architecture*). It deals with design objectives, art and technology. The only building Vitruvius mentions having designed himself is a pagan basilica. Most of his experience was in matters far beyond the scope of what we call 'architecture': military structures, defensive plans, harbours, clocks, aqueducts, pumps, siege engines and harbours. He makes few remarks on the design of outdoor space. After using the preface as an opportunity to fawn on his emperor, Vitruvius divides the subject into ten parts. He does not give them names but we may do so:

1 Design theory and landscape architecture
2 Materials
3 Temples (Part 1)
4 Temples (Part 2)
5 Public projects: squares, meeting halls, theatres, parks, gymnasiums, harbours
6 Private houses
7 Finishes and colours
8 Water supply
9 Sundials and clocks
10 Engineering.

1.6 Towns, like gardens, should be a composition of landform, vertical structures, horizontal structures, vegetation, water and climate (Aranjuez, in Spain)

1.7 Isfahan was planned like a garden with the pavilion on Khaju Bridge giving a view and catching the breezes

1.8 The grand axis of Paris was formed by extending Le Nôtre's axis from the Tuileries to la Défense. The foreground planting is by Dan Kiley

The best-known passage, from Vitruvius' Book 1, deals with design objectives. It is quoted below with the three key terms in latin and alternative English translations in square brackets:

> All must be built with due reference to *firmitas* [firmness, durability, strength], *utilitas* [commodity, utility, convenience], and *venustas* [delight, loveliness, beauty]. *Firmitas* will be assured when foundations are carried down to the solid ground and materials wisely and liberally selected; *utilitas*, when the arrangement of the apartments is faultless and presents no hindrance to use, and when each class of building is assigned to its suitable and appropriate exposure; and *venustas*, when the appearance of the work is pleasing and in good taste, and when its members are in due proportion according to correct principles of symmetry.[3]

Translation of the design objectives as 'Firmness, Commodity, and Delight', comes Henry Wotton's *Elements of Architecture*.[4] They are of central importance to the art of garden design. For landscape architecture, Ian Thompson has suggested 'ecology' and 'community' as alternatives for *firmitas* and *utilitas*.[5] Thompson also suggests the terms mono-valent, bi-valent and tri-valent for three categories of project. As examples of mono-valent garden projects, a Temple Garden would focus on *venustas*, a Domestic Garden on *utilitas* and a Plant Garden on *firmitas*. Estate gardens, as described below (p. 13), tend to be tri-valent.

Firmitas is necessary to all design and construction. *Utilitas*, the rationale for undertaking a design, has primacy in gardens which provide for bodily comfort and mental satisfaction. *Venustas*, deriving from Venus, the goddess of love, was used to describe objects and places which shared her characteristics: grace, charm, beauty and loveliness. 'Utilitarian' gardens may lack these characteristics. Venus and Diana remain the most commonly represented deities in traditional gardens, symbolising beauty and action respectively. Apollo, symbolising the sun, and therefore divine distance, is associated with spirituality. He still appears in collections of cast statuary offered for sale, but less frequently than Aphrodite (Venus).

Vitruvius has disappointingly little to say about enclosed outdoor space. In the case of temple enclosures, this may result from the fact that Roman temples, unlike their Greek predecessors, were more often in towns than in sacred groves. In the case of dwellings, it may be because Vitruvius' life had been spent on campaign, giving him little experience of domesticity. Book 5, on public projects, has most comment on outdoor space. The following recommendation is for athletics enclosures:

> This kind of colonnade is called among the Greeks *xystus* because athletes during the winter season exercise in covered running tracks. Next to this *xystus* and to the double colonnade should be laid out the uncovered walks into which, in fair weather during the winter, the athletes come out from the *xystus* for exercise. The *xysta* ought to be so constructed that there may be plantations between the two colonnades, or groves of plane trees, with walks

1.9 Venus lives still, in gardens: the Veiled Lady at Borde Hill, Sussex

laid out in them among the trees and resting places there, made of *opus signinum* [i.e. paved]. Behind the *xystus* a stadium, so designed that great numbers of people may have plenty of room to look on at the contests between the athletes.[6]

The Romans used the word *xystus* to mean a garden court but noblemen, like Pliny, would also have exercise grounds on their private estates. Roofed colonnades (peristyles) had many purposes in the Graeco-Roman world. They were used, like trees, to create shelter and shade. Cloister gardens in European monasteries and the forecourts of West Asian mosques and madrasahs are examples of their use to make spiritual space. It is surprising that their popularity has declined, since roofed outdoor space has both utility and beauty.

Location

Where to make gardens is a central issue, following the consideration of objectives and preceding a design. Since few owners have left records of how their decisions were made, the analysis of garden location is closer to archaeology than history. It is at once apparent that great gardens have significant locations, often including:

- A significant topographical location
- A favourable microclimate
- A planned relationship to water
- Rich soil.

In the modern world, the planning of gardens in relation to sites is woefully neglected. Officials and developers seem to care only about the relationship of buildings to flows of vehicles and money. Historically, however, the relationship between gardens and landscapes was fundamental. Queen Hatshepsut's Temple on the edge of the Nile Valley (p. 39) can be described as the first great example of landscape architecture. The sanctuary at Delphi (p. 72) stands between the Gulf of Corinth and the woods of Mount Parnassus, providing a sense of mystery as well as fresh air and wonderful views. The Alhambra (p. 92) sits on a low hill overlooking a river valley surrounded by the Sierra Nevada. The Medici chose sites on the hills round Florence for their houses and gardens. Blenheim (p. 204), like all Lancelot 'Capability' Brown's designs, uses the site as the chief feature of the layout.

Vitruvius explains the classical approach to site planning, in Book 1, Chapter 4:

First comes the choice of a very healthy site. Such a site will be high, neither misty nor frosty, and in a climate neither hot nor cold, but temperate, without marshes in the neighbourhood. For when the morning breezes blow toward the town at sunrise, if they bring with them mists from marshes and, mingled with the mist, the poisonous breath of the creatures of the marshes to be wafted into the bodies of the inhabitants, they will make the site unhealthy. Again, if the town is on the coast with a southern or western exposure, it will not be healthy, because in summer the southern sky grows hot at sunrise and is fiery at noon, while a western exposure grows warm after sunrise, is hot at noon, and at evening all aglow.[7]

1.11 A good location – the south–easterly aspect favoured by Repton, together with elevation, shelter and water: Caerhays, Cornwall

Landscape architects continue to argue that garden and open space design should receive priority in housing layout and that the character and qualities of the existing site, the Genius of the Place (see p. 63 and p. 195), should be respectfully consulted on all occasions. Chip Sullivan reviews the influence of climatic design on Italian gardens in his book, *Garden and Climate*.[8]

Garden types

What type of garden to make rests on decisions about objectives, with owners and designers often looking to pre-existing types. Table 1 relates garden types to more familiar categories used for music and architecture.

Table 1 Comparisons can be made between categories of music, architecture and outdoor space

Music	Architecture	Gardens and parks
Romantic	Domestic	Domestic gardens serve family needs. This use has not changed.
Religious	Religious	Aesthetic gardens, like other works of art, provide intellectual and spiritual rewards. These aims generated the temple gardens of the ancient world, the palace gardens of the Renaissance and some of the competition-winning designs of the modern era.
Martial	Defensive	Parks can be places to take exercise and interact with the environment. In the ancient world this inspiration led to walled enclosures for exotic animals and plants, including paradise gardens and hunting parks. In the modern world it led to the making of sports parks, zoos and botanical gardens.

Philosophers continue to discuss whether mind, body and spirit are one thing (monism), two things (dualism) or three things (a trinity). Table 2 suggests a threefold classification of garden types.

Gardens can have one or more categories of objective. Temple gardens and beer gardens tend to be single-purpose. Versailles was both a work of art and a meeting-place for high society. The Villa Lante, described by Georgina Masson as 'one of the most beautiful in existence',[9] served each of the three main objectives of garden design: it was a work of art, a hunting park and a place for outdoor parties; Sissing-hurst, perhaps the best-loved garden of the twentieth century, served the three objectives in a different manner: it was a work of art, it accommodated family needs and it was a place for the owners to exercise their minds and bodies.

Table 2 Three classes of motivation have led to the evolution of primary garden types

For the body	For activity	For the spirit
	Primeval enclosure	
Palace Garden	Paradise	Sacred Grove
Domestic Garden	Hunting Park	Temple Garden
Vegetable Garden	Animal Garden	Academy Garden
Hofgarten	Botanical garden	Ceremonial Avenue
Medicinal Garden	Zoological Garden	Cloister Garth
Public Garden	Sports Park	Sculpture Court
Beer Garden	Arboretum	Grotto
Café Garden	Alpine Garden	City Park
City Garden	Flower Garden	National Park

Table 3 Analysis of types applied to parks and extended from open space types to open space characteristics (from T. Turner, *Landscape Planning and EID*)

OPEN SPACE PLANNING CHART

Ownership	Central government	Local government	Trust	Company	Utility	Local people
Colour theme	Red	Yellow	Blue	Green	Brown	White
Mood	Calm	Exciting	Solemn	Sensuous	Sensual	Gloomy
Age group	0–10 years	10–20 years	20–30 years	30–40 years	40–60 years	60+ years
Ethnicity	Anglo-Saxon	Latin	African	Central Asian	SE Asian	East Asian
Culture	Radio 1	Radio 2	Radio 3	Radio 4	Radio 5	World service
Religion	Christian	Confucian	Jewish	Hindu	Buddhist	Islamic
Landform	Hill	Mountain	Valley	Plateau	Beach	Meadow
Habitat	Marshland	Grassland	Maquis	Forest	Lake	Ocean
Climate	Sunny	Shady	Windy	Humid	Dry	Sheltered
Special use	Fine Art	Sport	Swimming	Nature study	Food	Courting

The analysis of open space types can be extended to sub-characteristics, as in Table 3, which analyses the characteristics of urban parks. Some of the considerations are domestic, some relate to plants and animals, some concern the spirit.

Great parks and gardens combine use with beauty, pleasure with profit and work with contemplation:

Utile quimiscens, ingentia Rura,
Simplex Munditis ornat, punctum hic tulit omne.

He that the beautiful and useful blends,
Simplicity with greatness, gains all ends.[10]

Domestic gardens

Domestic gardens contribute to our wellbeing. We value places where the old can sit, the young can play and parents can rest. We relish succulent vegetables, ripe fruits and fresh herbs and scents. On hot days we seek shady places that catch the breeze. On cool days we prefer an outdoor seat with full sun and shelter from the wind. Good domestic gardens meet these design objectives in ways that have not changed during the four millennia covered by this book. The best policy is that when land for housing becomes available, gardens and parks should be planned before roads and buildings.

Palace gardens were made by kings and nobles as adjuncts to their living quarters. It was natural to gather officials and hold parades in such places, which became known as the court (or hof). The words court-yard and hof-garten are compounds

1.12 The provision of space for sitting outdoors is an ancient garden function

1.13 Dining may be the oldest domestic use of enclosed outdoor space: riverside café in Prague

1.14 The Hofgarten, Munich. T. S. Eliot captured the atmosphere of a court garden:
'Summer surprised us, coming over the Starnbergersee

With a shower of rain; we stopped in the colonnade,
And went on in sunlight, into the Hofgarten,
And drank coffee, and talked for an hour.'
('The burial of the dead',
The Waste Land, 1940)

1.15 (right) Upper courts are still used for military ceremonies: Horse Guards Parade, London

1.16 (far right) The Orto Botanico in Padua is said to be the oldest botanical garden in the world

1.17 (left) Labelled plants attract botanists: the Botanical Garden, Vienna

1.18 (centre) The Zoological Garden at Schönbrunn is said to be the oldest in the world

1.19 (right) The Temple of Hephaistos in Athens is the oldest surviving example of a temple garden in Europe

which, etymologically, mean 'enclosed-enclosure', a secular parallel to 'holy of holies'. In the baroque period court gardens were opened to the public as acts of conspicuous consumption, and became available as public open spaces. In the nineteenth century specialised city gardens, tea gardens, beer gardens, and café gardens were made to satisfy the domestic objectives of garden design.

Plant and animal gardens

People have always sought to understand the natural world and enclosures have assisted the quest by containing collections of plants and animals. The earliest spaces of this type were known as *pairidaeza* (literally 'around-wall'). Paradise took on a religious meaning at a later date (see p. 82). Early West Asian kings used their *pairidaeza* for exotic species brought back from military campaigns. Animals could be hunted and guests served with their meat, or vice versa.[11] Rare plants were used in cooking and medicine. Roman emperors kept animals to entertain crowds by fighting, a tradition which lives on in the public bull-fighting arenas of Spain. Monasteries and then universities made infirmary gardens, herb gardens and botanical gardens. With the rise of post-Renaissance science, zoological gardens became fixtures on royal estates, as did aviaries. The blue peacock, from India, became a popular adornment in western gardens. New types of plant garden were made in the nineteenth century, including American gardens, Japanese gardens, alpine gardens, arboretums and pinetums. Animals recovered something of their place in garden design with the reintroduction of aviaries in the nineteenth century and the creation of wildlife gardens in the twentieth century.

1.20 Berlin's Tiergarten ('Animal Garden') retains more of the character of a wild place than most parks in other capital cities in Europe

1.21 A superbly-named botanical garden: the Eden Project, Cornwall

Spiritual gardens

The Bible explains the Creation as God breathing life into dust and making a garden:

> And the Lord God formed man of the dust of the ground, and breathed into his nostrils the breath of life; and man became a living soul.
>
> And the Lord God planted a garden eastward in Eden; and there he put the man whom he had formed.
>
> And out of the ground made the Lord God to grow every tree that is pleasant to the sight, and good for food; the tree of life also in the midst of the garden, and the tree of knowledge of good and evil.
>
> And a river went out of Eden to water the garden; and from thence it was parted, and became into four heads.[12]

The Koran records that Allah 'seated Himself upon his throne, and imposed laws on the sun and moon'.[13] Scientists explain the creation more prosaically: life on earth began 4 billion years ago and human life began 4 million years ago. The word 'spirit', from the Latin *spiritus* meaning 'breath', is still used to describe the life-force which drives humans and animals. In a religious context, the spirit is associated with the soul. It is that aspect of humans which, because it is immaterial, can survive bodily death. Religions have used gardens as symbols of paradise and, seeking immortality, men have often sought to create things which will survive them: reputations, families, empires, buildings, inventions, works of art – and great gardens.

Ninian Smart identified six dimensions of religious belief:[14]

1.22 Exotic animals have long had a place in gardens: peacocks on Isola Bella

1.23 Gardens can be places in which to contemplate nature (Nymphenburg)

- a ritual dimension
- a mythological dimension
- a doctrinal dimension

- an ethical dimension
- a social dimension
- an experiential dimension.

In ancient times the ritual, mythological and doctrinal aspects of spiritual space were prominent. In the design of Christian and Islamic enclosed outdoor space, the ethical, social and experiential dimensions of spirituality became more significant. Religious objectives lie behind the oldest surviving garden types, which can be described as sacred landscapes. In current usage, 'sacred' means 'made holy by religious association, hallowed'.

In Egypt, a temple compound with a sacred lake and a sacred grove was conceived as a home for a god-king (pharaoh) to use after his bodily life (Chapter 2). In Greece, a bounded sanctuary with a sacrificial altar was used for religious ceremonies (Chapter 3). In Rome, where religion centred more on the home, altars were placed in courtyard gardens and towns. In the Islamic world, as in Ancient Egypt, the entire religious compound (mosque) was sacred to Allah (Chapter 4). In Christendom, an indoor church altar became the ceremonial focus but meditative 'cloister' gardens were made by religious communities (Chapter 5). The association of gardens with perfection is found in Judaism, Christianity and Islam.

The temple enclosures of Egypt and Mesopotamia are the oldest surviving examples of spiritual outdoor space. They were planned in relation to the path of the sun, flood plains and other significant astronomical and geographical considerations. This helped people understand the nature of the world, the social structures which maintain order, and humankind's place in the firmament. Art developed as a means of explaining truths to non-literate peoples. When art separated from religion, it retained the role of helping people comprehend the nature of the external world and of the internal world through which it is perceived. This was the 'nature' which artists learned to 'imitate', as will be discussed below ('Aesthetics', p. 14 and Chapter 3). In the modern world a spiritual dimension has become an aspect of certain gardens, rather than a specialised garden type, leading us to speak of gardens as 'works of art'. Two of the last gardens discussed in this book were made for museums, one of which is a museum of art (Gallery of Modern Art, Edinburgh and Jewish Museum, Berlin).

Estates

The rich can afford gardens-with-everything: to satisfy body, mind and spirit. This was true in ancient West Asia and also in the gardens made by Europeans who visited that region. Alexander the Great's generals formed estates in Macedonia. Roman emperors, following their example, made private villas. The word *villa* was used to describe a country dwelling together with its farm and outhouses. As *ville*, the word continues to mean 'town' in French. Luxurious villas had domestic gardens, groves of trees and hunting parks. When Roman emperors proclaimed themselves gods, the villas they commissioned had characteristics in common with religious sanctuaries.

1.24 Egyptian temples were planned in relation to the path of the sun and the course of the Nile, helping to explain the nature of the world

1.25 The Villa Lante, seen here from the town gate (left) and looking towards the town (right), is widely admired as a work of art and, like paintings from the same period, can be subjected to iconographic analysis

1.26 Medici villas on the hills round Florence

1.27 Some parks still permit horse-riding: Rotten Row in Hyde Park, London

Hadrian's villa can be understood as a representation of the world he knew. Emperors also had a fondness for grottoes (see pp. 68–9).

During the Renaissance, Roman villas were studied and excavated. This led to the making of new villas outside the walled castles and towns of medieval Europe. The Medici family were prolific builders and the hills round Florence became dotted with palatial estates. One of the most celebrated, at Pratolino, had a mannerist garden extending into a hunting park. Francis I made a comparable estate at Fontainebleau, outside Paris; Henry VIII followed his example at Hampton Court, outside London. George Washington was a superb horseman and made a hunting park at Mount Vernon, outside the capital city that bears his name. These are the ancestors of the suburban villas which ring modern cities, often aspiring to characteristics shared with the three classical garden types. The word 'estate' (from the Latin *status*) refers to the categories of a man's property which define his status.

Aesthetics

After decisions about design objectives and types of space, the next set of design issues involves the branch of philosophy known as aesthetics.[15] How a garden is formed clearly relates to ideas and beliefs, which brings us to an apparent paradox: gardens made by man using natural materials to represent ideas about nature, are as much influenced by the actions of man as by the forces of nature. The paradox arises from the many meanings encompassed by the word 'nature'. Different design approaches result from conceiving nature as:

- The forms which shape the real world (Ancient Greece)
- A Great Chain of Being, extending from God on high to the humblest organism (medieval Christianity)

- Human nature (the Enlightenment)
- Everything which is not man (Romanticism).

These views are associated with schools of philosophy and attitudes to aesthetics. Bertrand Russell began his *History of Western Philosophy* with the statement that 'Philosophy, as I shall understand the word, is something intermediate between theology and science'. As a mode of thought, he believed philosophy to have begun in Greece during the sixth century BC.[16] The first philosopher to be treated in a separate chapter is Pythagoras, 'intellectually one of the most important men that ever lived'.

The Pythagorean School originated the belief that 'all things are number' and that mathematics should be 'the fundamental study in physics *as in aesthetics*' (my italics).[17] Pythagoras' discovery of harmonic proportion, in music, was an example of mathematics being used to explain an aspect of nature with aesthetic consequences. Russell wrote that 'those who have experienced the intoxicating delight of sudden understanding that mathematics gives' will understand 'that the pure mathematician, like the musician, is a free creator of his world of ordered beauty'.[18] Designers creating worlds of 'ordered beauty' have similar experiences.

Plato, doubtless enjoying the same 'intoxicating delight of sudden understanding' as Russell, came to believe in the existence of a perfect world, accessible only to those who reason about nature. This became known as the Theory of Forms and is explained by Russell as follows:

1.28 Plato believed that universal forms (the 'ideal' cat) must exist before particular individuals can exist

This theory is partly logical, partly metaphysical. The logical part has to do with the meaning of general words. There are many individual animals of whom we can truly say 'this is a cat'. What do we mean by the word 'cat'? Obviously something different from each particular cat. An animal is a cat, it would seem, because it participates in a general nature common to all cats. Language cannot get on without general words such as 'cat', and such words are evidently not meaningless. But if the word 'cat' means anything, it means something which is not this or that cat, but some kind of universal cattiness. This is not born when a particular cat is born, and does not die when it dies. In fact, it has no position in space or time; it is 'eternal'. This is the logical part of the doctrine. The arguments in its favour, whether ultimately valid or not, are strong, and quite independent of the metaphysical part of the doctrine. According to the metaphysical part of the doctrine, the word 'cat' means a certain ideal cat, 'the cat', created by God, and unique. Particular cats partake of the nature of the cat, but more or less imperfectly; it is only owing to this imperfection that there can be many of them. The cat is real; particular cats are only apparent. In the last book of the Republic, as a preliminary to a condemnation of painters, there is a very clear exposition of the doctrine of ideas or forms.[19]

1.29 Plato's cave analogy suggests we live as prisoners, able to see nothing but shadows on the walls of caves

1.30 The central portal of the west façade of Nôtre Dame, Paris, was arranged in a platonic hierarchy to explain the nature of the world

Plato used an analogy between the human condition and life in a cave to explain his theory. Our knowledge of nature is comparable to that of troglodytes, able to look only at shadows cast on a cave wall, never at the forms which cast the shadows. Since artists paint these 'shadows', their work is at a third remove from reality. This led Plato to a low opinion of art, and Iris Murdoch to write a book on *Why Plato banished the artists*.[20] Plato believed there is something deceptive about art: 'A painter . . . may deceive children or simple persons, when he shows them his picture of a carpenter from a distance, and they will fancy that they are looking at a real carpenter.'[21] One doubts if he knew many children who had been deceived but his theory of art was, to say the least, influential.

Plotinus and St Augustine developed a philosophical theory, described as Neo-platonic, from Plato's Theory of Forms. It resolved Plato's objection to painting and had a deep influence on European art (see Chapter 5). The idea was that artists should view many particulars in order to gain the clearest possible impression of the eternal Forms. This became known as the Ideal Theory of Art. The Elder Pliny, writing before Plotinus' time, related that when Zeuxis was commissioned to paint Helen of Troy he organised a parade of naked girls, chose the most beautiful and reproduced the best parts of each in his painting.[22]

Encapsulated in the axiom that 'Art should imitate nature', the Theory of Forms came to have a pervasive influence on western culture. By 'nature' the Neoplatonists meant the world of the Forms, not the everyday visible world. During its long history the consequences of this axiom have varied according to different interpretations of the words 'art', 'imitation' and 'nature'. Developments in religion and science caused an endless succession of changes. Before discussing the influence of the axiom on garden design it is worth pausing to look at some of its consequences for architecture.

Erwin Panofsky explains that 'the High Gothic cathedral sought to embody the whole of Christian knowledge, theological, moral, natural, and historical, with every-thing in its place' and arranged to manifest the 'uniform division and subdivision of the whole structure', and the separate identity of each part.[23] 'Nature' was understood as a Christian version of the hierarchy of Forms, 'the whole of Christian knowledge . . . with everything in its place'. 'Imitation' was interpreted as the process of manifesting this body of knowledge in the fabric and ornamentation of the cathedral. Thus the central portal of the west façade of Nôtre Dame in Paris was arranged, visually and structurally, to show the hierarchical relationship between the Damned, the Resur-rected, the Apostles, the Virtues, the Saints and the Wise and Foolish Virgins.

Plato's works were studied afresh during the Renaissance by scholars concerned with the roots of Greek philosophy. In 1439 Lorenzo de Medici founded a Platonic Academy in his garden at Carregi, outside Florence. It was an event with important consequences for garden design. After the meeting, Plato's influence shifted from the background to the foreground of western art. Humanists concluded that Greek and Roman architecture must have been based on mathematical proportions. The relationship between the width of a column and its height, for example, was taken to be based on the mathematics of harmonic proportion. Architecture was made to imitate the Platonic Forms.

Wittkower has shown how the interests of the mathematician, the artist and the designer were linked in the work of Alberti, and has explained the degree to which Palladio was influenced by Plotinus and Neoplatonism.[24] Palladio's architecture was based upon the circle, the square and harmonic proportion because they represent the Forms of Goodness, Justice and Harmony. The imitation of these essential Forms was a way of producing buildings which partook of the essence of the universe: they imitated the nature of the world. A. N. Whitehead characterised western philosophy as 'a series of footnotes to Plato',[25] thus reducing the history of aesthetically-designed gardens to the status of a footnote to a footnote to a footnote.

Neoplatonic ideas lie behind the Islamic and Christian square designs of the Middle Ages and the mathematically calculated 'Cartesian' gardens of the Renaissance. Descartes did not write either on aesthetics or gardening but his use of the 'geometrical method' (i.e. deduction) in reasoning led philosophers and artists to seek self-evident axioms on which to base design. The axiom that art should imitate nature fitted perfectly with a Cartesian approach. 'Nature' was understood, once again, as the essential and universal forms which shape the visible world. We can find the 'geometrical method' in Poussin's use of grids, in Racine's plays, in Le Nôtre's garden designs, and in the formulas which Jacques Boyceau (1560–1633), gardener to Louis XIII, gave for calculating the correct relationship between the length, height and width of an avenue. The latter correspond to the formulas used by Palladio to work out the mathematical relationship between pavements and arcades.

Neoplatonic ideas were current in seventeenth- and eighteenth-century England. They permeate the writings of Dryden, Shaftesbury, Pope, Johnson and Reynolds. These authors tell us that art should imitate nature (see pp. 189–190). Pope expressed the belief as follows in his *Essay on Criticism*:

> First follow Nature, and your judgement frame
> By her just standard, which is still the same:
> Unerring NATURE, still divinely bright,
> One clear, unchang'd, and universal light,
>
> . . .
>
> Those Rules of old discover'd, not devis'd,
> Are Nature still, but Nature Methodiz'd;
> Nature, like Liberty, is but restrain'd
> By the same Laws which first herself ordain'd.[26]

In these verses Pope uses 'Nature' to mean the universal forms and rules of proportion which, in Neoplatonic and neoclassical theory, it is the artist's task to

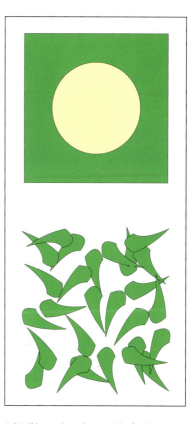

1.31 'Nature' as the world of universals (above) and as the world of particulars (below)

17

1.32 The geological specimens in Pope's grotto at Twickenham, west of London, are a survival of Nature, at once 'unadorned' and 'Methodiz'd'

imitate. But Pope also wrote of 'the amiable Simplicity of unadorned Nature, that spreads over the Mind a more noble sort of Tranquillity, and a loftier Sensation of Pleasure, than can be raised from the nicer Scenes of Art'.[27] Here, he uses 'Nature' in a sense close to 'wild nature'. Inserting 'unadorned Nature' into the Neoplatonic axiom revolutionised the art of garden design during the eighteenth century.

The use of 'nature' to mean empirical reality was not an eighteenth-century innovation. J. D. Hunt explains that Cicero thought of the wild landscape as a First Nature and the agricultural landscape as a Second Nature so that, in sixteenth-century Italy, gardens could be seen as a Third Nature.[28] In eighteenth-century England, study of the First Nature was given renewed significance by the philosophical school known as empiricism. There was a steady swing from Cartesian rationalism to the empiricism of Bacon, Hobbes, Locke and Hume. In the nineteenth century, this led to a botanical appreciation of plants. Gardens became an example in the discussion of man's relationship to nature. T. H. Huxley, whose advocacy of evolutionary theory earned him the sobriquet 'Darwin's Bulldog', regarded his garden as a work of art, in contrast to the state of nature which preceded its design.[29]

Summary

The kiss of the sun for pardon,
The song of the birds for mirth,
One is nearer God's Heart in a garden
Than anywhere else on earth.[30]

Her theology can be questioned but Dorothy Frances Gurney's ever-popular poem reflects a truth about gardens: their design has been influenced by views of the inter-relationships between God, man and nature. The following list gives instances of these relationships and, in brackets, examples of the resultant approach to the design of enclosed outdoor space:

- If gods control the natural world, they should be propitiated through ritual and sacrifice (religious/astronomical compounds)
- If it is natural for kings to become gods after death, they should be provided with temples and gardens for use in the afterlife (temple and pyramid compounds in the Ancient World)
- If the gods of nature intervene in our daily lives, sacrificial offerings should be made in a sacred place, such as an altar in a wood (sacred groves, classical temples, domestic garden shrines)
- If the natural forms have a godlike existence in a perfect world they should be incorporated into architectural and garden design (Graeco-Roman and Islamic sacred geometry)

- If the nature of the world is revealed to mankind through religion, then gardens, as places for contemplation, should symbolise the perfection of nature (medieval gardens)
- If the best knowledge of nature comes from the ancients, then modern gardens should be made in the style of ancient gardens (Renaissance gardens)
- If the natural order is revealed to man through reason, then gardens should be based on mathematical ideas and perspective (baroque gardens)
- If nature is best interpreted through empirical science, then gardens should exhibit a great range of phenomena: natural, artificial and emotional (Romantic gardens)
- If nature is best understood through scientific analysis, then gardens should be based on the principles of abstraction (modern/abstract gardens)
- If our understanding of nature depends on our conceptual framework, then concepts should have a central place in the design of gardens (postmodern/conceptual gardens).

Modified and combined, the above ideas have generated many of the styles of garden design which are the subject of this book. The stylistic progression is summarised by the diagrams on p. 20.

Organisation of the book

Succeeding chapters trace the development of gardens through 40 centuries. For the period from 2000 BC to 1400 AD the discussion is mainly of garden types (e.g. 'temple garden' and 'castle garden'), because there are too few records and too few examples for detailed stylistic analysis. For the period from 1400 to 1700 gardens are placed in the art-historical categories to which they belong (e.g. Renaissance and baroque). For the period from 1700 to 2000 names relating to styles of garden design are used (e.g. Picturesque and gardenesque), this being possible because of the fuller records of gardens made in modern times. Art-historical categories are used in the chapter titles to relate garden design to the other arts. It must, however, be recognised that most of the categorisations can be – and have been – deconstructed. As long ago as 1915 Wölfflin wrote that 'We denote the series of periods with the names Early Renaissance, High Renaissance, and Baroque, names which mean little and must lead to misunderstanding in their application to south and north, but are hardly to be ousted now'.[31]

The geographical coverage of the book centres on Europe but with significant excursions. We begin in the region known to Europeans as the Middle East. Dealing

Domestic
Garden

Palace
Garden

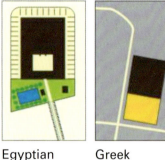

Egyptian
Sanctuary

Greek
Court

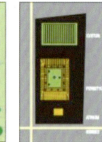

Greek
Sanctuary

Roman
Court

Roman
Villa

West Asian
Palace

Hunting
Park

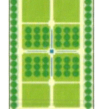

Paradise
Garden

Mosque
Court

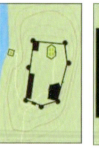

Medieval
Garden

Castle
Garden

Cloister
Garden

Early
Renaissance

High
Renaissance

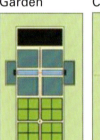

Mannerist

Early
Baroque

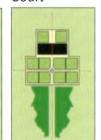

High
Baroque

Forest
Style

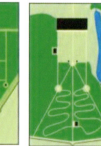

Augustan
Style

Serpentine
Style

Picturesque
Style

Landscape
Style

Mixed
Style

Arts and Crafts
Style

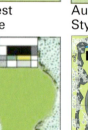

Abstract
Style

Post-abstract
Style

1.33 Garden design 2000 BC–2000 AD. The early diagrams show garden types and the later diagrams show garden styles

with Islamic gardens requires that we visit India. In looking at twentieth-century gardens, work in North and South America is included. Other periods in history and parts of the world, including China, Japan, Africa south of the Sahara, Oceania and Pre-Columbian America, are not covered because they belong to different traditions: this book is concerned with gardens made under the influence of 'Western' philosophy. Reference to national characteristics is underemphasised, partly because garden design has long been an international art and partly because nation-states are of recent origin. Empire-builders, marriage-brokers and travellers have always roamed the world and have often been able to make themselves understood in a widely-spoken tongue. At the start of the Roman era they could use Greek in Southern Europe and Celtic in Northern Europe. Persian and Arabic have been international languages in West Asia. After the fall of Rome, Latin could be used everywhere in the West for 1,000 years. Eventually, it was replaced by French, English and American.

The nine historical chapters are in two parts with subsections. The first part of each chapter outlines the ways in which social, geographical, philosophical and artistic ideas have interacted to create gardens. The second part of each chapter contains an analysis of garden plans, commencing with a style diagram and giving selected examples. The style diagrams are intended to parallel the elevational diagrams used in synoptic histories of architecture with sections and elevations to show the six compositional elements of buildings (walls, doors, windows, floors, roofs and stairs). Plans with north points show the six compositional elements of gardens (landform, water, vegetation, horizontal structures, vertical structures and climate). Garden and landscape design can be defined as the arts of composing these elements to create commodity, firmness and delight in outdoor space. Key dates are given for examples, relating to their inception, completion, high point or (in the case of Pompeii, for example) their destruction. The date ranges given in chapter titles are also regrettably arbitrary. Readers are advised to consult the *Oxford Companion to Gardens*, edited by my colleagues, for more detail.[32]

Since the book covers a wide geographical region and a long period of time, it is sure to contain errors. There is also a little guesswork. As Barry Kemp wrote of his work at El-Amarna, 'It has proved impossible to write a history of Akhenaten's reign which does not embrace an element of historical fiction'.[33] Speculations of my own, inserted into text or plan, are identified as such. Sources are given and the examples are accompanied by quotations which readers can use to find famous accounts of the gardens.

Generally, new plans and new photographs have been used instead of old plans and drawings. Contours are included where they could be obtained. I love old illustrations but they are widely reproduced elsewhere and, because they were drawn in different styles for different purposes, it is less easy to use them to conduct a narrative. The use of colour on plans makes it easier to identify the six great compositional elements of gardens and landscapes.

Notes

1   This reference, and the etymological notes which follow, are based on van Erp-Houtepen, 'The etymological origin of the garden', *Journal of Garden History*, Vol. 6, No. 3, pp. 227–31.

2   Kipling, R., *The Serving Men*: 'I keep six honest serving men/(They taught me all I know);/Their names are What and Why and When/And How and Where and Who.'

3   Vitruvius, *The Ten Books on Architecture*, Transl. Morris Hicky Morgan, 1914 and reprinted Dover Books, Inc., 1960. UK edn, Constable & Co., p.17.

4   Wotton, H., *The Elements of Architecture*, London, 1624.

5   Thompson, I., *Ecology, Community and Delight,* London: Spon, 2000.

6   Vitruvius, op. cit., pp. 161–2.

7   ——, op. cit., Chapter 4, p. 17.

8   Sullivan, C., *Garden and Climate*, London: McGraw-Hill, 2002.

9   Masson, G., *Italian Gardens*, London: Thames & Hudson, p. 168.

10 Horace, *Ars Poetica*. The quotation and its translation are from Hussey, C., *English Gardens and Landscapes 1700–1750,* London: Country Life, 1967, p. 11.

11 The practice has not entirely ceased: it was reported at the time of writing (*Sunday Times*, 27 July 2003) that Saddam Hussein's son, Uday, fed two men to lions, in Mesopotamia, because they had competed for his girlfriend's favours.

12 *Book of Genesis* Ch. 2, v. 7–10 (Authorised version).

13 The Koran, Surah XIII, 2.

14 Smart, N., *The Religious Experience of Mankind*, London: Fontana, 1971, p. 15ff.

15 The term 'aesthetics' was coined by Alexander Baumgarten, a disciple of Leibniz, in his book *Aethestica* (Pt. I 1750, Pt. II 1758).

16 Russell, B., A *History of Western Philosophy*, London: Allen & Unwin, 1946, pp. 13–14.

17 ——, op. cit., p. 54.

18 ——, op. cit., p. 53.

19 ——, op. cit., p. 136.

20 Murdoch, I., *The Fire and the Sun: Why Plato banished the artists*, Oxford: Clarendon Press, 1977.

21 Plato, *Republic,* Book X (transl. Benjamin Jowett).

22 Pliny, *Natural History* XXXV, 64.

23 Panofsky, E., *Gothic Architecture and Scholasticism*, London: Thames & Hudson, 1957, pp. 44–5.

24 Wittkower, R., *Architectural Principles in the Age of Humanism*, London: Academy Editions, 1962, pp. 22–32.

25 Lovejoy, A. O., *The Great Chain of Being*, New York: Harper, 1965, p. 24.

26 Pope, A., *Essay on Criticism*, London, 1711.

27 ——'On gardens', *The Guardian*, London, 1713.

28 Hunt J. D., *Greater Perfections. The practice of garden theory*, London: Thames & Hudson, 2000, pp. 32–75.

29 Huxley, T. H., *Evolution and Ethics and Other Essays*, London: Macmillan, 1893.

30 Gurney, D. F., *A Little Book of Quiet,* London: Country Life and George Newnes, 1915.

31 Wölfflin, H., 'Principles of art history' (1915) in D. Preziosi (ed.), *The Art of History*, Oxford: University Press, 1998, p. 115.

32 Jellicoe, G., Jellicoe, S., Goode, P. and Lancaster, M., *The Oxford Companion to Gardens*, London: OUP, 1986.

33 Kemp, B. J., *Ancient Egypt: Anatomy of a Civilization*, London: Routledge, 1991.

Chapter 2

Ancient gardens
2000 BC–1000 BC

History and philosophy

The first nomads to reach the Lower Nile found an extraordinary paradise: a green-blue ribbon running in a deep valley through a yellow-brown desert. The valley was lush and sheltered. Even the desert was a source of good things: safety, precious stones and wild animals. A great river came from the heart of Africa. Once a year, from July to September, the Nile flooded and fertilised the valley. As the waters rose, Egyptians withdrew to higher land. At the valley edge, they found cliffs which could be quarried to make stone buildings. There was every reason to settle in this place, and every opportunity to found a great civilisation, which they did.

Egypt had a vital strategic position as a conduit between the prehistoric world of Africa, where man evolved, and the colonisation zones of Asia, Europe and beyond. The Nile facilitated transport. Boats could drift downstream with the current and sail upstream with the prevailing wind. Annual floods created a summer season when hands and minds could turn to other things besides subsistence agriculture. Since the surrounding desert was hostile to invaders, the valley was comparatively easy to defend. It thus became home to a stable society: Egyptian law and religion endured longer than those of any other civilisation. They were maintained by pharaohs who were both gods and kings. The dynastic history of Egypt is divided into nine periods:

- Early Dynastic Period   2920–2575 BC
- Old Kingdom   2575–2040 BC
- First Intermediate Period   2134–2040 BC
- Middle Kingdom   2040–1567 BC
- Second Intermediate Period   1567–1550 BC
- New Kingdom   1550–1070 BC

2.1 The valley of the Nile was a blue-green conduit through a red-yellow desert

2.2 A waterside quarry on the Upper Nile

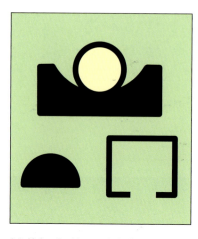

2.3 Heiroglyphic symbols for the setting sun, bread and a tomb

- Third Intermediate Period   1070–712 BC
- Late Period   712–332 BC
- Graeco-Roman Period   332 BC–395 AD.

Egyptians interpreted the world through religion, making little distinction between the divine and everyday spheres. Some gods represented abstract ideas, some were natural features, and some were powers of nature. Most could partake of each other's capabilities and characteristics.

The pharaoh's task was to uphold *Ma'at*, which is translated as order, truth and justice. His responsibilities therefore extended across what we distinguish as society, nature and religion. He had, for example, to ensure a regular annual flood ('annual' was easy; 'regular' was difficult). Laws and rituals assisted pharaohs in their task of protecting Egypt from danger. Since the duties did not end with his human life, the pharaoh required a mortuary temple with priests, worldly goods and gardens for his afterlife, which lasted for millions of years. Some objects, including furniture and jewellery were placed in tombs for use in the afterlife. Others were painted, or written, on tomb walls and papyri. Knowledge of Egyptian gardens thus comes from tombs, archaeological investigations and texts. The oldest settlements with garden-type spaces date from *c.* 6000 BC but the oldest records of designed gardens date from *c.* 2000 BC. Since Egypt is the most popular field in ancient archaeology, the material has been studied by many scholars.

Without the plans and drawings on tomb walls we would know no more of Egyptian gardens than we do of contemporary examples in Mesopotamia (see Chapter 4). But the plans are not easy to read. Wilkinson explains that 'the ancient Egyptian artist represents space and time in his compositions. Space could be shown as one place only, or as several views of the same place. Time could also be indicated as a sequence of events in cartoon style, or by the addition of an inscription, or as one significant moment'.[1] Ancient Egyptian artists did not understand or use linear perspective. Objects are represented 'as known' rather than 'as seen'. This convention has some similarities with the use of symbols in medieval art but was more sophisticated. A hippopotamus in an Egyptian river scene might be drawn small to indicate either that it was deep in the water or far away.

Hieroglyphs were used as symbols or sounds or as both. The word 'sun' was shown as a circle and the word 'lotus' by a pictogram of its flower. The setting sun, together with the symbols for bread (the half-circle) and house (the open rectangle) form a hieroglyph which 'could mean "horizon" as well as "tomb"'.[2] The way in which symbols could be used to express sounds is illustrated by the hypothetical English example of using 'bee-leaf' to write 'belief'.[3] The word 'garden' was written with symbols for three water pots, a ripple and the bread loaf sign. This gave the phonetic sound 'hnt-s/hent-esh'.[4] On garden drawings some elements are shown in plan, some (e.g. flowers or buildings) are in elevation and some are symbols. The sycamore fig, drawn as though lying flat on the ground, could be used as a hieroglyph for any tree or could also represent an actual fig tree. These conventions allowed pictorial richness with many layers of meaning.

Egyptian gardens

There was a clear distinction between domestic space, made for the body at rest, and temple space, made for the mind and spirit (*ka*). The emotion produced by temples was religious awe: they drew attention to the splendour of the universe, man's place in creation and the important role of pharaohs. Hunting was the royal sport, and the proximity of deserts and swamps made the creation of hunting parks unnecessary. Five Egyptian garden types can be distinguished:

- Fruit and vegetable gardens
- Small domestic gardens
- Palace gardens
- Temple gardens
- Plant and animal gardens.

Logic suggests that domestic gardens predated palace gardens, that the first large gardens belonged to kings and that dwellings predated temples. Garden types will therefore be discussed in this order.

2.4 (top) The Colossi of Memnon were surrounded by water during the season of inundation, before the Aswan High Dam was built. Floods were welcomed as givers of life and tokens of god's love. The painting is *c.*1900 (from R. Talbot Kelly, Egypt)

2.5 (above) Photograph of the Colossi of Memnon, *c.*2000

2.6 The Ramesseum comprised: a home for a deceased pharaoh, a palace for a living pharaoh, a massive food store, a small garden, a sacred lake and a sacred grove. The complex assisted in the task of maintaining order (Ma'at). Hatshepsut's Temple and the Valley of the Kings are in the upper right section of the photograph

2.7 An avenue of sphinxes joined the temple compounds of Luxor and Karnak

Fruit and vegetable gardens

Vegetables benefit from walled enclosures and require intensive care, including the classic horticultural activities of weeding and watering. In Egypt, horticulture began in early times. A fifth-dynasty (2465–2323 BC) tomb at Saqqara shows the irrigation and cultivation of lettuce. The plant was sacred because its milky sap symbolised the semen of a fertility god, Min. The same tomb has an illustration of a gardener watering the vegetable patch in the royal garden. Another tomb records that the owner was granted 'land property 200 cubits long and 200 cubits wide, enclosed by a wall, equipped, and planted with useful trees; a very large pond is to be made in it, and fig-trees and vines are to be planted'.[5] The property was about the size of nine tennis courts – a large space for vegetables but small for cereals.

Domestic gardens

Even royal dwellings were made of mud brick, not stone, because they were only needed for a lifetime, not for eternity. By the close of the Pre-dynastic period (2920 BC) Egypt had rectangular houses comprising a room and a yard. Except when built outside the cultivated zone, almost all these structures have been washed away, ploughed or pulverised for use as manure. Egypt is sometimes described as a land without cities because of the dearth of information on private houses and gardens. The main sources are a few small settlements on non-agricultural land, some models of houses placed in tombs and some paintings of houses which also show private gardens. Archaeologists have, understandably, been more interested in non-domestic architecture. Aufrère and Golvin describe Amarna as 'without doubt the most interesting urban site in Egypt',[6] but in three volumes of reconstructions of Egyptian

2.8 Ancient Egyptian houses were not unlike modern agricultural dwellings, though better use was made of the roof-space. In Ancient Persia, a man was allowed to shoot an arrow at another man if he caught the latter spying on his womenfolk as they slept on the roof

buildings, their only view of the town is drawn from too great a height to show houses or gardens. Wildung observes that, 'the closet equivalent today of everyday Egyptian architecture can be seen in the mud-brick houses in the Yemen'.[7]

The New Kingdom (1550–1070 BC) craftsmen's village of Deir el Medina at Luxor is a rare example of a surviving village. It is in the desert because its inhabitants were builders of tombs in the Valley of the Kings. Water had to be carried to the village by donkey and there was little to spare for plants. For reasons of security, it was a tightly-walled settlement with a single gate, narrow streets and houses with minute rooms. Kitchens were not roofed, and stairs led to flat roofs used for cooking and for sleeping in hot weather. An even more regimented craftsmen's village was made near the pyramids at Giza. They are not good places for learning about Egyptian domestic gardens.

Models and paintings deposited in tombs as grave-goods show one-, two- and three-storey dwellings with rooms and yards. Outdoor steps lead to flat roofs. They correlate with evidence from Amarna to give a picture of Egyptian houses and gardens.

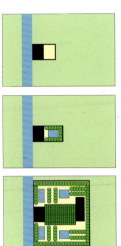

2.9 Conjectural evolution of the Egyptian domestic garden. Poorer people would have used enclosed outdoor space for utilitarian purposes

2.10 Looking across the Nile from Luxor to western Thebes

2.11 (above) A drawing of Edfu, commissioned by Napoleon *c.* 1800, gives an idea of the relationship between royal temples and private houses in Ancient Egypt, though houses were never built within temple compounds (from E. F. Jornard's *Description de l'Egypt* 1809–28)

2.12 (right) The houses of early nineteenth-century Edfu have now been cleared away

2.13 A mud-brick house with steps to the roof and gardens beyond (in Iran)

Outer walls provided security and privacy. Garden doors opened onto streets. Roofs were brick-vaulted or flat. Columns and beams were made from timber, which was scarce. Open courts were often on the north sides of houses, for shade. Small courts had space only for cooking and eating. Animals were kept in yards at night. Craftsmen used yards as workplaces. Wealthy families had several courts, pools and areas for different kinds of plant. Servants and animals, including cats, donkeys and cows, probably slept in lean-to shelters. Outdoor living areas were shaded by vines and mats. Water was brought into gardens for horticultural use. At Amarna, many houses had circular wells in their yards (see p. 42).

Pools were the first necessity and first luxury of gardens. They had functional and aesthetic roles. Water irrigates plants and cools air through evaporation. Keeping fish provides entertainment, food and a means of eliminating the larvae of biting insects. Texts from the Old Kingdom summarise the role of domestic gardens and their features: 'I returned from my estate. I built a house and set up doorways. I dug a pool and planted trees.' Gardens could also be places for lovers to meet:

I belong to you like this plot of ground
That I planted with flowers
And sweet-smelling herbs.

Perhaps the most surprising fact about the domestic gardens of Ancient Egypt is their similarity to modern courtyard gardens. The plants are also familiar. As in European gardens of the Middle Ages, there was a greater representation of functional than of purely decorative species. Plants known to have been cultivated in Ancient Egyptian gardens include those shown on the facing page.

2.14 A coffin text. It shows Osiris on a throne with Maat's hand on his shoulder. In front of them are Nakht, his wife and his property. Their garden pool is surrounded by sycomore figs.

Coffin texts, known collectively as the *Book of the Dead*, were inscribed in tombs for guidance in the afterlife. A famous illustration shows a royal scribe, Nakht, and his wife. They stand in front of their house. It has a flat roof and triangular devices to catch the wind. The owners' hands are outstretched in the hieroglyphic gesture signifying worship. Beyond the pool, surrounded by nine sycomore fig trees and four date palms, sits Osiris, god of the dead and of resurrection, with Maat, the goddess of truth and justice, behind him. A tomb was a realm of peace, truth and justice in which to dwell for eternity. The Egyptians believed heaven to be on earth.

Flowers
- Corn poppy (*Papaver rhoeas*)
- Cornflower (*Centaurea depressa*)
- Madonna lily (*Lilium candidum*)
- Mallow (*Althaea ficifolia*)
- Mandrake (*Mandragora officinarum*)
- Papyrus (*Cyperus papyrus*)
- Water lily (*Nymphaea caerulea*)

Food
- Apple (*Malus sp.*)
- Argun palm (*Medemia argun*)
- Carob (*Ceratonia siliqua*)
- Castor oil plant (*Ricinis communis*)
- Christ's thorn (*Ziziphus spina-christi*)
- Common fig (*Ficus carica*)
- Date palm (*Phoenix dactylifera*)
- Doum palm (*Hyphaene thebaica*)
- Egyptian plum (*Balanites aegyptiaca*)
- Juniper (*Juniperus oxycedrus*)
- Olive (*Olea europea*)
- Pistachio (*Pistacia vera*)
- Pomegranate (*Punica granatum*)
- Stone pine (*Pinus pinea*)
- Sycomore fig (*Ficus sycomorus*)
- Vine (*Vitis vinifera*)

Herb
- Chervil (*Anthriscus cerefolium*)
- Coriander (*Coriandrum sativum*)
- Peppermint (*Mentha piperita*)
- Thyme (*Thymbra spicata*)

Perfume
- Henna (*Lawsonia inermis*)
- Myrtle (*Myrtus communis*)

Vegetables
- Broad bean (*Vicia faba*)
- Chick pea (*Cicer arietinum*)
- Cucumber (*Cucumis melo*)
- Garlic (*Allium sativum*)
- Lentil (*Lens culinarus*)
- Lettuce (*Lactuca sativa*)
- Onion (*Allium cepa*)
- Watermelon (*Citrullus lanatus*)

Palace gardens

Palace gardens were larger than private gardens but were similar in design and use. The word 'pharaoh' means 'great house' (from the Egyptian *per aa*)[8] but few archaeological remains of palaces have been found and almost all are from the New Kingdom. The few include the palaces within the temple compounds of Rameses II (the Ramesseum) and Rameses III (at Medinet Habu) which were probably used only for short periods, during coronations and royal visits. More is known of Akhenaten's palace and gardens in his capital city, Amarna (see p. 24). It was built as a new town on virgin land and remains the best surviving example of Ancient Egyptian town planning, despite being having been inhabited for only 15 years. Akhenaten worshiped Aten, the sun god, and is thought to be the originator of monotheism. His city stands on the east bank of the Nile, half-way between the modern cities of Cairo and Luxor. The waterside strip was within the zone of cultivation but the greater part of Amarna was in the desert. This allowed more space for gardens but made pools essential. Fragments of mud-brick buildings and courts survive. Akhenaten explained the layout of the town he called Akhetaten:

2.15 The Temple of Rameses III at Medinet Habu had a small palace and garden. They were built in mud brick and located to the left of the stone temple

I build the great temple for the Aten, my father, in Akhetaten in this place. And I build the small temple for the Aten, my father, in Akhetaten, in this place. I build the sun-shadow chapel for the great royal consort Nefertiti of the Aten, my father, in Akhetaten in this place. I build a jubilee temple for the Aten, my father, on the island of the Aten in Akhetaten in this place . . . I build for myself palaces for the pharaoh, and I build a harem for the royal consort in Akhetaten in this place. I have a tomb built in the mountain of Akhetaten, where the sun rises, where I shall be buried after the millions of years' reign, that the Aten, my father, has allocated to me.[9]

The 'great temple' for the sun-god was aligned on an east–west axis. The 'palaces for the pharaoh', during his earthly life, had outdoor courts and gardens. They were distributed along a 5 km south–north Royal Road which was also a Sacred Way. It was used for the king and queen's chariot ride, south of the ceremonial area of the Central City. This area had a King's House and a Great Palace with sunken garden courts, pools and overhead shading. The walls were painted and, in roofed areas, so were the pavements. The King's House had a Window of Appearance from which he and Queen Nefertiti could show themselves and distribute gifts.[10] A bridge crossed the Royal Road to a harem palace.

'Harem' derives from an Arabic word, meaning prohibited, and acquired its modern association with sexual pleasure at a later date. In Egypt, the harem was the residential palace for women and children. Life was precarious and kings needed many wives because they needed many children, in whose veins ran the blood of gods. When his son, the future Rameses II, came of age, Seti presented him with a delicious harem of 'female royal attendants who were like unto the great beauties of the palace'.[11] Rameses was able to boast of fathering 79 sons and 59 daughters, four of whom he married (since royal daughters could not marry commoners, this may have been an act of charity). A harem palace was a safe residence for the royal women, their children, the old and the unmarried. It was a dormitory establishment with fertile women, productive gardens, fields and orchards. Dwellings within the harem compound had internal courts, often with plants and pools:

The physical setting of the more modern harem was very firmly focused inwards towards the central open space which became the scene of the daily activities of the harem-women. Here food was prepared, cosmetics applied, and the days and evenings were spent singing, dancing and telling stories.[12]

The royal harem was also the most important school in Egypt. It was run by the Teacher of the Royal Children and attended by children of noble families. Officials boasted of having been 'a child of the Palace of the Royal Harem'. Garden courts in the king's palaces were used for official gatherings, receptions and private life. Christian Jacq turned his imagination to an exotic garden scene:

The twelve dancers had chosen a vast lotus pond as their torchlit backdrop. Wearing pearl-studded netting beneath short tunics, triple-braided wigs, strands of beads and lapis lazuli bracelets, the young women swayed suggestively . . . Suddenly, the dancers discarded their wigs, tunics and netting. Hair in a strict chignon, bare-breasted, clad in a wisp of kilt, they each tapped their right foot, then executed a breathtaking back flip, perfectly timed. Arching and bowing gracefully, they performed more acrobatic feats, all just as spectacular.[13]

The most famous Egyptian garden painting was found, by an Italian Egyptologist in the nineteenth century, in the funerary chapel above Sennufer's burial chamber (Tomb 96 in the Western Valley). Today, the chapel is closed and the painting destroyed. Fortunately, a careful copy was made. Sennufer was an important man, 'Mayor of the Southern City' (Thebes) and 'Overseer of the Gardens of Amun', but it is not likely that

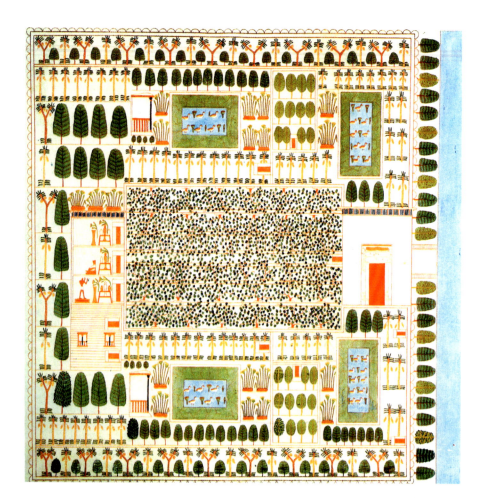

2.16 The most famous painting of an Egyptian garden. Sennufer was responsible for the garden but is not thought to have been its owner. As a type, it is astonishingly similar to a modern domestic garden in a hot country

the painting depicts his private garden. More probably, Sennufer had responsibility for the garden's care, and perhaps its design, as part of the Karnak temple complex. A pharaoh could have used it during his afterlife but would have needed a similar space for his bodily life. The plan shows an enclosed court bounded by a mud-brick wall topped with glazed tiles. Gothein analysed the plan as follows:

> You enter from the front by a large entrance gate, or by one of two side wicket-gates. A shady avenue follows the outside wall, and a canal, outside that; this adds to the feeling of complete seclusion which the picture suggests. You step through the door straight into the house, which is shown much too large in comparison with its surroundings, the doors being the only break in the façade. No doubt the artist wished to suggest that the owner was a very rich person, by emphasising the beauty of his front gate. Here too was the porter's lodge, perhaps also a reception-room for such visitors as were not allowed in the main building, which was hidden away in the garden. Between the gate and the house, occupying the whole of the middle space, was the vineyard. It consisted of four arched arbours, their rafters supported by posts. A path is left open in the middle forming the chief approach to the house from the gate; and from this path two side-walks lead directly to the covered ways.[14]

Gothein writes as though it were a private garden. Wilkinson believes it to have been a temple garden.[15]

Temple and tomb gardens

Origins

The oldest religious site in Egypt is the stone circle at Nabta Playa (*c.* 4500 BC),[16] which appears to have been used for astronomical observations. It may also have had a religious role. The oldest temple to a known god is that of Neken in the 'city of the falcon', Hierakonopolis in southern Egypt.[17] It was an enclosure containing a paved floor and a flagpole. Settled societies require cohesive beliefs and customs to maintain order. In Egypt this was provided by an integrated system of religion, government, laws and defence. Cities allowed protection and communication. Modern societies maintain a separation of powers but in the ancient world they were fused. The hierarchy of power had a god-king at the top and slaves at its base. Priests, scribes, soldiers, craftsmen and farmers occupied intermediate ranks. During his bodily life, a pharaoh's duty was discharged from a string of palaces along the Nile. During his afterlife, the duty was performed from a tomb-temple. At the transition from bodily life to afterlife a pharaoh changed from one incarnation of a god to another, just as the land he ruled changed with the annual cycle of inundation.

2.17 Hieroglyph for a burial mound, planted with sycomores and with ideograms for flag, building and Osiris inside

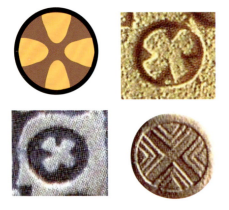

2.18 Hieroglyph for a city, perhaps symbolising the need for protection (the defensive circle) and communication (the connecting lines)

When tombs are distinguished from temples it is more a matter of emphasis than essence. In the Old and Middle Kingdoms, the mortuary role appears stronger because the dominant structure was a pyramid. In the New Kingdom, the ceremonial role was emphasised, with tombs placed in the Valley of the Kings for reasons of security against tomb-robbers. The Egyptian word for all types of temple was *hut* ('mansion'). Cult temples were known as 'mansions of the gods' and mortuary temples as 'mansions of millions of years'. Cults were systems of worship expressed through ceremony. Gods were expected to inhabit their mansions for millions of years. For three millennia, extending through the Old, Middle and New Kingdoms, the planning of tombs and cult temples was governed by a creation myth inspired by Egypt's unique landscape.

When the flood reached its zenith, the Nile valley became a serene composition of water and desert. Swirling currents produced uneven surfaces. As the flood ebbed, mounds appeared before flats and hollows. Everything was coated in black mud. Then the land was replanted and repopulated. The creation myth held that the earth itself was formed in this way: after the primal mound emerged from the waters, a reed grew and a falcon, representing Horus, landed. Divine powers, not unlike 'laws of nature', ruled the world. Concepts and aspects of the creation were represented by a family of gods with overlapping roles. Atum was father of the gods. Amun was king of the gods. Ptah was creator of the universe. Nun, being the god of the primordial waters, was old and wise. Re was father of mankind and, as Amun-Re, identified with the sun god. Osiris was the giver of civilisation, ruler of the dead and god of fertility. Osiris' son by Isis was Horus. Osiris' family extended from the father of the gods to the 'Living Horus', Egypt's reigning pharaoh. The word for god (*netjer*) used a hieroglyph of a flag, which was derived from the flags that were always placed at entrances to shrines and temples.

Osiris' tomb was made of sycomore wood and shaded by sycomore trees. The sycomore fig (*Ficus sycomorus*) was the abode of Hathor. These figs grow directly on branches. Botanically they are inside-out flower clusters that depend on a pollinator wasp. Without fertilisation, the fig falls to the ground and shrivels. The tree can bear up to seven crops a year – a good symbol for a fertility god. Sycomore wood, which is easy to work, was used for making royal coffins.

An eighteenth-dynasty hymn to Osiris celebrates his powers:

Thou hast made this earth by thy hand, and the waters thereof, and the wind thereof, the herb thereof, all the cattle thereof, all the winged fowl thereof, all the fish thereof, all the creeping things thereof, and all the four-footed beasts thereof. O thou son of Nut, the whole world is gratified when thou ascendest thy father's throne like Ra. Thou shinest in the horizon, thou sendest forth thy light into the darkness, thou makest the darkness light with thy double plume, and thou floodest the world with light like the Disk at break of day. Thy diadem pierceth heaven and becometh a brother unto the stars,

O thou form of every god. Thou art gracious in command and in speech, thou art the favoured one of the great company of the gods, and thou art the greatly beloved one of the lesser company of the gods.[18]

The central feature of a temple sanctuary was first an Osirian mound (*benben*), then a pyramid and then a 'mansion'. Each was a house of Amun. Temples were not places for the faithful to gather and pray, as we do in synagogues, churches and mosques. They were exclusive places in which high priests performed sacred rites. Statues of gods were dressed, anointed and given food and drink, at fixed times determined by the sun. Priests, some full-time and many part-time, provided assistance. They helped to predict floods, resolve disputes and regulate water by forming basins and opening dykes. A temple door keeper was the 'Door Opener of Heaven'.[19]

Development
In the Old and Middle Kingdoms the features of a sanctuary were:

- a significant place in the landscape
- a protective wall, often wavy in plan, to symbolise the primordial waters
- a sacred mound or pyramid, to symbolise the emergence of land from water
- a path from the mound to water.

The New Kingdom was established after an Intermediate Period in which Egypt had been ruled by an Asiatic people, the Hyksos, probably from Palestine. A 'standard' temple layout developed, redeploying the above symbolic elements as follows:

- a small 'valley temple' beside the water, to house a barge, used for the pharaoh when he died and for transporting effigies of gods at subsequent festivals
- a ceremonial route from the water (river, pool, or T-shaped canal-end) to the temple. Gardens could be made along the route
- an outer wall of mud brick, bounding the temple compound; the latter contained a lake, a grove, a mansion of god and stores
- a pylon gateway marked by flagpoles and leading to the mansion itself
- an open peristyle court, to admit the sun
- a hypostyle hall, to symbolise the created world
- the holy of holies (an inner sanctuary with a plinth for the god's statue).

Later temples were sited on the boundary of life and death: the edge of the floodplain. Ceremonial routes were then walled, roofed, planted, lined with sphinxes, or given significance by colossal statues. Pylon gates were positioned so that the sun rose between the towers, creating the hieroglyph for horizon. A sacred lake and a sacred

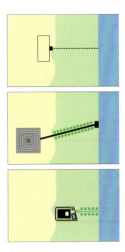

2.19 Diagrams of an Osirian Temple in Predynastic Egypt (top), the Old Kingdom (centre) and the New Kingdom (bottom)

2.20 Borchardt's drawing of the pyramid at Abusir shows a processional route to a 'valley temple' beside the Nile during the period of inundation (from L. Borchardt *Das Grabdenkmal Ne–User-Re*, 1907)

2.21 The sacred lake at Karnak (painting from R. Hichins *Egypt and its monuments*, 1909)

grove were contained within the sanctuary. The grove was planted with sycomore fig, native to water margins, and tamarisk, native to desert margins. A flight of steps led into the water from the temple side of the lake. It was a place for priests to bathe at dawn to purify themselves. The sacred lake at Karnak had a tunnel from which geese, symbolising Amun, could emerge onto the water surface, as Amun himself had done at the beginning of time. The pharaoh, an incarnation of Amun and of Horus, was rowed on the lake.

At Malkata, near Medinet Habu, Amenhetep III made a ceremonial lake (2 km by 1 km) and shaped the spoil into 'rows of artificial hills'.[20] Kemp describes Malkata as 'Egypt's largest earthwork' and the mounds as an 'early example of landscaping'. They stood at the meeting point of the Nile floodplain and the desert. At royal jubilees (*Sed* festivals), the lake was traversed by Morning and Evening Barges, representing the journeys of the sun-god. A New Kingdom temple was a model of creation. The ceiling represented the sky; the columns represented plants; the floor, occasionally flooded by the Nile, represented the primordial waters from which land emerged. The processional axis lay along the sun's daily path from east to west. The inner sanctuary was at the point nearest the setting sun. The temple compound was a meeting place of heaven, earth and underworld. It was a gate, allowing gods and kings to move between the here-and-now and the hereafter. Blank doors defined exit and entry points. Temples were tombs; tombs were temples.

Location and planning

At Thebes, New Kingdom temples for state gods were placed on the east bank of the Nile, the side over which the sun rose. They were built on levees and on the remains of older buildings. Temples for gods of the afterlife were placed on the side of the Nile over which the sun set, on levees or, as with Hatshepsut's temple, on the border of the Red Land (*Deshret*, desert) and the Black Land (*Kemet*, agricultural land). Floods were welcomed as symbols of the primal condition from which the earth emerged. Temples were planned in relation to significant landscape features (e.g. cliffs, mountains, buildings, springs), places associated with myths and traditions (e.g. a god's birthplace) and lines of sight to other temples. They were connected to the Nile by a canal ending in a T-shaped dock. The T-shape was also used for pools containing pure water for rituals[21] and probably represented quays used by sacred barges. Temples owned fleets. Ships brought construction materials and the produce amassed within temple compounds. Stores filled up if there were 'seven fat years' and emptied in periods of 'seven lean years'.

Some temples (e.g. on Elephantine island) were aligned with the stars. Slots were made in walls and slits in roofs so that sunlight illuminated significant features. A temple's location was fixed at a foundation ceremony which included 'stretching the cord' (*pedj-shes*). This involved laying the first bricks and placing ritual offerings in foundation pits. North–south was favoured for the temple's short axis and east–west for the long axis. Prime axes could be fixed in different ways and a slightly new line was often adopted when a new king extended an old temple. Most temples used east–west as the long axis so that the sun arose over the pylon gate and set over the sanctuary of a departed pharaoh-god.

Temples were dimensioned in cubits. The Egyptian royal cubit was equal to the length of a god-king's forearm (524 mm). Multiples of ten cubits (5.24 m) were preferred for key temple dimensions. Subsidiary dimensions, as shown on the ruler (Figure 2.26) were one finger, two fingers, three fingers and a hand. Temples had large land holdings, from which they drew tribute. In the time of Rameses III, the Domain of Amun had over 2,300 sq km of land and 80,000 personnel, most of whom were engaged in agriculture and horticulture. It is recorded that in a period of 1,057 days a total of 4,786,184 floral offerings were made in the Temple of Amun at Karnak.[22] Such a tribute required many skilled gardeners.

Festivals

The Domain of Amun (see p. 47) united the world of the living (the east bank) with the world of the departed (the west bank). Festivals marked seasonal and mythological events. The Festival of Opening the Dykes took place when the flood arrived and refilled pools. There were three seasons, related to the agricultural cycle:

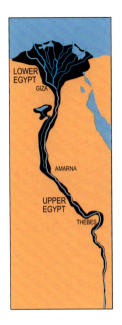

2.22 Ancient Egypt: the Red Land and the Black Land

- Inundation (*Akhet*): the flood lasted approximately mid-July to mid-November
- Growing (*Peret*): the winter growing season was from mid-November to mid-March
- Drought (*Shemu*): the dry summer period was from mid-March to mid-July.

Memphis was an administrative capital. Thebes (now Luxor) was a religious capital and festival city. It was called Waset and described simply as 'The City':

Waset is the pattern for every city. Both the flood and the earth were in her from the beginning of time. The sands came to delimit her soil, to create her ground from the mound when earth came into being. Then mankind came into being within her. To found every city in her true name (The City), since all are called 'city' after the example of Waset.[23]

Like its temples, Luxor was inspired by the Osiris myth. The temple of Karnak is built on a Nile levee and the mound of the pre-New Kingdom city. It was planned on what Nims calls 'river north', a theoretical north–south line but actually a north–east south–west line at a right-angle to the Nile.[24] The inner sanctuary, or 'holy of holies', housed the divine boat-shrine and a statue of Amun. Carved reliefs show him, as

2.23 The Red Land, the Nile, and the Black Land

2.24 Queen Hatshepsut's Temple, the oldest masterpiece of landscape architecture, once had a sacred grove and sacred lake

Amun-Min, with penis erect to create the world. A T-shaped quay and canal led to the Nile. Festivals were occasions when the gods from the east bank of the Nile (both pharaohs and statues) visited the departed gods on the west bank. Processional routes, often paved and lined with statues, defined the Domain of Amun. From Karnak, routes led over the river to Western Thebes and up the river to Luxor.

The Festival of the Valley took place in the second month of summer, at the time of the new moon. Amun dwelt at Karnak. At the start of the Festival his statue, in its ship, was carried from its home by torchlight procession, escorted by priests, dancers, musicians and incense-bearers. He followed a processional way to the Nile, crossed the river and travelled by canal to a small temple on the edge of the Libyan Desert. Another processional route, centred on Karnak and lined with pairs of painted sphinxes, led to Hatshepsut's Temple, then known as *Djeser-Djeseru* ('Holiest of the Holy'). The temple compound was surrounded by a thick limestone wall:

2.25 Kalabasha Temple, before it was moved

> Once through the gate, Amun passed immediately into a peaceful, pleasantly shaded garden where T-shaped pools glinted in the sunlight and trees – almost certainly the famous fragrant trees from Punt – offered a tempting respite from the fierce desert sun. Looking upwards, Amun would have seen the temple in all its glory; a softly gleaming white limestone building occupying three ascending terraces set back against the cliff, its tiered porticoes linked by a long, open-air stairway rising through the centre of the temple towards the sanctuary. Amun's route lay upwards. Passing over the lower portico he reached the flat second terrace where his path was marked out by pairs of colossal, painted red-granite sphinxes, each with Hatshepsut's head, inscribed to 'The King of Upper and Lower Egypt Maatkare, Beloved of Amun who is in the midst of *Djeser-Djeseru*, and given life forever'.[25]

Festivals thus joined temple compounds to the wider landscape. They are the ancestors of garden avenues and urban avenues in the modern world.

Plant and animal collections

Temples were surrounded by gardens, outside the wavy wall. Productive gardens had orchards, pools, vineyards, vegetables and flower gardens. Ornamental gardens were located on processional routes. Special gardens had names.[26] Aten was the solar disc and Akhenaten's garden at Amarna was 'The Seeing-Place of the Aten'. The garden to a shrine on the processional route between Karnak and Luxor was called 'Hatshepsut is united with the perfection of Amun'. A pyramid had a grove called the 'the soul of Sahure appears in splendour'.

Animals with symbolic significance were kept in temple and palace gardens. Carved lions decorated the king's throne and live lions were kept in cages at the entrance to the gardens at Karnak. Paintings show pharaohs being presented with giraffes, monkeys and tigers. Plants with symbolic significance were grown.

At Pi-Ramesse there was a large garden filled with plants and animals, on a similar principle to contemporary Mesopotamian gardens (see Chapter 4):

> The abundant supply of water allowed Pi-Ramesse to become a garden city, planted with pomegranate and date orchards and vineyards. Around the royal palace were ornamental gardens, a lake and even a zoo; lion, giraffe and elephant bones have all been discovered in the remains of the grounds.[27]

Sycomore fig and tamarisk were grown within temple compounds because of their symbolic significance. The Egyptian Lotus (*Nymphea lotus*) was sacred to the goddess Isis and appears in more tomb pictures than any other flower. Girls gathered flowers in the marshes, to place on banqueting tables, in vases, and in their hair, or to offer as gifts to their gods.

The influence of Ancient Egyptian gardens

Archaeology reveals the garden tradition of Ancient Egypt to have developed over 3,000 years. One cannot detail its influence on Europe, nor can one doubt it. The features listed below are common to the Egyptian and Graeco-Roman traditions. Some may have originated in Mesopotamia and some may have been reinvented:

- Sacred lakes and groves
- Processional ways
- Peristyle courts with fresco decoration
- Columns inspired by plant forms
- Terracing
- Rectangular pools and plant beds in walled enclosures
- Symbolic use of plants
- Stone and terracotta pots
- Vine pergolas
- Plant and animal gardens.

2.26 The Egyptian royal cubit used fingers, hands and forearms as units of measure

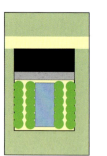

2.27
Egyptian
domestic
gardens

Types and examples

Domestic gardens

Use: Small domestic gardens functioned as part of the dwelling, meriting the description 'outdoor rooms'. Garden pools held fish and served as a water supply. Climbers and trees were needed for shade.

Form: House and garden walls were made of mud brick. Outdoor stairs led to flat roofs with rush sunshades. The roof space could be used for cooking, eating and sleeping. Since dwellings were on higher land, to avoid the floods, water had to be carried in or drawn from wells.

Amarna 1350 BC

Amarna is one of the few Ancient Egyptian settlements to have survived. The layout of dwellings, garden walls and wells was excavated by Barry Kemp. Nothing is known about the planting of its gardens. One of the dwellings belonged to the sculptor who made the famous bust of Nefertiti and it is likely that most of the spaces shown on the plan were working yards for craft and horticultural activities.

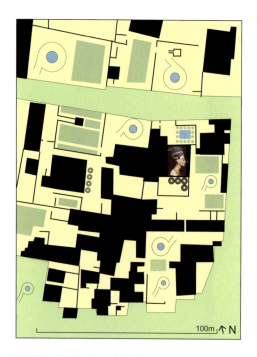

2.28 The famous head of Queen Nefertiti is positioned over the house of the sculptor in which it was found

Palace gardens

Use: Egyptian palace gardens appear to have been more domestic than courtly. They were used for relaxation, outdoor eating, children's play and the cultivation of plants, both beautiful and edible. Our knowledge of palace gardens comes from tomb paintings, made so that pharaohs could enjoy in the afterlife comforts similar to those enjoyed in the earthly phase of their existence.

Form: Palace compounds, like temple compounds, were rectangular enclosures bounded by high walls. Tomb paintings show gardens with fruit trees, flowers, pools, pot plants, vine-clad pergolas and places to sit in winter sun or summer shade. Excavations reveal substantial buildings with internal courts that are likely to have been treated in this way. The geometry of gardens is more symmetrical than that of temples but this may indicate only the way they were drawn: regularity comes naturally to the draughtsman and less easily to those who work directly on the ground. The diagram shows a building with an internal court (based on Sennufer's garden).

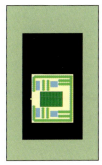

2.29
Egyptian palace garden

Sennufer's garden 1400 BC

The most famous painting of an Egyptian garden was found in the funerary chapel of Sennufer, above his burial chamber (Tomb 96 in the Western Valley). Sennufer lived in the reign of Amenophis II and is more likely to have been designer than owner of the garden, which is palatial in scale and may have belonged to a pharaoh. The original painting has been lost but a careful copy was made in the nineteenth century. Buildings and trees are drawn in elevation, as though flat on the ground, but other features are shown in plan. The garden is surrounded by a high mud wall capped with clay tiles, which are represented by hoops on the plan. Visitors could arrive by boat at the garden entrance, which is shown on the right of the drawing. A causeway leads to a gate lodge with a decorated door; one passed through this to a central, vine-shaded court. The master's house, shown with three rooms, is on the opposite side of the garden from the entrance. There are lines of palm trees on the other two sides. Four small garden pools can be seen, with ducks and flowers in their midst; two of these pools are overlooked by shelters with clumps of lotus flowers, possibly in pots, nearby.

Its mile-long canal, imposing entrance gate, numerous trees, and large vineyard all suggest great wealth . . . the roof of the villa is shaded by awnings, and small garden pavilions overlooking the storage pools invite relaxation.[28]

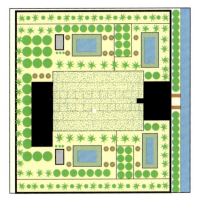

2.30 Sennufer's garden

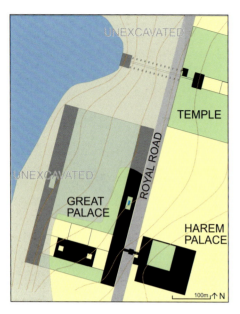

2.31 Akhenaten's palace, Amarna

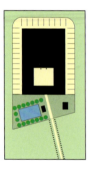

2.32 Egyptian sanctuary

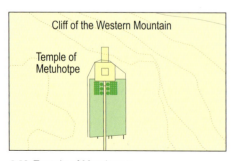

2.33 Temple of Metuhotpe

Amarna Palace 1350 BC

Akhenaten's palace and garden were excavated by Barry Kemp after 1977, revealing the layout of buildings, courtyards and pools, but not planting. Something of its character can be imagined by inserting the drawing of Sennufer's garden (Figure 2.15) into the layout uncovered by archaeology.

The desolate and deserted appearance of the plain of Amarna should not deceive the modern visitor, however. In the days of Akhenaten, this was a vast garden, dotted with plants, flowers, splendid palaces with magnificent painted decorations depicting natural subjects, and even a lake.[29]

Temple gardens

Use: The oldest 'garden' survivals are the temple compounds of ancient Egypt. They were used by priests and pharaohs, though some members of the public might be admitted on festival days. The design of temples explained the nature of the world and the social order, as we now do through science, religion, art, history and political theory. Temple compounds are the oldest surviving manifestation of the quest to design outdoor space as what we now call works of art. Sacred groves and lakes were formed within temple compounds.

Form: Axial lines were used but the overall geometry was non-symmetrical. Temples were built in compounds bounded by wavy walls. The internal space was in part ceremonial and in part laid to gardens. Temples were linked by avenues, lined with trees, sphinxes and statues. The line of the avenue ran into the compound and led through a series of processional gates to a hypostyle hall and then an inner sanctum, the holy of holies. Much of the enclosed land was used to accommodate storehouses. Compounds also held sacred lakes, pools, statues, shrines, flower and vegetable gardens. The construction material was stone for the temple and mud brick for other structures

Temple of Metuhotep 2065 BC

The Temple of Metuhotep at Dêr el-Bahari was made for the pharaoh who re-united Egypt and established the Middle Kingdom. Described as 'entirely novel in its multi-level construction',[30] Mentuhotep's Temple has a forecourt, once planted with trees, and a ramp leading to a platform on which stood a temple with a view over the Nile Valley. A decoy burial chamber was dug beneath the Temple and the king's actual burial chamber was dug into the cliffs.

Its unknown architect showed a remarkable eye for the picturesque exploitation of a site with his use of terraces and colonnades.[31]

Domain of Amun 1100 BC

The Domain of Amun comprised land on both sides of the Nile. It was a sacred landscape with cult and mortuary temples linked by processional routes. Festival processions began in the land of the living, on the east bank of the Nile, crossed the river by royal barge and visited the mortuary temples in the land of the dead, on the west bank. Routes were treated in various ways: canals, roofed causeways and pavements lined with trees and statues. Temples were built on the margin of the Red Land (mountain and desert) and the Black Land (agricultural land within the flood zone).

> On the western bank of the Nile, dominated by the Sacred Peak, devoted to the goddess Meretseger, 'She Who Loves Silence', stretched the great necropolis of Thebes, the final resting place for all eternity of kings and royal princes and princesses, of functionaries and courtiers. Here, between the Nile and the Mountain, every pharaoh ordered the construction of a 'Temple of Millions of Years', for the celebration of his cult. Each year, the god Amun paid a visit, in solemn procession, on the occasion of the 'Beautiful Feast of the Valley'.[38]

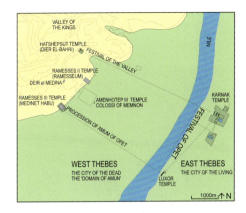

2.34 Domain of Amun, Luxor

Temple of Queen Hatshepsut 1450 BC

The Temple of Queen Hatshepsut is the first masterpiece of western landscape architecture: structure and setting are united. It was known as *Djeser-Djeseru* (Holiest of the Holy) to the Ancient Egyptians and is now known as *Deir el-Bahri* (Monastery of the North), after the Coptic monastery which occupied the site from the fifth century to the nineteenth century. Queen Hatshepsut (also known by her throne name *Maat-ka-Re*, 'Justice is the soul Re') ruled from 1479 to 1458 as 'God's Wife' (high priestess) of Amun. Her tomb and mortuary temple are in different locations. The tomb, where the treasure lay, is the oldest dateable tomb (KV 20) in the Valley of the Kings. Her temple was designed by Senenmut, governor of the Domain of Amun. There are three great rectangular courts, connected by ramps and commanding outward prospects. A handrail in the form of a serpent with a falcon's head followed the ramp. Tree pits in the lower court reveal the outline of a sacred grove which had two T-shaped pools abutting the central path. The *Book of the Dead* (Chapter 186) shows Hathor, as a cow, coming from a sacred mound in a clump of papyrus, representing the margin between life and death.

A processional route to the Nile, used for the Festival of the Valleys, was lined with sphinxes placed at 10 m intervals; each of these was 3 m long and 1 m high. Napoleon's experts saw traces of their positions. There is no doubt that, 'approaching from the valley up a processional way lined with sandstone sphinxes, the visitor would have been conscious from far away of the great painted limestone Osiride statues of the queen fronting the colonnade of the upper terrace'.[32]

Djeser-Djeseru is a deeply symbolic place:

> Here there stands out for the very first time in the history of art a most magnificent idea – that of building three terraces, one above the other, each

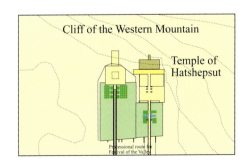

2.35 Temple of Hatshepsut

of their bordering walls set against the mountainside and made beautiful with pillared corridors.[33]

Karnak 1350 BC

The temple precinct of Karnak is on the east bank of the Nile in the town known today as Luxor. It had a ceremonial dock for use during festivals but the layout shown on the diagram is conjectural.

Temples were used by priests and pharaohs for the religious and sexual rites on which the continued stability of the world was believed to depend. Pharaohs did not live in temples, but, being gods, had a central role in religious rites. The outer walls gave secrecy and mystery to the proceedings. Internal walls articulated the space and created compartments for different activities. Within the precinct, some of the land was managed as a sacred garden, but no details of this have survived. A 'holy of holies' lay at the centre. The Sacred Lake was a symbol of the eternal ocean from which the earth was created; the priests of Amun purified themselves in holy water. Avenues of sphinxes linked temple compounds.

> The processions of images of the holy family of Thebes and of other sanctified beings (including statues of kings of olden times) setting forth from the huge, brightly painted temples, and making their slow progress along formally arranged avenues with carefully stage-managed halts at intermediate stations, and the occasional excitement of a 'miracle': all this brought to the city as a whole spectacle and munificence which regularly reinforced the physical and economic dominance of the temples.[34]

Temple of Rameses II [Ramesseum] 1200 BC

The temple and palace of Rameses II (Rameses the Great) was the greatest project of one of Egypt's greatest builders. His throne name, *User-Maat-Re*, was rendered by Diodorus Siculus as 'Ozymandias' and used by Shelley in his famous lines, 'My name is Ozymandias, King of Kings: Look on my works, ye Mighty, and despair'.

Much of the temple's structure has decayed: stone was removed for building, statues were smashed, the site was used as a church, and foundations were undermined by the Nile floods. Yet the layout and some of the structures survive. In plan, the temple is a parallelogram, not a rectangle, and half the space is occupied by storerooms. There was a palace and several garden courts and probably a sacred lake within the temple compound. A garden illustrated in the tomb of Nezemger (TT 138) 'Overseer of the Garden in the Ramesseum in the Domain of Amun', shows what these gardens may have contained.

The decoration of the site celebrates the arts of war and of peace: Rameses led the charge at Kadesh on the Orontes river that changed the course of history, and details of his victory are emblazoned on the Ramesseum. The 'astronomical room'

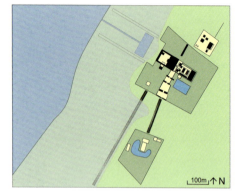

2.36 Karnak

shows the night sky and is decorated with scenes from the 'Beautiful Feast of the Valley'. There is a drawing of a sacred ished tree. The scale of the site is impressive: the head of an enormous statue (its nose the size of a grown man) lies on the ground. This colossus was cut from a single block of limestone, brought from Aswan, 400 km away. Another colossus from this site was taken to the British Museum.

> The Ramesseum . . . Most noble and pure in Thebes as far as great monuments are concerned.[35]

Temple of Rameses III at Medinet Habu 1150 BC

As the last great king of the New Kingdom, Rameses III revived Egypt's glory. There are remains of houses and vaulted stores built of mud brick. The eastern perimeter wall is battlemented and there is a palace beside the temple. A contemporary account describes a sacred pond: 'In front of it [the temple] I dug a pool copious with water, planted with trees and verdant as the Delta . . . It was surrounded by arbors, courtyards, and orchards laden with fruit and flowers for thy [Amon's] countenance. I built there pavilions . . . and I excavated a pool before them, adorned with lotus blossoms.'[36]. Rameses' sacred pond lay where the ruined Saite Chapels are today. Another sacred pond, made after 330 BC, still contains water and gives life to the Temple compound. One can see the distinctions between temple, palace, citadel and garden starting to dissolve. A ceremonial route, used for the festival of Amun of Opet, led from Luxor to Medinet Habu. The sites and design of the canal and dock are conjectural.

> Medinet Habu is no more than a tourist attraction today. It has long since stopped functioning in any of its past roles as fortress, shrine, or administrative headquarters. Yet, with imagination, the place can fleetingly live again. Here, in the city of the dead, silent with the memories of over five millennia, we can re-create the bustle of a living community of priests, workmen, and officials, whose everyday transactions, preserved in the surviving ostraia and papyri, speak to us today with a refreshing and poignant directness.[37]

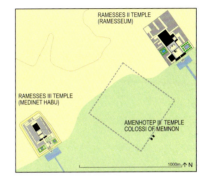

2.37 The temples of Rameses II, Rameses III and Amenhotep III in West Thebes

Notes

1   Wilkinson, A., *The Garden in Ancient Egypt,* London: Rubicon Press, 1998, p. 16.
2   McDermott, B., *Decoding Egyptian Hieroglyphs*, London: Duncan Baird Publishers, 2001, p. 43.
3   ——, op. cit., p. 20.
4   ——, op. cit., p. 38.
5   Malek, J., *In the Shadow of the Pyramids: Egypt during the Old Kingdom*, Little, Brown & Co., 1986, p. 43.
6   Aufrère, S. and Golvin, J-C., *L'Egypte Restituée,* Tome 3, Paris: Errance, 1991, p. 236.
7   Wildung, D., *Egypt from Prehistory to the Romans*, Cologne: Taschen, 2001, p. 12.
8   Verner, M., *The Pyramids. Their archaeology and history*, London: Atlantic Books, 2001, p. 23.
9   Wildung, D., op. cit., Cologne: Taschen, 2001, p. 121.
10 Kemp, B. J., *Ancient Egypt: Anatomy of a Civilisation*, London: Routledge, 1989, p. 276 ff.
11 Tyldesley, J., *Rameses*, London: Viking, 2000, p. 113.
12 ——, *Hatchespsut, the Female Pharaoh*, London: Penguin, 1998, p. 54.
13 Jacq, C., *Rameses, the Son of Light*, London: Simon & Schuster, 1997, p. 32.
14 Gothein, M-L., *A History of Garden Art*, London: J. M. Dent, 1928, pp. 9–10.
15 Wilkinson, A., op. cit., p. 131.
16 Wilkinson, R. H., *The Complete Temples of Ancient Egypt*, London: Thames & Hudson, 2000, p. 16.
17 ——, op. cit., p. 17.
18 An English translation was published in *Records of the Past*, 1st series, vol. iv, p. 99 ff.
19 Wilkinson, A., op. cit., p. 119.
20 Kemp, B. J., op. cit., p. 215.
21 ——, op. cit., p. 214.
22 Wilkinson, R. H., op. cit., p. 97.
23 Nims, C. F., *Thebes of the Pharaohs, Pattern for Every City*, London: Elek, 1965, p. 69.
24 ——, op. cit., p. 13.
25 Tyldesley, J., *Hatchepsut*, pp. 170–1.
26 Wilkinson, A., op. cit., p. 8 and pp. 148–56.
27 Tyldesley, J., op. cit., p. 97.
28 Berral, J. S., *The Garden*, London: Thames & Hudson, 1966, p. 13.
29 Siliotti, A., *Egypt*, London: Thames & Hudson, 1994, p. 150.
30 Wilkinson, R. H. op. cit., p. 180.
31 Aldred, C., *The Egyptians*, London: Thames & Hudson, 1961, p. 132.
32 Smith, W. S., *The Art and Architecture of Ancient Egypt*, Pelican History of Art, 1958, p. 133.
33 Gothein, M-L., op. cit., p. 15.
34 Kemp, B. J., op. cit., p. 206.
35 Champillion, F., *Egypte Ancienne*, 1835, p. 291.
36 Papyrus Harris I.
37 Murnane, W. J., *United with Eternity: A concise guide to the monuments of Medinet Habu*, Cairo: American University in Cairo Press, 1980.
38 Siliotti, A., op. cit., p. 161.

Chapter 3

Classical gardens
1400 BC–500 AD

History and philosophy

Greece

H. J. S. Maine believed that 'except the blind forces of Nature, nothing moves in this world which is not Greek in its origin'.[1] His adulation of Greece is typical of the nineteenth century. Historians now believe that Greek civilisation flourished in the context of Mediterranean-wide flows of trade and civilisation. The Minoans, from Crete, established a maritime kingdom which functioned as a stepping-stone between the already-ancient civilisations of West Asia and the emergent civilisation of mainland Europe. By 600 BC the Greeks had acquired a phonetic alphabet, from the Phoenicians, and were familiar with the Egyptian use of stone for sculpture and for building temples. The defeat of the Persians at Marathon in 490 BC led to a surge of confidence, and Pericles' leadership, from 444 to 429 BC, saw Greek civilisation reach a climax.

But Classical Greece did not enjoy settled times of the kind which favour garden-making. Though its plains were rich and its seas convenient for summer navigation, Greece did not lend itself to the centralisation of power. It had high mountains, steep valleys and rocky islands. Cities were well able to maintain their independence and were as often at war with each other as with invading armies. People therefore lived in walled towns for safety. The hill of Acrocorinth, inhabited for some 5,000 years, was impregnable as a fortress but no place for a garden culture. Farmers commuted from walled towns to the fields and enjoyed a countryside where, in peaceful times, they could escape the closeness of city life. Pastoralism and the joy of being a 'happy husbandman' were celebrated in prose and poetry. Flowers were loved and garlands made.

Religion was a bond between warring city states. In the early days, Greek gods were symbolised by natural objects, including plants and animals. Later, they took human forms and a pantheon of gods was assembled. With Zeus as father of the

3.1 The city of Acrocorinth, on this hill, had a well but was unsuited to garden-making, for obvious reasons

3.2 The Acropolis of Athens is the most famous classical landscape. Places with caves, springs and particular groupings of hills were regarded as sacred, leading to the placement of altars, statues and temples

family, they were believed to live on Mount Olympus in Northern Greece. Many gods symbolised concepts and forces of nature. Homer and Hesiod explained their roles and relationships. Gods were more powerful than men but had human characteristics – and, like humans, they appreciated gifts. The places with which they were associated became sacred. According to Vincent Scully:

> All Greek sacred architecture explores and praises the character of a god or a group of gods in a specific place. That place is itself holy and, before the temple was built upon it, embodied the whole of the deity as a recognised natural force . . . Therefore, the formal elements of any Greek sanctuary are, first, the specifically sacred landscape in which it is set, and, second, the buildings that are placed within it.[2]

Temenos, the Greek word for a sanctuary, has the literal meaning 'cut out' (i.e. from the landscape).[3] Sanctuaries were marked by boulders, cliffs or walls and used for ceremonies and animal sacrifices. Temples housed cult statues, not congregations. Altars were located out of doors so that smoke could drift to the realm of gods. The most sacred landscapes, taken by Scully to symbolise the anatomy of the Earth Mother, had horned hills and pure springs arising from deep caves. Important sanctuaries became walled compounds with temples and treasuries (a little like Victorian cemeteries). There is some evidence that sanctuaries in Greece had ornamental planting and 'the adornment of temple precincts with groves was also common practice in Roman Italy'.[4] In Athens, planting pits and irrigation channels have been found beside the Temple of Hephaistos (Figure 1.16).[5] Pausanias (*c.* 160 AD) observed that

3.3 The Temple of Apollo in Delphi has an altar, beyond the columns, overlooking a landscape that was sacred for ages before the Temple was built

3.4 The Sacred Lake at Delos may have been near a sacred grove. Both features would have had a particular significance on such a small, dry, windy, sun-baked island

in the sanctuary at Gryneum, in Ionia, 'there is a most beautiful grove of Apollo, with cultivated trees, and all those which, although they bear no fruit, are pleasing to smell or look upon.'[6] A palm tree has been planted in the Sacred Lake on Delos, which, following Egyptian precedents, is likely to have had a sacred grove. The sanctuary was dedicated to Apollo as god of wisdom, awe and divine distance. Sanctuaries were also places where traders and leaders could meet in comparative safety. Christians later described ancient Greek beliefs as 'pagan' – a reference to their association with the countryside (*pagus*, country district).

Ancient Greek religious rituals included 'processions, dances, dramatic performances and athletic contests'.[7] Sanctuaries and gods were associated with particular cities. The sanctuary of Athena was in the centre of Athens, surrounded by a town and a prosperous agricultural zone. Delphi and Delos developed as towns because they were sacred to Apollo. Festivals were held with a presiding deity: Dionysus for the wine harvest, Artemis for hunting, Aphrodite for love. Statues were placed in sacred groves, as they were later placed in gardens. Copies of Greek statues can still be found in most of Europe's historic gardens and even in modern garden centres, often with their Roman names:

3.5 A stampede of Greek gods, at Charlottenburg, Berlin

3.6 Plato is famed for having taught philosophy in a garden: a tiled mural at Evora

- Athena (Roman name, Minerva): goddess of wisdom and learning
- Artemis (Diana): goddess of hunting
- Poseidon (Neptune): god of the sea
- Dionysus (Bacchus): god of wine, feasts and revelry
- Demeter (Ceres): goddess of earth and agriculture
- Aphrodite (Venus): goddess of love and beauty.

Adophrodite's lover was Adonis, a youth of exceptional beauty whose life and death symbolised the cycle of the seasons. Girls sowed seeds in pots to watch the cycle:

> At the festivals of Adonis, which were held in Western Asia and in Greek lands, the death of the god was annually mourned . . . At Alexandria images of Aphrodite and Adonis were displayed on two couches; beside them were set ripe fruits of all kinds, cakes, plants growing in flower-pots, and green bowers twined with anise. The marriage of the lovers was celebrated one day, and on the morrow women attired as mourners, with streaming hair and bared breasts, bore the image of the dead Adonis to the sea-shore and committed it to the waves. Yet they sorrowed not without hope, for they sang that the lost one would come back again.[8]

The Adonis cult is one of the scraps of evidence for plants having been grown in pots within walled towns, possibly on flat roofs and in paved yards.

The intervention of human-like gods in everyday affairs directed philosophers' attention to the nature of the relationship between man and the world. This was of fundamental importance for the advance of European civilisation. Plato, in the *Republic*, argued that the often-immoral behaviour of Homeric gods set a bad example to the young. His Theory of Forms identified abstract concepts, rather than anthropomorphic gods, as the fundamental means of explaining nature. Reason thus came to supplant tradition and belief as the ultimate criterion of truth. Mathematics was developed and applied to practical affairs, including art and architecture. Groves outside cities became significant meeting-places in which to debate relationships between man, nature and the gods. Plato's Academy was in an olive grove, near a sanctuary and a gymnasium. Greeks also took to the sea, studied geography, and established colonies in the lands around the shores of the Mediterranean. They traded in knowledge as well as in material goods.

Alexander the Great was born in Macedonia in 356 BC and extended the Greek empire to India before his death at the age of 33. He and his generals saw the luxurious gardens of West Asia; they found exotic parks, rich palaces and courtyards filled with flowers, succulent fruits and graceful women. They rode home with dreams of sumptuous palace gardens, beyond anything they had known in Greece, and their foot

3.7 The walking place (*peripatos*) in Plato's Academy, outside the walls of Ancient Athens

soldiers struggled home with booty. Towns grew, and as security improved, Macedonian nobles began making palaces outside the town walls. These palaces are thought to be the first European examples of what became a predominant urban form: a country estate on the edge of town, with house, garden, farm and woods.

Greek gardens

Less is known of Greek gardens in its Golden Age than of Egyptian gardens made a thousand years earlier. This is partly because Greek towns were constantly rebuilt and partly because so little Greek painting has survived, except on ceramics. The archae-ological evidence for sculpture having been used in Greek domestic gardens is 'virtually non-existent'.[9] Yet Pierre Grimal felt able to write that 'no garden art worthy of the name could have developed in Rome without Greek influence.'[10] Homer, the father of Greek literature (and thus of European literature), is the key to the paradox.

Homeric courts, gardens and groves

Homer describes three categories of designed outdoor space: courts, gardens and groves. His poems, believed to have been written *c.* 800 BC, were set in the Heroic Age of Mycenae, Troy, Agamemnon and Ulysses. This was the period in which Indo-European invaders, the Dorians, ended the Mycenaean Bronze Age, giving Greece a Dark Age (*c.* 1200–800 BC) and then a Golden Age (*c.* 500–338 BC), in which classical literature, philosophy and architecture flowered. Greek school children learned history from the *Iliad* and *Odyssey*. Virgil (70–19 BC) based the *Aeneid* on these poems and they were learned anew in Roman times and from the Renaissance until the twentieth century. Since Greek civilisation drew upon that of Egypt, Mesopotamia and Crete, it is likely that we are reading, in Homer, about how outdoor spaces were conceived and used in earlier cultures with a less extensive literary heritage. George Steiner wrote that 'what is inescapable in the *Odyssey* is a sense of the Oriental. That the poet knew the Babylonian Gilgamesh epic is probable.'[11] (See p. 82.)

A selection of Homeric references to courts, gardens, groves and forests is given in Table 4. Though few, they may be the most the influential garden comments in the entire corpus of European literature. Sacred groves are associated with gods, altars, offerings, nymphs, burials, caves, springs and the drawing of water. Palace courts are outdoor rooms associated with domesticity (and with threats to domesticity). Productive gardens, outside town walls, are used to grow fruits and flowers. Hunting forests are associated with masculinity, excitement and mountains. Homer's account of the garden of Alcinous – a palace court within a citadel, with productive gardens below its walls – 'became famous in antiquity as the ideal'.[12] Neglecting the Homeric distinctions between types of outdoor space leads to confusion about Greek 'gardens'.

Table 4 Homeric references to groves, gardens, courts and hunting

Sacred groves	
Iliad Book VI	When he had burned him in his wondrous armour, he raised a mound over his ashes and the mountain nymphs, daughters of aegis-bearing Jove, planted a grove of elms about his tomb.
Iliad Book XX	There was not a river absent except Oceanus, nor a single one of the nymphs that haunt fair groves, or springs of rivers and meadows of green grass.
Iliad Book VIII	After a while he reached many-fountained Ida, mother of wild beasts, and Gargarus, where are his grove and fragrant altar.
Iliad Book XXIII	I returned home to my loved native land . . . to sacrifice to you there at your springs, where is your grove and your altar fragrant with burnt-offerings.
Odyssey Book XVII	When they had got over the rough steep ground and were nearing the city, they reached the fountain from which the citizens drew their water. This had been made by Ithacus, Neritus, and Polyctor. There was a grove of water-loving poplars planted in a circle all round it, and the clear cold water came down to it from a rock high up, while above the fountain there was an altar to the nymphs, at which all wayfarers used to sacrifice.
Iliad Book II	Holy Onchestus with its famous grove of Neptune;[13] Arne rich in vineyards; Midea, sacred Nisa, and Anthedon upon the sea.
Odyssey Book VI	As the sun was going down they came to the sacred grove of Minerva[14], and there Ulysses sat down and prayed to the mighty daughter of Jove.
Palace courts	
Iliad Book IX	Nine whole nights did they set a guard over me taking it in turns to watch, and they kept a fire always burning, both in the cloister of the outer court and in the inner court at the doors of the room wherein I lay; [the Penguin translation is 'and keeping two fires burning, one under the colonnade of the walled yard, and the other in the forecourt'[15]] but when the darkness of the tenth night came, I broke through the closed doors of my room, and climbed the wall of the outer court after passing quickly and unperceived through the men on guard and the women servants.
Odyssey Book VI	'If, therefore, you want my father to give you an escort and to help you home, do as I bid you; you will see a beautiful grove of poplars by the road side dedicated to Minerva; it has a well in it and a meadow all round it. Here my father has a field of rich garden ground, about as far from the town as a man's voice will carry. Sit down there and wait for a while till the rest of us can get into the town and reach my father's house. Then, when you think we must have done this, come into the town and ask the way to the house of my father Alcinous. You will have no difficulty in finding it; any child will point it out to you, for no one else in the whole town has anything like such a fine house as he has. When you have got past the gates and through the outer court, go right across the inner court till you come to my mother. You will find her sitting by the fire and spinning her purple wool by firelight. It is a fine sight to see her as she leans back against one of the bearing-posts with her maids all ranged behind her. Close to her seat stands that of my father, on which he sits like an immortal god. Never mind him, but go up to my mother, and lay your hands upon her knees if you would get home quickly. If you can gain her over, you may hope to see your own country again, no matter how distant it may be.'
Odyssey Book XXII	As for Melanthius, they took him through the cloister into the inner court. There they cut off his nose and his ears; they drew out his vitals and gave them to the dogs raw, and then in their fury they cut off his hands and his feet.
Iliad Book XXIV	She went to Priam's house, and found weeping and lamentation therein. His sons were seated round their father in the outer courtyard, and their raiment was wet with tears.

Productive gardens	
Iliad **Book XXI**	As one who would water his garden leads a stream from some fountain over his plants, and all his ground-spade in hand he clears away the dams to free the channels.[16]
Odyssey **Book VI**	You will see a beautiful grove of poplars by the road side dedicated to Minerva; it has a well in it and a meadow all round it. Here my father has a field of rich garden ground, about as far from the town as a man's voice will carry.
Odyssey **Book VII**	Outside the gate of the outer court there is a large garden of about four acres with a wall all round it. It is full of beautiful trees-pears, pomegranates, and the most delicious apples. There are luscious figs also, and olives in full growth. In the furthest part of the garden there are beautifully arranged beds of flowers that are in bloom all year.
Hunting forests	
Odyssey **Book XVII**	This was Argos, whom Ulysses had bred before setting out for Troy, but he had never had any work out of him. In the old days he used to be taken out by the young men when they went hunting wild goats, or deer, or hares.
Odyssey **Book XX**	And indeed as soon as she began washing her master, she at once knew the scar as one that had been given him by a wild boar when he was hunting on Mount Parnassus with his excellent grandfather.
Iliad **Book XXIII**	Achilles was still in full pursuit of Hector, as a hound chasing a fawn which he has started from its covert on the mountains, and hunts through glade and thicket.

3.8 Mount Parnassus is mentioned by Homer as a place with good hunting

3.9 Tiryns was a citadel with a coastline to the south and productive gardens to the north

Homer's words probably relate to the Mycenaean towns of mainland Greece and the west coast of modern Turkey, including Troy, where Homer is thought to have lived. Tiryns and Mycenae, which flourished until the twelfth century BC, are hill-top citadels with Cyclopean outer walls. Gated paths led to outer and inner colonnaded courts of the types described by Homer (only their foundations survive). Tiryns had an inner palace and court, assumed to be the women's quarters, where one could expect to follow the instructions given to Ulysses, to 'go right across the inner court till you come to my mother' (see Table 4 excerpt from *Odyssey* Book VI). Looking over the Argolid Plain from either citadel, seeing productive groves and hazy mountains, one can populate the landscape with rich gardens, sacred groves, satyrs and departing heroes. Physically and conceptually, this was the seedbed of European garden design.

From Tiryns, it is 12 km to Mycenae and 140 km to Athens. Settlements developed into fortified towns as western civilisation trod this path. An acropolis is a town on a hilltop (from *akron*, summit and *polis*, town). The most famous acropolis, in Athens, began as a fortified settlement on a plateau but became a religious sanctuary with a walled town beneath its walls. Caves and springs round the Acropolis became shrines. In the town, houses opened onto paved internal courts for living and working. The courts may have had pot plants and statues but no physical evidence for this survives. Few Greek houses survive, because they were built of mud brick. At Delos, Olynthos and Prienne there are stone houses with small rooms and paved outdoor

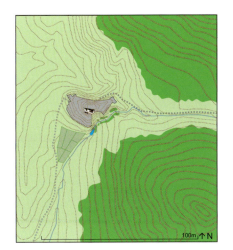

yards. At Delos many of the yards drain to underground cisterns. Towns also had a public space, the *agora*, for meetings and markets. Many of these had roofed colonnades and were planted with trees beneath which philosophers could sit while formulating the concepts which led to the development of western civilisation. In Athens, the Greek *Agora* had colonnades attached to individual buildings (*stoas*) and the Roman *Agora* had a continuous colonnade enclosing an outdoor space.

Sanctuaries

In classical times the Greeks continued to use land outside fortified towns in the ways described by Homer. Individual landowners commuted to their fields and gardens, some only 'as far from the town as a man's voice will carry'. Young men hunted in the woods. A good spring 'from which the citizens drew their water' often became a sacred grove with a 'fragrant altar'. One could find 'a beautiful grove of poplars by the road side dedicated to Minerva' with 'a well in it and a meadow all round'. Both Greeks and Romans had sanctuaries for Isis, wife of the Egyptian god Osiris. Conjecture provides the following development path for classical sanctuaries:

- The idea of a sacred grove derives from the religious sanctuaries of Egypt (see Chapter 2) and Mesopotamia (see Chapter 4)
- Springs and caves were especially valued, because the water was fresh, pure, cool, healthy – and miraculous
- Groves associated with a presiding god were marked by boundary stones
- Offerings were made at outdoor altars
- Statues were erected and treasuries built to house gifts
- Shelters built to protect statues became temples
- Boundary walls provided security
- Sacred groves outside walled towns became places of resort for exercise (gymnasiums) and rest (stoas)

3.10 Palace courts have been excavated at Mycenae: plan of the citadel, with conjectured forests on the hills and gardens in the valley. One can envisage the other types of open space described by Homer: hunting grounds on the hills, a sacred grove in the valley, and productive gardens beneath the walls

3.11 Mycenae: looking out from the palace to the Argolid Plain

3.12 Mycenae: looking up the valley to the palace walls, with probable garden sites on the valley floor

3.13 Greek houses on Delos consisted of small rooms with paved yards, opening onto narrow streets (left). There were productive gardens outside towns (a vegetable garden on Mykonos, right)

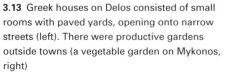

3.14 The Roman Agora in Athens was a peristyle court, used as a meeting and market place

3.15 An artist's reconstruction of a sacred grove in Athens. The temple housed a statue of a god. It was not a place for congregation, prayer or ritual

- Philosophers and students came to these places to experience nature and learn about the natural order.

This evolution took place as the Homeric Age developed into the Classical Age. Two-and-a-half thousand years later the sacred grove evolved into the English landscape garden, laying the basis for the natural parks and national parks of modern times.

The sacred groves of Greece had some characteristics in common with modern sports parks and universities. Olympia had the most famous games and Delphi the most famous oracle. Sparta emphasised physical prowess, Athens, intellectual skills. Glistening young men, clad only in oil, exercised in groves which became known as gymnasiums (from the Greek *gumnos*, naked and *gumnazo* exercise). Wrestling schools (known as *palaestra*, from the Greek *palaio*, to wrestle) were established, stadiums were built for races, and shelters, baths and specialised yards were added. Open colonnades provided for summer shade and winter exercise. A gymnasium had moral, therapeutic and educational roles. Plato wrote that for a citizen to tell a lie is 'a more heinous fault than for the patient or the pupil of a gymnasium not to speak the truth about his own bodily illnesses'.[17]

Philosophers seeking conditions more suited to calm reflection than those offered by a public *agora* turned to quiet groves. The most famous 'grove of Academe', the Academy, was founded by Plato among the olive trees some 2 km from the walls of Athens and named after the hero Academus. Aristotle, himself the 'pupil of a gymnasium', was peripatetic: he paced his grove while discoursing on philosophy. The grove was called The Lyceum, from (*Lukeion*, an epithet of Apollo) and may have been near the site now occupied by Syntagma Square.[18] There are fine examples of gymnasiums at Delphi, Delos, Ephesus and Pergamon. European high schools continue to be known as Gymnasiums, Academies, and Lycées.

In Ancient Greece, the curriculum centred on gymnastics, poetry, rhetoric and music. Theophrastus is famed for teaching philosophy in a garden and wrote in his will: 'The garden and the *peripatos* and the buildings adjoining the garden I leave to my

friends, named below, who wish to pursue the study of philosophy together'.[19] Diogenes described Epicurus as 'A philosopher and a great lover of gardens'.[20]

Grottoes

> Water is best, and gold, like a blazing fire in the night, stands out supreme of all lordly wealth.[21]

Essential for life on earth, water is most pure and most fascinating when it springs from rock. Caves were associated, as in Neolithic times, with the Earth Mother, Gaia. According to Hesiod, life originated from a union between Gaia and the sky god, Uranus. Nymphs lived in caves, Naiads lived in springs, Dyrads lived in trees. Zeus was said to have been born in a cave grotto (still a tourist attraction on Crete). Thus, caves were places in which one could reflect on the creation and make offerings to the gods. Marble statues of gods, dwarfed by the powers of nature, were placed in small temples outside caves, and wreaths were laid.

There are sacred caves at Eleusis, Delos and in the cliffs round the *peripatis* of the Acropolis. Hadrian was initiated into the mysteries at Eleusis and, at his Villa outside Tivoli, made both a sacred cave and an underground room overlooking the Canopus.

Since we return to Mother Earth at the end of our days, a grotto could also be a gateway to the underworld, ruled by Hades. Caves were used for burials.[22] Offerings

3.17 The sanctuary at Olympia became famous for its games

From Greece to Rome, the grotto evolved from a sacred cave to a garden feature.

3.18 (top left) The grotto on Delos

3.19 (top right) The Caves of Apollo and Pan on the north slope of the Acropolis

3.20 (second left) Hadrian's cave at Tivoli

3.21 (second right) The so-called Villa of Tiberius at Sperlonga

3.22 (third left) The sacred cave at Eleusis

3.23 (third right) The Castalian Spring at Delphi

3.24 (bottom) Grotto Ninfa Egeria

3.25 (bottom) Fountain of Peirene at Corinth

3.26 This relief, found on the north slope of the Acropolis, is thought to have come from the Cave of Pan and to show Pan with three nymphs

3.27 Relief showing a young man placing a wreath at a temple beside a sacred tree

were made for proud mothers, newborn children and departed spirits. Later, the Romans used family shrines in gardens for these purposes. Cicero planned a shrine to his daughter, Tullia, who died in February 45 BC, 'to ensure her apotheosis'.[23]

Caves might also house medicinal waters. The Romans valued mineral springs and hot springs. Bath, in England, has a sacred healing spring dedicated to Minerva from which water bubbles out at 46°C.

Caves are the origin of garden grottoes: the word 'grotto' derives from the Greek *kruptos* (hidden), as does the word 'crypt'. James Lovelock's Gaia Hypothesis[24] may yet produce a new interest in the design of grottoes.

Hellenistic gardens

Greek cities lost their independence to Macedonia in the Hellenistic Period (332–330 BC) but saw their culture influence a geographical area extending from France to India. Macedonia had the land, wealth and security which garden-making requires. Gothein sees this period as 'the beginning of garden craft in Greece' and notes that 'the raids of Alexander the Great opened to the Greeks the whole of Asia and all its elaborate garden culture'.[25] Longus' story, *Daphnis and Chloe*, written *c.* 200 BC, linked gardens to romantic adventure in the country outside towns.

Macedonians placed residential palaces in 'a commanding position above the city'[26] with 'enclosed gardens in the courtyards'.[27] Owners wanted to view their fields and gardens, together with the city, its temple and gymnasium. The Romans were

3.28 The hot spring at Bath was dedicated to Minerva (Athena)

3.29 The Roman villa at Oplontis (on the coast near Herculaneum, south of Naples) has a peristyle and a gymnasium-style pool (see plan, p. 77)

profoundly influenced by this approach to residential planning and used it in all parts of their empire – and one need look no further than the suburbs of the nearest modern city to find estates of this type. They may still have outdoor courts, flower-filled urns, ornamental ponds, vegetables, woods and, if the owner can afford it, a gymnasium with a hot tub and a cold pool. Great cities with gardens began to develop throughout the Hellenistic world, including Byzantium, Syracuse, Naples, Marseilles, Pergamum, Alexandria and Antioch.

Rome

> The glory that was Greece
> And the grandeur that was Rome.[28]

The glory of Greece lay in original thought, the grandeur of Rome in the vast application of new ideas to the establishment of a civil society under the rule of law. The two cultures were linked, first by Greek settlements in Italy, later by Roman annexation of the Hellenistic empire. In the period of Greek supremacy, Italy had a relatively primitive society and 'no Homer or Hesiod to tell us what men, their dwellings, and their altars, were like'.[29] The Romans undertook wholesale adoptions of Greek religion, philosophy, art, architecture and literature. Initially, they even wrote in Greek. The lack of information on pre-Roman Italy is consequential upon the lack of literature, though something is known of the Greek-influenced Etruscan culture.

Legend dates the foundation of Rome to 753 BC. A Republic was declared in 509 BC and the rapid expansion of Roman power began. The Etruscans were defeated by 273 BC. Carthage and Greece became provinces in 146 BC. Spain fell in 133 BC, Syria in 64 BC and Egypt in 30 BC. Rome became the great cultural melting pot. The rule of Augustus, from 27 BC to 14 AD, saw the end of the Republic but also the birth of a new Golden Age. In Roman eyes it stood comparison with Greece's Age of Pericles. Suetonius records Augustus' justifiable boast that 'I found Rome built of sundried bricks; I leave her clothed in marble'.[30] The Empire was marked by extravagant excess with intervals of reform, brilliance, chaos, madness and terror. Hadrian, a Spanish emperor who ruled from 117 to 138, loved peace, architecture, religion and gardens. His *pax Romana* allowed extensive building, including the construction of Rome's most famous temple, the Pantheon, and his own palace-garden at Tibur (Tivoli), 40 km from Rome. Rome was sacked by Alaric in 410 and the last Western Emperor was deposed in 476. The western historical tradition, heavily influenced by Gibbon, still tends to view the Empire's decline and fall as a triumph of 'barbarism and religion' over a classic period of political, intellectual and religious freedom.[31]

The old religion of Italy was more practical than that of Greece but equally polytheistic. Strict observance of ritual (*pietas*) fostered a sense of awe (*religio*) and was expected to result in divine assistance of a timely and practical nature. Mythology, ethics and metaphysics had minor roles. The spirit (*numen*) which inhabits a place and the procreative power (*genius*) which sustains a family were revered. A spirit associated with a particular place, such as a river or wood, was known as a *genius loci* ('genius of the place'). Providing rituals were observed, the Romans were a tolerant people and found it easy to import religious and other ideas from around the empire. The Greek pantheon of personal gods was renamed and adopted, as were Greek statues and the idea of making sacred ways and temples. Caesars became gods, as pharaohs had been. Statues were erected to the *genius* of the nation and its leader.

Small gardens contained shrines. Every substantial house in Pompeii had such a place, used for offerings and prayers to mark family events. The Isis and Mithras cults, deriving from Egypt and Persia respectively, brought sacramental and mystery elements to Roman religion. Public temples were erected in towns, following Etruscan and Greek precedents. The Roman Forum had a shrine to Janus. London had a temple to Mithras. *Lares* (Roman household gods) were honoured at property boundaries and crossroads. The circular temple of Vesta, goddess of the hearth, contained an eternal fire attended by the vestal virgins. Hercules had a Great Altar in Rome's cattle market. Ancestors were revered and entombed. Statues were imported from Greece and, having lost their original significance, were used as ornaments on the Palatine and in lavish villa gardens.

Roman civilisation established garden design as a pan-European art. Those famous Roman roads helped transmit knowledge throughout the Empire. Near towns, roads were lined with tombs, so that they resembled sacred groves. Roman governors made gardens wherever they were posted. This required a vocabulary, which also travelled. The Latin word *topiarius* is the name for a workman employed in an ornamental garden. In modern English 'topiary' is used to describe clipped hedges of the

3.30 (left) The Sacred Way through Rome's Forum, now thronged with tourists, led past temples and public buildings

3.31 (right) A re-created Etruscan temple in the garden of the Villa Giulia, Rome

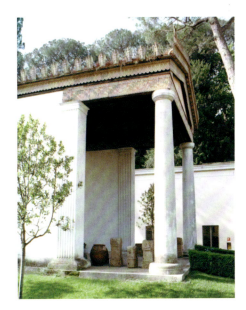

3.32 (top left) The vestal virgins had a garden beside the Sacred Way in the Roman Forum

3.33 (top right) Pagan shrines placed in gardens resembled the wayside shrines still found in Roman Catholic countries

3.34 (right) The Romans spread gardening skills throughout Europe: model of a Roman gardener at Fishbourne, Sussex

type loved by Roman gardeners. *Hortus* was the Latin word for a planted garden, as opposed to a paved court, and the art of growing plants in gardens came to be described, in English, as horticulture. '*Hortus conclusus*' is used by garden historians to mean 'an enclosed garden' in contrast to an open estate garden.

Roman garden types

Too few Roman gardens have been excavated but those that have, appear to show that gardens throughout the Empire made little response to local conditions: regularity was always the Roman way. One can, however, distinguish between palace gardens, villa gardens and town gardens.

Palace gardens

The word 'palace' derives from the Palatine Hill, where the Emperors Augustus, Tiberius, Caligula and Domitian built palaces and gardens, creating a citadel with open courts. 'The predominating characteristic of the whole palace was the close association – interpenetration is a better word – of house and gardens. The great open courtyards, with their fountains and flower beds, were evidently used as out-of-doors saloons merging, through porticoes and colonnades, into the rooms themselves.'[32] One can reconstruct their character, in one's imagination, by remembering Pompeii (see p. 75) and strolling through the archaeological wastes of the Palatine.

The house of Augustus (now called the House of Livia) confirms this interpretation. There are paintings on the walls and Suetonius wrote that 'In summer [Augustus] slept with the bedroom door open, or in the courtyard beside a fountain, having someone to fan him'.[33] Augustus watched official games from the palace windows, walked in the grounds and played hand-ball with his friends.[34]

Nero's Golden House resembled a modern dictator's palace or billionaire's retreat. It was 'a fanciful landscape garden' with a lake, open glades, groves, statues and numerous buildings: a '*rus in urbe*'.[35] After his death, the Coliseum was built on the site of Nero's 'sea' and the Imperial Baths on the site of his Golden House, a fragment of which has been excavated.

Villa gardens

Emperors also had country villas, which can be viewed as privatised Greek sanctuaries and gymnasiums. The best surviving example is Hadrian's Villa at Tivoli. Though this site was pillaged over the centuries, enough survives to reveal the immensity of the emperor's ambition. In our terms it was a museum complex, a sculpture park, a sports park, a banqueting suite and a vast pleasure ground with water features and a sacred cave. The amazing opulence of villas may have contributed to the decline and fall of the Roman Empire. Pliny believed that the taste for large estates ruined Italy; Gibbon observed that: 'The rich and luxurious nobles, . . . as long as they were indulged in the enjoyment of their baths, their theatres, and their villas, . . . cheerfully resigned the more dangerous cares of empire to the rough hands of peasants and soldiers.'[36]

The urban villa (*villa urbana*) was 'urban' in the sense of 'civilised' rather than in terms of location. It was a comfortable place for a comfortable life. Scipio's villa at Liternum, often cited as the earliest example of the type, was made with detailed knowledge of Egyptian civilisation. Urban villas with luxurious rooms and gardens have been excavated in and around Herculaneum, with the Villa at Oplontis the most fully

3.35 A model of the Palatine Hill with the Circus Maximus in the foreground. Several garden courts, with colonnades and fountains, have been excavated

3.36 Looking across the Circus Maximus, still used as an exercise ground, to the Palatine

3.37 A view from the roof of Nero's Golden House to the Coliseum built on the site of his private lake

3.38 Hadrian planned and built the largest and most opulent of all Roman Villas. Much survives – but the planting arrangement on this model is entirely speculative

3.39 'Villa di Plinio' at Laurentum. The identification of the site has been challenged, but Pliny's Laurentian Villa had this character and was near this spot

researched example. The suburban villa (*villa suburbana*), as the name suggests, shared characteristics with urban and rural villas. Seaside villas were popular on the coasts south of Rome and Naples.

The rural villa (*villa rustica*), exemplified by Virgil's retreat in the Sabine hills, was a farm which provided some urban refinements, but with less extravagance. Virgil shared the Greek dream of a happy husbandman retreating to a life of rural bliss, caring for his bees, his grapes and his soul. It was a pagan dream, in the religious sense and also in the physical sense that it was set 'in a country district'. Cato used *hortus* to mean the part of a farm which was watered and used for growing vegetables.[37]

The freshest picture of how villa gardens were used comes from the letters of Pliny. His uncle, Pliny the Elder, had written a treatise on natural history. Pliny the Younger had a villa at Laurentium on the coast south of Rome. The following quotations reveal his delight in villa life. He speaks of modesty but was immensely rich.

Table 5 Pliny's references to gardens

Letter III To Caninus Rufus	How is that sweet Comum of ours looking? What about that most enticing of villas, the portico where it is one perpetual spring, that shadiest of plane-tree walks, the crystal canal so agreeably winding along its flowery banks, together with the lake lying below that so charmingly yields itself to the view?
Letter XXIII To Gallus	You are surprised that I am so fond of my Laurentine, or (if you prefer the name) my Laurens: but you will cease to wonder when I acquaint you with the beauty of the villa, the advantages of its situation, and the extensive view of the sea-coast . . . My villa is of a convenient size without being expensive to keep up. The courtyard in front is plain, but not mean, through which you enter porticoes shaped into the form of the letter D, enclosing a small but cheerful area between. These make a capital retreat for bad weather, not only as they are shut in with windows, but particularly as they are sheltered by a projection of the roof. From the middle of these porticoes you pass into a bright pleasant inner court, and out of that into a handsome hall running out towards the sea-shore . . . The gestatio [an avenue for exercise either on horseback on in a horse-drawn vehicle] is bordered round with box, and, where that is decayed, with rosemary: for the box, wherever sheltered by the buildings, grows plentifully, but where it lies open and exposed to the weather and spray from the sea, though at some distance from the latter, it quite withers up. Next the gestatio, and running along inside it, is a shady vine plantation, the path of which is so soft and easy to the tread that you may walk bare-foot upon it. The garden is chiefly planted with fig and mulberry trees, to which this soil is as favourable as it is averse from all others. . . . Before this enclosed portico lies a terrace fragrant with the scent of violets, and warmed by the reflection of the sun from the portico, which, while it retains the rays, keeps away the north–east wind; and it is as warm on this side as it is cool on the side opposite: in the same way it is a protection against the wind from the south–west; and thus, in short, by means of its several sides, breaks the force of the winds, from whatever quarter they may blow.
Letter LII To Domitius Apollinaris	You descend, from the terrace, by an easy slope adorned with the figures of animals in box, facing each other, to a lawn overspread with the soft, I had almost said the liquid, Acanthus: this is surrounded by a walk enclosed with evergreens, shaped into a variety of forms. Beyond it is the gestatio laid out in the form of a circus running round the multiform box-hedge and the dwarf-trees, which are cut quite close. The whole is fenced in with a wall completely covered by box cut into steps all the way up to the top. On the outside of the wall lies a meadow that owes as many beauties to nature as all I have been describing within does to art; at the end of which are open plain and numerous other meadows and copses.
Letter XXXIX To Mustius	I shall perform an act both of piety and munificence if, at the same time that I build a beautiful temple, I add to it a spacious portico; the first for the service of the goddess, the other for the use of the people. I beg therefore you would purchase for me four marble pillars, of whatever kind you shall think proper; as well as a quantity of marble for laying the floor, and encrusting the walls. You must also either buy a statue of the goddess or get one made; for age has maimed, in some parts, the ancient one of wood which stands there at present.

Town gardens

Roman town houses, unlike their Greek predecessors, had sufficient outdoor space for horticulture. This is best seen at Pompeii and Herculaneum. Drawing on Etruscan, Samnite, Greek and West Asian precedents, they provide much of our knowledge about Mediterranean garden culture. To a greater degree than anywhere else in the ancient world, these towns give one the sense of visiting a garden in the owner's temporary absence.

Pompeii is a walled town with stone-paved streets, raised sidewalks, stepping stones and deep grooves cut by chariot wheels. When it rained, the streets must have been torrents of liquid filth. Pompeian dwellings were windowless for reasons of security, privacy and stench-avoidance. Many of the internal courts were surrounded by colonnades (peristyles) which acted as ventilated corridors between rooms and courts. Vitruvius specifies the correct proportions for such colonnades as follows:

3.40 Though over 2,000 years old, Herculaneum resembles the towns found in Mediterranean countries today. Volcanic debris secured its preservation

Peristyles, lying athwart, should be one third longer than they are deep, and their columns as high as the colonnades are wide. Intercolumniations of peristyles should be not less than three nor more than four times the thickness of the columns. If the columns of the peristyle are to be made in the Doric style, take the modules which I have given in the fourth book, on the Doric order, and arrange the columns with reference to these modules and to the scheme of the triglyphs.[38]

Within the scheme of proportions described here with such precision, garden courts were richly coloured, well-planted and intensively used. The *atrium* was a family space in which the central portion of the roof was open to the sky. Larger dwellings had a paved enclosure surrounded by a row of columns, known as a *peristyle*, which integrated indoor and outdoor space. The *peristyle court* was used for outdoor living and entertaining. Even larger town houses also had a rectangular space at the rear, known as a *hortus*, or *xystus*, used for vegetables and flowers. Sometimes the *hortus* became a private pleasure garden with statues, grottoes and topiary, as shown in the figures on p. 69.

Shrines to family gods (*aediculae*), were decorated with mosaic tiles. When dedicated to a nymph the shrine was known as a *nymphaeum*. Fountains were fed by lead pipes, which permitted larger and more complex designs than could be achieved by earlier civilisations that had used terracotta ducts. Grottoes were made on large

3.41 The atrium, in the foreground, was a small paved court which allowed light and water to enter. There is a peristyle beyond the atrium (Pompeii)

3.42 A peristyle graden with fresco painting used to increase its apparent size (Pompeii)

estates, the best surviving examples being those associated with Tiberius, including the Blue Grotto on Capri and the wonderful seaside grotto at Sperlonga.[39]

Marble, bronze and terracotta statues were extensively used in Roman gardens. Cicero wrote of a villa that had 'Greek statues, soon to be gardeners themselves, offering their ivy for sale'.[40] His own villa was at Pompeii,[41] where the statuary was of 'garden centre' quality; the Oplontis villa, which is thought to have belonged to Nero's wife Poppaea Sabina, had much better statues.[42] The typical subjects for garden sculpture were Greek gods: Ceres, Venus, Flora, Bacchus, Cupid, Diana, Apollo and Pan. Sundials were decorative and functional. Paintings of garden scenes on the walls of colonnades enlarged the apparent size of peristyle courts: frescos show men in togas, dancing girls, fountains, trellis-work, pergolas, nymphs, flowers, children playing games and parents offering wine to visitors. Birds were prized, whether painted, wild, caged, cooked or as a source of manure.[43] Fish were kept in pools and eaten.

Stone seats and tables were used for outdoor meals. They may look harsh without cushions but most of us would find more comfort in a small Roman court than in the typical suburban garden of today. They were secure and sheltered. Plants were grown: for the kitchen (e.g. cabbage, parsley, fennel), for making medicines (mustard), for making drinks (grapes, apples, medlars), for feeding bees and keeping them healthy (rosemary), for making perfumes (roses), for making garlands (ivy, myrtle), for decoration (acanthus, periwinkle, laurel, rose) and for shade (pine, cypress).

3.43 A fresco painting of a fountain, fence, flowers and birds, with a small garden shrine (Pompeii)

3.44 A hortus, or xystus, was an ornamental area used to grow fruit and vegetables (Pompeii)

Byzantine gardens

Byzantium was founded as a Greek colony, *c*. 660 BC, at the point where Europe meets Asia. Emperor Constantine named the city Constantinople and it became capital of the Empire in 330 AD. Greek remained the official language and Constantinople became the most resplendent city in the western hemisphere. Its prosperity enabled its classical traditions, art and books to survive the Dark Ages of Northern Europe. To travellers from the benighted north, Constantinople was amazingly large, beautiful, bureaucratic and opulent. Like a pot of gold, it attracted visitors – and invaders. The latter were resisted with strong walls, sea power, military governors and occasional help, or hindrance, from the Crusaders. By the eleventh century, Constantinople was little more than a fortified zone but within its walls the old tradition of garden-making survived and prospered. Indeed, the city survived as an outpost of Graeco-Roman culture until it fell to the Turks in 1453; it is now Turkish-speaking Istanbul.

Constantine ordered the building of the first church of St Peter in Rome (330), on the site of the present St Peter's. It had a large peristyle entrance court, originally planted as a garden and later paved. The great domed church of St Sophia in Constantinople, begun in 532 and known as Hagia Sophia, also had a peristyle court. The Palace of the Emperors had a garden which included the site of what is now the Blue Mosque and extended from the Hippodrome to the Sea of Marmara. These projects influenced the Islamic gardens discussed in the next chapter.

MacLagan writes of the Emperor's Palace in Constantinople that 'efforts can be made to reconstruct the sites of some of the main features, but nothing will fully recreate the courtyards and the fountains, the corridors and vaulted chambers'.[44] The only area to have been excavated has 'a large cloistered courtyard' with floor mosaics. Information on other Byzantine gardens is mainly literary and difficult to interpret. Irrigation channels encouraged the planting of flowers and shrubs in rectangular blocks. Paths appear to have alternated with lines of vegetation and water. Changes of level were utilised to create terraces and sunken gardens. Flowers (rose, violet, lily, iris, narcissus) were cherished, as were evergreens (ivy, myrtle, box, bay), fruit trees (apple, pear, pomegranate, fig, orange, lemon, grape) and shade trees (pine, palm, oak, elm, ash). As in Pompeii, the sounds of birds, fountains and rustling leaves was much appreciated.

Since Byzantine culture continued to flourish through the Dark Ages, future archaeology is the best hope of discovering more about this great missing link in garden history. Venice was the port through which Byzantine influence entered Europe: as Robert Byron argued in 1942, Byzantium was the source of many Renaissance ideas.[45]

Types and examples

Sacred groves

Use: Believing that gods intervene in daily life, people bestowed gifts, either in thanks or in the hope of securing good fortune. In Greece, sacred landscapes were places to make offerings and sacred precincts were defined by boundary stones or walls. A place for discussion, education and exercise, such as a gymnasium or *palaestra*, would often be created near a sanctuary. As places of spiritual enlightenment, Greek sanctuaries are related to the temple compounds of Egypt. Roman sanctuaries were usually within towns and shrines were often within gardens.

Form: The first sacred grove was probably an altar in a wood, perhaps near a cave with a clear spring. Groves were later furnished with a statue of the god and architectural elements, including temples and treasuries to contain gifts. Important groves became walled sanctuaries. There is textual and archaeological evidence that sanctuaries had ornamental planting. A settlement might develop near a sanctuary or a sacred grove might be established outside an existing town. A *palaestra* might have a roofed colonnade (peristyle) enclosing a rectangular court and a stadium for races. There were rooms, pools and lines of trees. Seats were placed in alcoves (exedra). Philosophers used the gardens for teaching.

3.45
Greek santuary

Classical Athens 400 BC

The Acropolis was a fortified settlement in Mycenaean times, when the caves and springs below its cliffs became the shrines which were later dedicated to Apollo and Pan. In classical times the plateau became a sanctuary and a walled city developed beyond the cliffs. The Walls of Themistocles enclosed what Herodotus called a 'wheel-shaped city'. It had a diameter of less than 2 km, with one spoke extending to the port of Piraeus and another, the Sacred Way, proceeding west through the Agora to the Dipylon Gate and Eleusis. Academy Way branched north, through Kerameikos, to Plato's Academy. Trees grew in the Agora and the surrounding buildings had roofed colonnades (stoas). The three famous gymnasiums with their associated schools of philosophy, and gardens, were outside the city walls, as were the city's productive gardens. Structures were placed in relation to landform and, since statues, columns and walls were painted, there was no distinction between the arts which later became sculpture, painting, architecture, landscape architecture and town planning. Knowledge (*techne*) of their practice was simultaneously technical and artistic.

> In the end the forms in the landscape there cannot be spoken of in terms of action or of time. Because of this it is possible they cannot be spoken of at all . . . There is only being and light.[46]

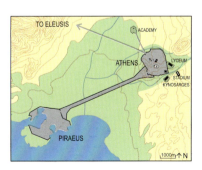
3.46 Classical Athens

Delphi 400 BC

Delphi occupies an extraordinary site: a cleft in the mountains beneath the horned cliffs of Phaedridae. As Vincent Scully has observed, 'entrance by land into the citadel of Parnassos involves passage between horned cliffs . . . a fastness is being penetrated.'[47]

The Sanctuary of Apollo is 600 m above the Gulf of Corinth and 1855 m below the peak of Mount Parnassos, although neither of these features is visible from the site. The aim, as with coquetry, was both to conceal and reveal. Apollo was the god of divine distance, light and wisdom. A sacred spring, dedicated to the Earth Mother, Ge, in Mycenaean times and now known as the Castalian Spring, was probably the landscape feature which led to the site being chosen. Even today, local drivers stop to fill their bottles with its health-giving water. Delphi was known as the centre of the world, its navel (*omphalodes*), a place of encounter between humankind, wisdom and Earth. Delphi remains a place of calm mystery, and – like a human navel – a reminder of the original creative drama. The Oracle's pronouncements were swathed by smoke from the sacred fire and profoundly ambiguous. The walled sanctuary contained a Temple of Apollo, an altar, a Sacred Way lined with Treasuries and a Theatre. Outside lay a Stadium, a town and a second Sanctuary, dedicated to Athena Pronaia. After the Acropolis in Athens, Delphi is the most visited archaeological site in Greece.

> Delphi must therefore have seemed to the Greeks the place where the conflict between the old way, that of the goddess of the earth, and the new way, that of men and their Olympian gods, was most violently manifest.[48]

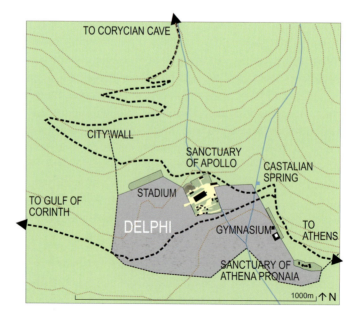

3.47 Delphi

Olympia 400 BC

Olympia lies amongst wooded hills and near two rivers, the Alpheus and Kladeos, which have changed course. The oldest remains at Olympia date from 2000 BC. Religious ceremonies later took place in a walled compound known as the *Altis*, or sacred grove of Zeus. It contained the Temples of Zeus and Hera and the Prytaneum with its perpetual fire and fountain. The inner Sanctuary of Pelops was a walled garden with trees and statues. Phidias the sculptor had his workshop at Olympia.

The Olympic Games were famed throughout the Hellenic world and held every four years from the eighth to the fourth century BC. A covered entrance used by athletes led from the *Altis* to the oldest stadium in Greece. Spectators sat on earth embankments, which survive. They probably slept in tents or in the open. Only men and unmarried girls were allowed to watch the athletics. Horse races took place in the hippodrome, south of the stadium. The Romans continued to use the Olympic site after their conquest of Greece in 146 BC. Nero built a small palace between the stadium and the hippodrome. Athletic facilities, sculptures and baths later became features of Roman villa gardens. Visitors may find it interesting to compare Olympia with the sports stadiums and park designed for the 1972 Munich Olympic Games (see p. 280). Great sports parks, whether from the fifth century BC or the twentieth century AD, demonstrate a harmony of intellectual, artistic and physical concerns. The modern series of Olympic Games began in 1896.

> [The Spartans] were the first to play games naked, and to rub themselves down with olive oil after their exercise. In ancient times even at the Olympic games the athletes used to have coverings for their loins.[49]

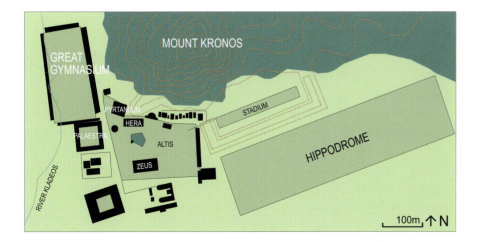

3.48 Olympia

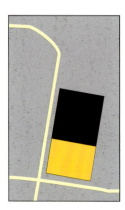

3.49
Greek
court

3.50
Roman
court

Classical courts

Use: Private outdoor space within walled cities was valuable: emperors had palaces with outdoor courts; wealthy nobles had houses with outdoor rooms; poor families lived in single, windowless rooms with doors opening onto narrow streets. In Greece, domestic courts were unroofed living rooms. In Roman Italy, courts were also used to house shrines, to grow plants and to display statuary and fountains. In towns, courts were enclosed by high walls for security and privacy.

Form: The Romans made three types of courtyard and some homes had one of each:

- a yard (*atrium*) in the centre of the dwelling giving access to other rooms and to the street. The atrium served as a lightwell and ventilation shaft. It was paved or slightly recessed to catch rainwater, which was stored in a cistern;
- a colonnaded yard (*peristyle*) ornamented and used as an outdoor living and dining room. The roofed colonnade on the perimeter functioned as a corridor giving access to bedrooms and living rooms. The enclosed yard had pools, fountains, shrubs, flowers, statues and a small shrine. Evergreens were favoured: bay, myrtle, oleander, rosemary, box and ivy. In flowers, the Romans liked the rose, iris, lily, violet, daisy, poppy and chrysanthemum;
- a horticultural space (*xystus*) was used for flowers and vegetables and might be decorated with statues, a pavilion and a water feature.

Delos 400 BC

The best-preserved examples of Ancient Greek domestic housing are at Olynthos in Northern Greece, Delos, an Aegean island, and Priene, in modern Turkey. At Delos, most of the houses consist of a room and an outdoor court, often with a cistern under the paving to store collected rainwater. The grandest houses at Delos have mosaic paving and elegant peristyles. They do not have any horticultural space but it is possible that plants were grown in terracotta pots.

> The better houses had a considerable number of rooms, some of them spacious and richly adorned, built round an elegant peristyle court . . . But there were many poorer simpler houses. The site on which most of the houses were built is irregular, sloping and rocky; and the narrow streets are very irregular.[50]

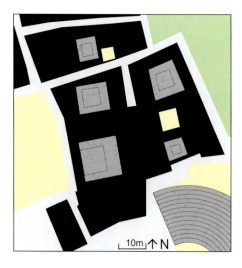

3.51 Houses at Delos

Pompeii 79 AD

Pompeii lay 10 km from the summit of Mount Vesuvius and 3 km from the sea. The eruption of Vesuvius in 79 AD was a disaster for the citizens of Pompeii but a boon for garden historians, since about 500 domestic gardens were preserved under the volcanic ash. The 1942 bombing of Pompeii, the post-war usage by tourists and the urbanisation of the Bay of Naples have been unmitigated disasters. Nevertheless, much survives and more is excavated every year. Pompeii had been a Greek city and a Samnite city before it was colonised in 80 BC by another Italian tribe, known to us as the Romans, and many Pompeian buildings pre-date the Roman conquest. Wall paintings (frescoes) were used to make small gardens appear large, often with a trellised fence in the foreground suggesting a barrier between the real garden and the garden painting.

> You then pass through the ancient streets; they are very narrow, and the houses rather small, but all constructed on an admirable plan, especially for this climate. The rooms are built round a court, or sometimes two, according to the extent of the house. In the midst is a fountain, sometimes surrounded by a portico, supported on fluted columns of white stucco; the floor is paved with mosaic.[51]

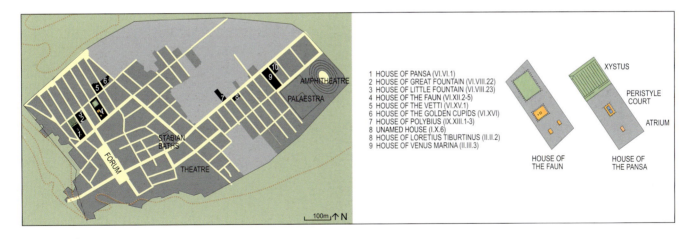

1 HOUSE OF PANSA (VI.VI.1)
2 HOUSE OF GREAT FOUNTAIN (VI.VIII.22)
3 HOUSE OF LITTLE FOUNTAIN (VI.VIII.23)
4 HOUSE OF THE FAUN (VI.XII.2-5)
5 HOUSE OF THE VETTI (VI.XV.1)
6 HOUSE OF THE GOLDEN CUPIDS (VI.XVI)
7 HOUSE OF POLYBIUS (IX.XIII.1-3)
8 UNAMED HOUSE (I.X.6)
8 HOUSE OF LORETIUS TIBURTINUS (II.II.2)
9 HOUSE OF VENUS MARINA (II.III.3)

3.52 Pompeii

Palace of the Emperors, Palatine Hill, Rome 100 AD

Several Roman emperors built palaces on the Palatine Hill. Deriving from earlier palaces in Macedonia, Mycenae, Crete and West Asia, the Palace of the Emperors was a complex of interpenetrating buildings, roofed colonnades and outdoor courts. The courts were the grandest gardens in Rome. Small patches of mosaic paving and the brilliant quality of the sculpture in the Palatine Museum give an idea of their ancient quality. Most of the statues were copies of Greek originals found in sanctuaries. The surviving courts are among the most easily identifiable features among the ruins of the Palatine: Augustus Court, in the House of Livia; the oval Nymphaeum in Augustus' palace, originally one of a pair; the Labyrinth Court, occupied by a maze-like garden feature; the Fountain Court, now viewed from above, with semicircular inner canals surrounded by a rectangular outer canal; the two Peristyle Courts, one of which contained a pool and fountain; the large Hippodrome, which may have been used as a stadium.

In the centre was an octagonal fountain, on the west side there were grottoes, where cool water flowed continuously into ornamental basins. Parallel with the great building devoted to the Emperor's private life stood a second [court], facing south and descending by two terraces to the edge of a huge amphitheatre. You can still see that in the upper peristyle was a rectangular sheet of water, in the middle of which stood a little temple joined to the land by a small bridge with seven arches. Round the lower peristyle was a maze of rooms, staircases and gardens, whose ornate fountains are now bare of the statues and white marble that once decorated them.[52]

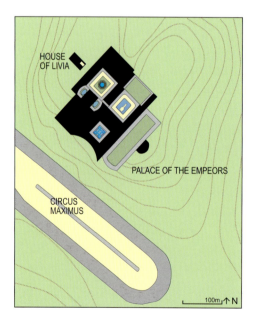

3.53 The Palatine Hill, Rome

Villas

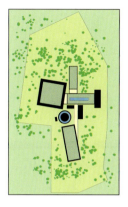

Use: Roman villas were palatial estates with dwellings, gardens and numerous subsidiary buildings. Both rural and urban villas were built. Their owners used them as places in which to relax, exercise, entertain friends and conduct pleasant business, – or, in Hadrian's case, run an empire. The villa incorporated elements from earlier outdoor enclosures: a domestic courtyard, a gymnasium (sacred grove), a temple garden (many emperors were considered gods) a park and grottoes.

Form: Buildings and gardens were grouped together within protected enclosures. The spaces adjoining individual buildings were axially planned but, by the standards of Renaissance villas, the lack of an overall controlling axis is surprising: structures were scattered like boxes on a table. The villa format was a persistent one: in southern Spain (*c.* 1250) the Moors built palatial villa-gardens, planned like their Roman predecessors but also drawing upon the eastern tradition of paradise gardens.

Poppaea's Villa at Oplontis 79 AD

A once-luxurious villa with extensive gardens has been excavated since 1974, with great attention paid to the gardens by Wilhelmina Jashemski. Soils were investigated to find planting positions and replanting has taken place. There were internal courts, a swimming pool and an external garden. Ownership of the villa is attributed to Nero's wife, Poppea, who was said to keep 500 asses to supply milk for her bath. The site is now hemmed in by cliffs of volcanic debris topped by ugly apartment blocks.

> Most important is the way in which the villa opened to the countryside, not only utilising the magnificent views of the sea and mountains but also looking out on its own parklike setting, embellished with formally planted exterior portico gardens that beckoned the visitor from both land and sea.[53]

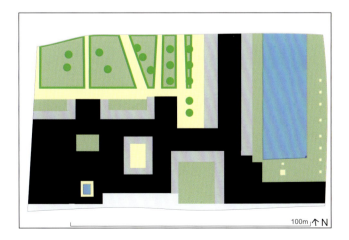

100m N

3.55 Poppaea's Villa at Oplontis

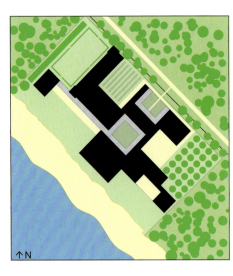

3.56 'Villa di Plinio', Laurentum

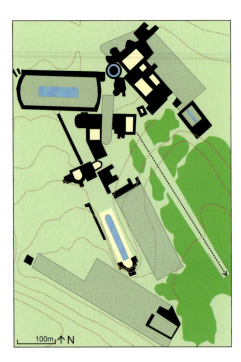

3.57 Hadrian's Villa, Tivoli

Pliny's Villa 100 *AD*

Pliny the Younger wrote about a seaside villa at Laurentum, east of Rome, and many authors have drawn garden plans based on his words. A possible site was found at Castel Fusano in 1935 and excavated. It is still marked on local maps as Villa di Plinio, and although it does not fit Pliny's words, it is of a similar age and type. The site contains features that evoke Pliny's words: sea air, sandy soil, a spring, pine trees and myrtles. In 1982 Ricotti argued that the real site of Pliny's villa is on the other side of Laurentum.

> He writes of garden practices, site planning, plant materials, and the enjoyment of leisure at that time. Pliny owned five hundred slaves divided between his town house and his two country places.[54]

Hadrian's Villa 130 *AD*

This is the most complete estate to have survived the fall of Rome. It is a larger and immensely grander version of the type of layout praised by Pliny the Younger. Though ruthless, Hadrian was a great emperor, an intellectual, a poet and a designer. His nickname 'Greekling' reflects his admiration for the source of Roman culture. Hadrian was probably born in Spain, near Seville, and, having travelled more extensively than any of his predecessors, made eclectic garden features representing places he had visited. In Greece, he could see the villas made after Alexander the Great's conquest of the East. In Egypt he could admire the 'land of wonders'. His own villa made lavish use of water. The Canopus is a pool representing a branch of the Nile, used for summer banquets and dedicated to Serapis, an Egyptian who was licentiously worshipped by the Romans. The Maritime Theatre is ringed by Ionic columns and a circular canal. A lyceum and academy were inspired by Athens. A stadium, like the hippodrome which Pliny describes, was used for state banquets. The Piazza d'Oro is a peristyle garden which was lavishly adorned with fountains and statuary. Hadrian also had baths, theatres, libraries and apartments. Most of the sculpture was removed during the Renaissance, when the site was excavated, but enough remains to enable visitors to appreciate the magnificence of a Roman imperial garden. Some spaces are enclosed and some give views over the surrounding countryside. The villa had six grottoes and occupied an area 1 km in length and 0.5 km in width.

> Hadrian's villa was really not a villa at all: it was a small town that had to contain everything that a great capital could offer. It was a dream translated into solid stone and marble, a miracle created by an emperor who was also an architect and an artist.[55]

Notes

1 Maine, H. J. S., *Village Communities in the East and West,* Rede Lecture, Oxford, 1876.

2 Scully, V., *The Earth, the Temple and the Gods*, New Haven: Yale University Press, 1962, p. 1.

3 Carroll, M., *Earthly Paradises: Ancient gardens in history and archaeology*, London: British Museum Press, 2003, p. 124.

4 —— op. cit. p. 69.

5 Scully, V., *op. cit.,* p.189.

6 Pausanias, 1.21.7. Gryneum is in Asia Minor (modern Turkey).

7 Tomlinson, R. A., *Greek Sanctuaries*, London: Paul Elek, 1976, p. 16.

8 Frazer, J. G., *The Golden Bough*, London: Macmillan & Co, 1890, Ch. 32.

9 Ridgeway, B. S., 'Greek antecedents of garden sculpture' in *Ancient Roman Gardens*, Dumbarton Oaks: Harvard University Press, 1981, pp. 7–28.

10 Grimal, Pierre, *Les Jardins Romains*, 2nd edn, Paris: Presses Universitaires de France, 1969, p. 63.

11 Steiner, G., and Fagles, R., *Homer: A collection of critical essays*, New Jersey: Prentice Hall, p. 10.

12 Farrer, L., *Ancient Roman Gardens*, Stroud: Sutton Publishing, 1998, p. 5.

13 Rieu, E. V. (transl.), *Homer: The Iliad*, Penguin Books, 1966, p. 53, has 'from holy Onchestus, with Poseidon's sacred wood'.

14 Lemprière, J., *A Classical Dictionary,* Routledge, 1904, p. 90: 'Athena, the name of Minerva among the Greeks; and also among the Egyptians, before Cercops had introduced the worship of the goddess into Greece (Pausanias 1, c, 2).

15 Rieu, E.V., op. cit., p. 173.

16 ——, op. cit., p. 387, has 'like a gardener who is irrigating his plot by making a channel in among the plants with fresh water from a spring'.

17 Plato, *The Republic*, Book 3.

18 Wycherley, R. E., *The Stones of Athens*, Princeton: Princeton University Press, 1978, p. 228.

19 ——, op. cit., p. 227.

20 ——, op. cit., p. 231.

21 Pindar, *Olympian Odes,* I.

22 Miller, N., *Heavenly Caves: Reflections on the garden grotto*, London: George Allen & Unwin, 1982, Ch. 3.

23 Littlewood, A. R., 'Ancient literary evidence for the pleasure gardens of Roman country villas', in MacDougal, E. B. (ed.), *Ancient Roman Villa Gardens*, Dumbarton Oaks: Harvard University Press, 1987, pp. 7–30.

24 Lovelock, J., *The Ages of Gaia*, 1989.

25 Gothein, M-L., *A history of garden art*, London: J. M. Dent, 1928, Vol 1 p. 72

26 Nielsen, Inge, *Hellenistic Palaces, Tradition and Renewal*, Denmark: Aarhus University Press, 1994, p. 81.

27 ——, op. cit., p. 96.

28 Edgar Allan Poe, *To Helen*, 1831.

29 Böthius, A., *The Golden House of Nero*, Ann Arbor: University of Michigan, 1960, p. 3.

30 Suetonius, *TheTwelve Caesars*, London: Penguin, p. 66.

31 Gibbon, E., The *Decline and Fall of the Roman Empire*. The phrase is from the final chapter (LXXI).

32 Masson, G., *Companion Guide to Rome*, Woodbridge: Companion Guides, 1998, p. 52.

33 Suetonius, op. cit., p. 95.

34 ——, op. cit., p. 96.

35 Böthius, A., op. cit., p. 105.

36 Gibbon, E., *Decline and Fall of the Roman Empire,* Vol. 1, Ch. 10, Part III, 1776.

37 Farrer, L., *Ancient Roman Gardens,* Stroud: Sutton Publishing, 1998, p. 14.

38 Vitruvius, *The Ten Books on Architecture*, Transl. Morris Hickey Morgan, 1914, p. 179.

39 Ricotti, E. S. P., 'The importance of water in Roman garden triclinia', in MacDougal, E. B. (ed.), op. cit., pp. 135–84. Ricotti believes Tiberius visited Sperlonga but was not the owner.

40 Littlewood, A. R., op. cit.

41 Ibid.

42 de Caro, S., 'The sculptures of the Villa of Poppaea at Oplontis: a preliminary report', in E. B. MacDougal (ed.), op. cit., pp. 77–134.

43 Littlewood, A. R., op. cit.

44 MacLagan, M., *The City of Constantinople*, London: Thames & Hudson, 1968, p. 67.

45 Byron, R. and Rice, D. T., *The Birth of Western Painting: A history of colour, form and iconography, illustrated from the paintings of Mistra and Mount Athos, of Giotto and Duccio and of El Greco*, London: Routledge, 1930.

46 Scully, V., op. cit., p. 185.

47 ——, op. cit., p. 108.

48 ——, op. cit., p. 109.

49 Thucydides, *History of the Peloponnesian War, c.* 400, transl. Rex Warner, Penguin Books, 1954, p. 38.

50 Wycherley, R. E., *How the Greeks Built Cities*, New York: W. W. Norton & Co., 1976, p. 194.

51 Jones, F. L., *The Letters of Percy Bysshe Shelley*, Oxford: Clarendon Press, 1964, Letter of 26 Jan. 1819.

52 Grimal, P., *Rome of the Caesars*, London: Phaidon, 1956, p. 24.

53 Jashemski, W. F., *Gardens of Pompeii*, 1979, p. 314.

54 Berral, J. S., *The Garden*, London: Thames & Hudson, 1966, p. 41.

55 Ricotti, E. S. P., op. cit., p. 174.

Chapter 4

West Asian and Islamic gardens
500 BC–1700 AD

History and philosophy

Chronologically, the ancient gardens of West Asia belong in Chapter 1. They are dealt with here, after Egypt, Greece and Rome, because of their subsequent relationship with Islamic gardens.

West Asia extends from India to Egypt and Turkey. The climate is predominantly hot and arid. Rainfall is spasmodic. There are long droughts and short floods. The mountains are harsh and dry, cold in winter and baked in summer. River valleys and coastal plains are lush and fertile. The region was occupied by migrants from Africa (*Homo erectus*) about 1–2 million years ago and by a later wave of African migrants (*Homo sapiens*) about 100,000 years ago.[1] Until *c.* 10,000 BC men lived by hunting and gathering. Agriculture probably began with herding animals and with the harvest of wild grain by settled communities in North–east Africa and South–west Asia. Larger settlements, the world's first towns, developed between 5000 and 3500 BC, probably in Anatolia and the East Mediterranean coastal plain. Urbanisation spread to the Persian Gulf and beyond. West Asia became a region of many languages, many cultures, many invasions and the first military empires known to history. Greek and Roman civilisation, as discussed in the previous chapter, grew from these roots.

The area between the rivers Tigris and Euphrates was named Mesopotamia by the Greeks and Al-Jazira ('The Island') by the Arabs. It is now within Iraq and geographers use 'Mesopotamia' to describe the whole area traversed by the rivers. The Sumerians, who built irrigation canals, towns, temples and ziggurats, probably migrated to the river delta from the Iranian highlands (*c.* 4000 BC). They were succeeded by the empires of the Akkadians (*c.* 2380 BC), Babylonians (*c.* 1900 BC), Assyrians (*c.* 1400 BC) and others. Innovations introduced by these peoples included the wheeled cart, cavalry, sailing boats, the plough, smelting and writing.

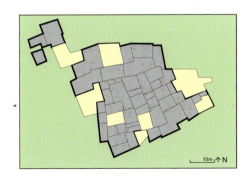

4.1 Catal Huyuk 6250–5400 BC. Houses abut one another; there are no streets and access to dwellings was from roof level. The courts may have contained animals

Early settlements were compounds with circular huts, as they remained in North Europe until Roman times. Later settlements were rectangular and had yards which probably contained plants and animals. Gods, represented by statues, were given temples with estates to supply produce. Temple stores were protected from floods by being raised up and were used to support the population in lean years. Priests were trained in cooking, baking, singing and other important arts. Temple compounds were open-air sanctuaries with artificial platforms and stepped ziggurats.

The *Epic of Gilgamesh*, written in Akkadian and one of the world's oldest literary works, has references to gardens and groves. It was found on clay tablets in the palace library of Nineveh, the Assyrian capital *c.* 1400 BC. Gilgamesh had ruled, at Uruk, 1,000 years earlier. The Epic tells of a warrior king who lived in a city where one-third of the land was garden or orchard. The gardens may have been yards near houses or fenced areas on the edge of the settlement. The Epic tells of Gilgamesh's friendship with Engidu and how they set forth together against Humbaba, guardian of the cedar forest. In the forest, 'the ways are straight, and the path is wrought fair. They see the cedar mount, the dwellings of gods, the sanctuary of the Irnini.' This grove compares with the religious sanctuaries and groves of Egypt, Greece and Rome. It was described as a perfect place: 'With crystal branches in the golden sands, in this immortal garden stands the Tree, with trunk of gold and beautiful to see'.[2]

Enclosed outdoor space became associated with perfection. Our word 'paradise' derives from the Persian word *pairidaeza* meaning 'an enclosure'. The first *pairidaeza* were probably animal and fruit gardens. But the word was taken into Greek to mean 'heaven' (the state of supreme bliss). It was later used by Christians for the Garden of Eden, the home of God and the place where virtuous people go after death. In the Koran, paradise is a reward for the faithful, symbolised by an ideal garden with shade, fruits, fountains and pavilions.

Mesopotamia

When first settled, parts of Mesopotamia were marshy, with lush vegetation. Other areas, lacking water, were open, dry and flat. Irrigating the dry land and clearing the wet land produced excellent conditions for agriculture and settlement. Luxuriant swamps provided additional food and fuel. Hunting, previously a necessity, became the royal sport which it remained ever after: exciting, spectacular and a way to learn the martial arts of riding a chariot and throwing spears at moving targets. It is reasonable to suppose that hunting reserves were first made when areas of wild vegetation became scarce. In Mesopotamia they may have been islands in swamps or fenced enclosures. Gothein remarks with justice that 'the Asiatics have the credit of being the real inventors of the park. A park must have a fence and can only come into being in a well-wooded land'.[3] Carved reliefs and ancient texts, recording their owners' heroic deeds, are the evidence for ancient hunting parks: there are no plans or archaeological remains. By the first millennium BC, Assyrian kings had large hunting parks outside their cities. King Tiglath-pileser I (1115–1077 BC) proclaimed:

4.2 Islands in the River Tigris (at Samarra) give an idea of Ancient Mesopotamia's marshy landscape

I carried off from the countries I conquered, trees that none of the kings, my forefathers, have possessed, these trees have I taken, and planted them in mine own country, in the parks of Assyria have I planted them.[4]

His boast reveals this type of park to be the ancestor of modern botanical and zoological gardens. Their role was not scientific in modern terms but it was linked to curiosity about the natural world. King Ashurnasirpal (833–859 BC) provided the city of Kalakh, which he rebuilt, with plant and animal collections. King Sargon II (721–705 BC), also of Assyria, laid out parks in conjunction with his new capital at Khorsabad. King Ashurbanipal (668–626 BC), who also assembled the first organised library in the Middle East, had the boast 'I killed the lion' inscribed on the walls of Nineveh. Lions, tigers, bears and cheetahs were native to West Asia but became scarce as agriculture intensified. Hunting remained popular and a seventeenth-century traveller recalled Xenophon's remark (c. 400 BC) that 'children in Persia are taught three things: to tell the truth, draw a bow and mount a horse', adding, 'this is really their whole practice to this very day.[5]

Literary and archaeological records of ancient cities reveal that buildings were arranged about internal courts. Tree pits have been found in and around the temple of the god Ashur, built by Sennacherib (705–681 BC).[6] Small houses had small courts; large palaces had great courts. Sumerian cities were dominated by religious temples, Assyrian cities by royal palaces. By the second millennium BC, palaces had protective walls incorporating rooms, and a variety of courts. Some courts were used for official functions and others had ornamental pools and flowers associated with women and children. Outward-looking gardens were also made. The most famous palace gardens of this type are the so-called Hanging Gardens of Babylon. The following two Greek accounts, written some 400 and 600 years after the construction of these gardens, are assumed to draw on earlier records:

Taking the Euphrates River as the centre, there was a wall with many big towers along it around the city. The wall was three hundred and sixty stades long [approx 65 km], according to Ctesias of Cnidos, but Cleitarchus and some of those who later crossed over to Asia with Alexander recorded that its length was three hundred and sixty-five stades long . . . The so-called hanging garden was by the Acropolis, built not by Semiramis but by a later Syrian king for one of his concubines. For they say that she was of Persian race and that, as she missed the meadows in the rolling hillside, she asked the king to imitate the distinctive features of her native Persia by means of a wonderfully designed garden.[7]

The Hanging Garden is in the shape of a square, each side four hundred feet long. It is surrounded by arched vaults which are positioned, one after the other, on cube-shaped boxes. The hollow boxes are filled with earth so that the biggest trees can grow in them. The slabs themselves, the vaults and the arches are all made from baked brick and bitumen. To get to the very top of

4.3 A hunting scene from Ashurbanipal's 'paradise'. Note the palm trunk and grape vine

4.4 The Temple of Ashur 705–681 BC was in a sacred grove. Actual planting pits are shown in dark green and conjectural planting pits in light green. Canals brought water to the trees

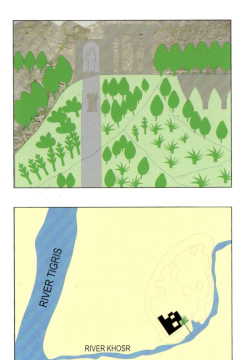

4.5 (top) An analysis of the British Museum relief showing what is believed to be the famous Hanging Gardens

4.6 (above) A hypothetical reconstruction, placing the garden shown on the British Museum relief onto the hill of Kuyunjic at Nineveh

the roof there are staircases and, running alongside these, there are spiral screws. Those whose job it was continually brought up water to the garden from the Euphrates through these screws . . . The garden is on the bank of the river.[8]

Dalley[9] has argued that the 'Hanging Gardens of Babylon' were in Nineveh, not Babylon, and that they belonged to Sennacherib, not Nebuchadnezzar. Sennacherib's palace was on the south–west section of the hill at Kuyunjic, opposite modern Mosul. Visitors to London can see a bas-relief of these gardens in the British Museum;[10] the illustrations (4.5 and 4.6) show a diagrammatic version of the bas-relief and a placing of this design at Nineveh . The hanging gardens were on the slopes of an acropolis. Water was brought up by rotating screws in wooden pipes. The position of the gardens on the slopes of a fortified town resembles that of the gardens on the Ramparts of Prague Castle, in the Czech Republic (Figure 5.18).

The Hanging Gardens of Nineveh, if this was their true location, were enclosed by a wall and supported by vaulted arcades. Within the outer wall were pavilions, flights of steps, trees, flowers, vegetables and channels with flowing water. The gardens were for walking in safety or for sitting in a pavilion, catching the breeze and admiring the view. They were not 'outdoor rooms' for cooking and eating: this was the role of palace courtyards. The Nineveh gardens had fruits and vegetables; a self-selected fruit tastes better than any other. They were closer to what is described below as a paradise garden than to the town gardens of Ancient Egypt. Pavilions became central features of Persian paradise gardens. Nineveh was burned by a Persian army in 612 BC and lost its importance. But a number of Mesopotamian outdoor space uses have survived into the modern world. They include hunting, collecting plants, collecting animals, growing choice fruits and holding parades.

4.7 Schönbrunn, outside Vienna, claims to have the world's oldest collection of exotic animals. Cheetahs were found in West Asia

4.8 Deer in an ancient hunting ground: Richmond Park, London

4.9 Orange trees in a Renaissance garden: the Boboli Gardens, Florence

4.10 A parade of boy soldiers in the Tivoli Gardens, Copenhagen

Persia

Persia had the good fortune, and the ill fortune, to bestride the Silk Road used by caravans and armies journeying between Europe and Asia. Parts of the plateau were under cultivation by 3000 BC, by Indo-European peoples. The name Iran ('Land of the Aryans'), adopted in 1935, reflects its ancient history. The Achaemenid Empire, founded by Cyrus the Great (c. 590–529 BC) and ruled by Darius I (550–486 BC), absorbed the cultures of Mesopotamia and, at its height, extended from Greece to India.

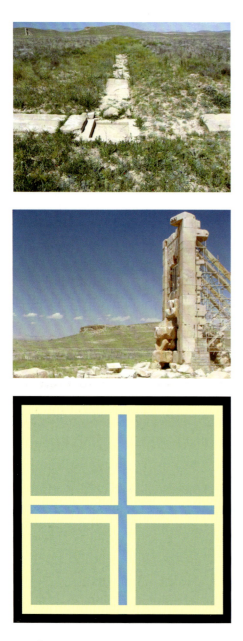

4.11 Pasargadae, Iran, has a Zoroastrian fire temple and the oldest surviving stone water courses

4.12 The origin of the classic 'four square' (chahar bagh) may never be determined. It could be up to 5,000 years old

Zoroastrianism was the religion of pre-Islamic Persia. Its founder, Zarathustra, was a pastoralist whose tribe suffered from marauding nomads. This gave him a keen sense of the contrasts between good and evil, order and chaos, desert and cultivation. The good man was seen as one who 'looks after his cattle and tills the soil in peace and neighbourliness'.[11] Nothing is known of Zoroastrian art but the stark contrast between order and chaos remained at the heart of Persian and Islamic garden design. Depending on whether their lives had been good or evil, Zoroastrians believed that people would reach paradise by crossing the Chinvat Bridge, or pitch into the hellish Abode of Lies.

Unlike Mesopotamia, Persia is predominantly mountainous and riverless. Buildings were therefore made of stone rather than mud brick. Water was highly valued and regarded as the source of life, symbolising the life force in Persian art. Irrigation canals and underground canals (quanat) made cultivation possible in desert regions. Surface channels were used for irrigation. The chahar bagh (quadripartite garden, from *chahar*, four, and *bagh*, garden) was an enclosed space divided into parts by water channels. Its origin is unclear.

Ceramic representations of the world divided into four quarters date from c. 4000 BC[12] and are thought to relate to the Buddhist mandala. The Book of Genesis recounts that 'a river went out of Eden to water the garden and became four heads'. The Koran describes the four rivers which flow through paradise as being of water, of milk, of wine, and of honey.[13] Wilber believes the four-square plan 'was crystallized at least as early as the Sassanian period (224–642 AD)'.[14] The oldest plan of a four-square religious space with crossing paths was drawn c. 820 by a monk who had visited Constantinople.[15] The oldest literary use of chahar bagh to mean a garden dates from c. 900 AD[16] and the oldest surviving four-gardens date from c. 1200 AD.[17] To conclude: the idea is old and its evolutionary path uncertain. Figure 4.12 shows a classic four-square pattern as it appeared in the second millennium AD.

Cyrus the Great had a palace within an enclosing wall at Pasargadae in the province of Fars from which Persia took its name. Stone watercourses defined the space between the main buildings. There were two pavilions and a fire temple. The garden had a geometrical plan, not unlike what became the classical Persian garden plan. Eating and other social activities would take place in the garden pavilions, catching the breeze but protected from the sun. As in the Hanging Gardens of Nineveh, the garden was a place to be viewed from a pavilion or in which to take an occasional walk. When necessary, the garden could be used as a military encampment, with the watercourses playing a functional role. Gardens contained fruit trees, including pomegranates and cherries, and also flowers, including lilies and roses. In 330 BC Alexander the Great saw Cyrus's tomb at Pasargadae, which survives, and recorded that it then stood in an irrigated grove of trees.

Darius I built a new ceremonial capital at Persepolis and an administrative capital at Susa. He favoured the Zoroastrian religion and consequently, towns were geometrically ordered. Emissaries from Darius's far-flung empire came to honour their king.

At Persepolis, ceremonial steps are inscribed with processions of tribute-bearers and lines of pointed trees. It is likely that avenues of trees marked the processional approaches to the palace. Susa was a walled and moated city, built for the defence of a settled society. Sardis, at the western end of Persia's royal road, near Izmir in modern Turkey, had another palace and garden. Cyrus the Younger called it a pairidaeza in 407 BC and told a Greek: 'All these things, Lysander, I measured out and ordered myself, and there are some of them that I even planted myself'.[18] Regularity was the outstanding characteristic of ancient Persian gardens and of subsequent Islamic gardens. Geometry was fused with a near-mystical love of trees, water and flowers – especially roses, which remain an important crop in Iran to this day.

After the Greek (Selucid) empire fell in 138 AD, Persia was ruled by Parthians and then Sasanians until 637 AD. Both were Persian tribes and what little remains of their gardens indicates that they were influenced by local traditions, not by Greece or Rome. As well as being places to be entertained by musicians, poets and dancing girls, Persian gardens were places to sleep on hot nights with slaves to fan the air and ward off insects. Attuned to environmental conditions, these cool, opulent and scented enclosures were protected by walls over 4 m high. After the seventh century AD, they were admired and imitated by Persia's Arab and Mongol conquerors.

Islam

Islam is a religion and a way of life. It transcends social, racial and national groups while having a pervasive influence on art, architecture and garden design. The flowering of Islamic culture after the sixth century drew upon many visual and literary sources, including Mesopotamian, Persian, Hebrew, Greek, Roman, and, later, Indian civilisations. As Gothein remarks, 'Scarcely ever has a people shown such aptitude for adopting foreign civilisation, and setting a common stamp on every art'.[19]

> God be their guide from camp to camp: God be their shade from well to well;
> God grant beneath the desert stars they hear the Prophet's camel bell.
> And son of Islam, it may be that thou shalt learn at journey's end
> Who walks thy garden eve on eve, and bows his head, and calls thee Friend.[20]

The word 'Islam' comes from the Arabic for 'surrender' (i.e. to the will of God). Islamic philosophers, influenced by Plato and Aristotle, argued that the more perfect something is, the more beautiful it is and the more pleasure it yields. God's beauty, being the most perfect, therefore yields the most pleasure. Artistic creativity was a means of communicating the truths of religion and philosophy, not an end in itself. Works of art aspiring to perfection give pleasure by aiding the contemplation of divine truth. Making a perfect place, or paradise, became the aim of Islamic garden design. Representation of the human form was forbidden as idolatrous, a ban which stimulated invention in other directions: abstract geometry and flowers were used decoratively, and mathematics was used to develop complex patterns.

4.13 At Persepolis, in Iran, the processional route is ornamented with tribute bearers and cypress trees

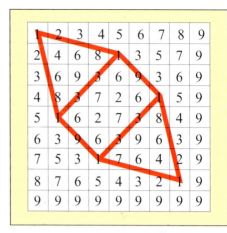

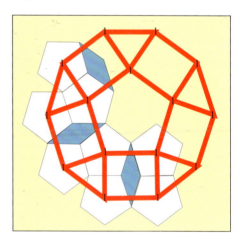

4.14 Islamic pattern design was rooted in mathematics

Islam originated in Arabia and spread as armies swept north to Syria and west to Egypt, joining with other pastoral peoples who were often Arabic speakers. The Byzantine Empire was pushed back and, in 642, the Persian Empire overrun. Arab armies advanced through the Roman towns of North Africa. Spain was partially occupied in 714. The Abbasid Caliphate had its centre in Iraq and its capital in Baghdad. Damascus, said to be the world's oldest continuously inhabited city, enjoyed a period of greatness. The Umayyad Caliphate moved its centre to Spain and its capital to Cordoba. Genghis Kahn created an Islamic empire in Central Asia and Babur established the faith in India. Becoming a world religion, Islam established a cosmopolitan, city-building, civilisation which retained its identity over 1,000 years and, from east to west, across 9,000 km. The gardens made under its influence will be reviewed in four sections (necessarily simplified along broad geographical and chronological lines):

- Middle East
- Spain
- Central Asia
- India and Pakistan.

Many Islamic gardens have decayed or vanished: although buildings and planting have deteriorated, in many cases they could be restored – and paving and tiles often survive in better condition. Since the princely families which made these gardens have been dispossessed, old paintings and traveller's tales have an important role in the history of Islamic gardens.

4.15 Islamic gardens often suffer from low maintenance budgets: grass-cutting in Lahore Fort

The Islamic Middle East

Mosque and madrasah courts

The importance of the spiritual motive in making enclosed outdoor space in Egypt, Greece and Rome was discussed in Chapters 2 and 3. Judaism, Christianity and Islam originated in the area now known, in the West, as the 'Middle East'. Of these, the religion most associated with making gardens was Islam. The Prophet Muhammad was born in Saudi Arabia *c*. 570 AD and died in 632 AD. His family worked in the ancient shrine of Mecca, a place-name which means 'sanctuary'. Mecca functioned as a town where nomadic and desert-living people could meet in safety to trade and to settle disputes. Muhammad's own garden, in Medina, became the first place of Islamic worship. His dwelling, following ancient precedents, was a partly-roofed enclosure. Basing their account on the Koran, Ettinghausen and Grabar describe this space:

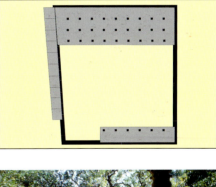

> It consisted of a square of sun-dried bricks approximately fifty metres to the side. On the east of the southern part of the eastern wall were rooms (nine of them by 632, when Muhammad died) for the Prophet's wives. On the southern and northern sides short colonnades (*suffa*) of palm trunks supporting palm branches were erected after complaints about the heat of the sun in the court. On each of the other sides was a door; the southern wall had become the *quibla* [the place towards which prayer is directed – Mecca]. The Prophet used to lean on a lance near the northern edge of the southern colonnade to lead prayer and deliver sermons.[21]

Mosques thus began as open spaces where men could gather in prayer, equal before God. It is wrong to think of the 'mosque' as the roofed part of the space. Early mosques were open courts with deep colonnades on the *qibla* (Mecca-facing) side and shallow colonnades on other sides. The roofed part of the court was a hypostyle, a roof supported by a grid of columns. Early mosques are likely to have been surfaced with beaten earth. Later mosques were paved or, as in Cordoba, planted with trees. Mosques were not residential, as Muhammad's house had been. But in Damascus and other Islamic cities they were often next to the governor's palace and closely associated with his administration. Because of the interest in geometry, and the concern for perfection explained above, later mosque courts were often perfect squares.

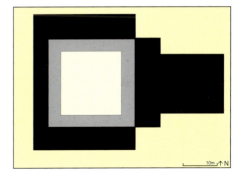

As the mosque-form developed, courts became more independent. In plan they resemble Roman peristyle courts and Christian cloisters. Large central domes, inspired by the church of Hagia Sophia in Constantinople, became a dominant feature of mosque buildings after the Turkish conquest of 1453. Courts then took on an increasingly separate spatial identity, defined by arcades. This created what many people think of the as the classic mosque form: a domed building, a minaret and a paved court with a fountain.

4.16 Plan of Muhammad's garden in Medina, based on Ettinghausen and Grabar. Nothing is known of its (possible) vegetation

4.17 The courtyard of the former mosque in Cordoba is planted with orange trees

4.18 Id der in Syria has one of the oldest mosque courts

4.19 The outdoor courts of mosques and madrasahs are among the finest examples of religious gardens; Emam Mosque, Isfahan

4.20 Madrasah–ye Chahar Bagh, Isfahan

4.21 Madrasah–ye Kahn, Shiraz

A visitor to Kesh in 1403 wrote: 'The whole of this mosque with its chapels is very finely wrought in blue and gold, and you enter it through a great courtyard planted with trees round a water tank. Here daily by the special order of Timur the meat of twenty sheep is cooked and distributed in alms'.[22] In *madrasahs* (theological colleges), courts for teaching and prayer are designed and used as religious gardens. In urban open spaces, courts and fountains were used, like paradise gardens, for rest and contemplation. Fountains in mosque courts were used for ceremonial ablutions. In later centuries the planning of mosques became geometrically integrated with the maidan, a public space. Shah Abbas (1587–1628) made Isfahan into a capital city with an intricate complex of gardens which Khansari *et al.* rightly compare with the urban structure of Versailles and Washington, DC.[23] Its development continued in the eighteenth century, with the Madrasah–ye Chahar Bagh. The Central Avenue, known as the Chahar Bagh is now a depressingly busy traffic artery.

Palace gardens

Having been predominantly nomadic in their homeland, the Arabs settled in the lands they conquered and employed local craftsmen, both Byzantine and Persian, to build palace homes. The design traditions came together under the geometrical discipline of what became Islamic art. Carpets were always important to nomads and the relationship between carpets and gardens was of particular interest. Khansari and Moghtader give an account of the Arabs' arrival in Persia:

> When in 637 Arab warriors swept down upon the famous palace of the Sasanian kings of Persia, they found treasures beyond compare, chief among them a carpet in the form of a garden. So curiously wrought was this carpet, so fairytale-like its splendor, that it surpassed all those wonders of the Sasanians that so delighted the chroniclers: the hundreds of elephants, the thousands of slaves and concubines, the vaults heaped with gold and silver . . . The carpet, modelled on a living royal garden, was 2,940 square feet (84' x 35' or 324 sq yds), with a ground, scholars believe, of heavy, woven silk. As in the real garden, this ground was divided into flower beds by water channels and intersecting paths. To represent earth, the royal craftsmen used threads of gold; the water in the channels was shimmering crystal; and the gravel in the paths was pearl. In the geometric plots were trees whose trunks and branches were shaped from silver and gold and whose fruits were precious gems. More jewels formed the flowers among the trees.[24]

The archaeological remains of early Arab palaces show them to have been semi-fortified buildings with internal courts. There are examples at Khirbat al Mafjar (745), Ukhaidir (780), Samarra (836) and elsewhere but no details of garden layouts survive.

Reports by European travellers at a much later date may be a reasonably close guide to the original use of palace gardens, particularly in Persia. Sir John Chardin had a good opportunity to view a Persian garden when waiting three hours for an audience with the Grand Vizir and Nazir in 1671. His account tallies with the above description of a garden carpet:

> There can be nothing more magnificent than the apartment where he [the Nazir] treated the king. It gives upon a garden that is not very large, but very fine; in the middle thereof is a great basin of water, lined with white transparent marble, the borders whereof are bored for spouts, four fingers distant from the other. Round the basin were spread tapestries of silk and gold, on which were placed cushions of very rich embroidery to sit upon ... On the four sides of the basin, were four perfuming pots of an extraordinary bigness, finely embellished with vermilion gilt, between eight little boxes of ivory, adorned with gold enamelled and full of sweets and perfumes ... At night there were fireworks played off in the middle of the garden. Nobody ever entertains the King of Persia, without giving him the diversion of an artificial firework. The king passed the whole night at the feast in drinking, drawing the bow and in other exertions ... He was carried away about the break of day, not being able to walk or ride.[25]

Vita Sackville-West visited Persia in 1927 and described its gardens as follows:

> All Persian gardens are walled in ... It would be churlish to complain of monotony in so graceful a sanctuary. But we may safely say that the layout was always more or less the same: the long avenues, the straight walks, the summer-house or pavilion at the end of the walk, the narrow canals running like ribbons over blue tiles, widening out into pools which oddly enough were seldom circular, but more likely to be rectangular, square, octagonal, cross-shaped, or with trilobed or shamrock-like ends. Sometimes these pools were reproduced inside the pavilion itself: a mirror of water beneath a domed roof, fantastically reflecting all the honeycomb elaboration of the ceiling.[26]

She could not resist adding that:

> I remember in particular one such pool with a kind of central throne on which some nineteenth-century Shah might sit, attired in the minimum of clothing, while the ladies of his harem, similarly attired or unattired, slithered down chutes from an upper gallery straight into the embracing arms of their imperial master.[27]

Vita's sexual romanticism is typical of the way in which Europe viewed 'the East'. Nor, remembering the erotic scenes depicted in Persian miniatures, can one say she was entirely wrong. Erotic art became popular after the ban on human representation was

4.22 Persian gardens are enclosed by mud brick (Bagh–e Doulat Abad, Yazd) and finished with canals (Bagh–e Fin, Kashan). Their relationship with Pasargadae (4.11) is evident

4.23 The Court of Lions in the Alhambra is one of the oldest four-square Islamic designs to have survived

4.24 (left) The Court of Myrtles in the Alhambra

4.25 (right) The Court of the Long Pond at the Generalife remains an Islamic space, though its detailed design has changed

relaxed during the sixteenth century. The Paradise Garden developed in Spain as a place to satisfy both the senses and the soul.

Islamic Spain

The best garden survivals from the Middle Ages in Europe are those made by the Umayyad caliphate in the south of Spain. Islamic civilisation, then at a peak, extended across the former colonies of Greece and Rome on the south and east shores of the Mediterranean. Coming from a poor and barren land, the followers of Muhammad learned as they travelled and built when they settled. On reaching Spain in the eighth century, they were familiar with the Roman gardening tradition. The gardens they made between the eighth and twelfth centuries have not survived. The Alhambra, which, though changed, survives in good condition, became a fort and palace in the mid-thirteenth century.

The perimeter of the Alhambra is fortified with towers which, seen from afar, remind one of an Assyrian city, a crusader castle or the walls of Constantinople. Within lay a palace, a fort, and a small town. The overall layout of the Alhambra is unlike a Persian paradise garden. It is closer to that of Hadrian's Villa. The decorative treatment of the buildings and courts make it 'one of the most famous monuments in all Islamic art'.[28] The Court of Myrtles has a perfect sheet of water and the Court of Lions has one of the oldest symmetrical chahar bagh layouts. Across the valley stands the Generalife. Its central courtyard is perhaps the most photographed garden scene in the world, but the long pool with arching jets and lush planting is not typical of West Asian gardens: such features derive from Roman gardens.

The Arabs took the Middle-eastern art of carpet-making to Spain and Sicily. Some Persian garden carpets had knot patterns, based on carpet knots, which may have inspired the knot gardens of the Italian renaissance and Northern Europe (see Chapter 6). Regrettably, no Islamic carpets survive from this period in Spain or elsewhere.

Islamic Central Asia

After the invasions of Genghis Khan (1219) and Timur Tamerlane (1381), a large proportion of Persia's population was massacred. The Mongols then adopted the culture and art of their victims. Timur Tamerlane transported craftsmen to his capital at Samarkand (now in Uzbekistan), where they built mosques, madrasahs palaces and gardens. Another Mongol ruler, Babur, occupied the city in 1497 and admired its design. He went on to become a great conqueror and introduced the same style to Afghanistan and then India. Later descendants of his gardens survive in Kashmir.

An ambassador from Spain viewed the splendour of Timur's Samarkand in 1403–1406. Six elephants stood near a garden entrance and performed tricks. Orchards contained deer and pheasants. A golden horde, of 20,000 nomads, camped in his park. Timur sat 'upon a raised dais before which there was a fountain that threw up a column of water into the air backwards, and in the basin of the fountain there were floating red apples'. Guests drank from gold cups. The emperor's younger wives played drinking games with the servants. Everyone, except Timur, was compelled to get drunk. A dragoman who drank too slowly was threatened with a cord being drilled through his nose so that he could be pulled round the garden. Timur's court travelled round the Samarkand palace gardens. The Spanish ambassador liked the New Garden best:

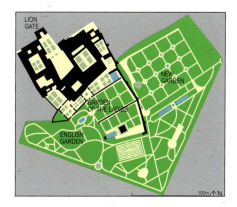

4.27 The Alcazar in Seville

4.28 Nishat Bagh, Kashmir, was an encampment garden for the summer season, with ample water for a chahar bagh

This orchard was surrounded by a high wall, four square enclosing it, and at each of the four corners was a very lofty round tower, and the enclosing wall going from tower to tower was very high built, and as strong as the work of the tower. This orchard in its centre had a great palace, built on the plan of a cross, and a very large water-tank had been dug before it. This palace with its large garden was much the finest of any that we had visited hitherto, and in the ornamentation of its buildings in the gold and blue tile work by far the most sumptuous. All these palaces with their surrounding gardens, as will be understood, are situated outside the actual city of Samarqand.[29]

Timur's gardens did not survive but Samarkand still has wonderful Islamic architecture clad with 'gold and blue tile work by far the most sumptuous'. As well as being places of pleasure, the Samarkand ring of gardens had political, symbolic and ceremonial roles. Gardens were named after areas of conquered territory (e.g. 'Damascus' and 'Shiraz').[30] As nomad encampments, they reminded the Turkish-speaking military elite of its past and the Persian-speaking proletariat of the power its rulers could draw from the steppes.[31] When a gathering of the golden horde turned the garden into an armed encampment, the ornamental canals provided water for drinking, cooking and washing.

In the plain here Timur recently had ordered tents to be pitched for his accommodation, and where his wives might come, for he had commanded the assembling of the great Horde, which hitherto and till now had been out in camp in the pastures beyond the orchard lands round and about the city. The whole of the Horde was now to come in, each clan taking up its appointed place: and we now saw them here, pitching the tents, their women folk accompanying them ... we saw near twenty thousand tents pitched in regular streets to encircle the royal camp, and daily more clans came in from the outlying districts ... there were baths and bathers established in the camp, who pitching their tents had built wooden cabins adjacent each with its iron bath that is supplied with hot water, heated in the caldrons which, with all the furniture necessary to their craft, they have there. Thus all was duly ordered and each man knew his place to go to before hand.[32]

Herat, in modern Afghanistan, also had encampment gardens and Cyrus's garden at Pasargadae must have been used in this way when the army assembled. Transported to India, the encampment garden's use and form were maintained. Shalamar in Lahore, was a camp for the court entourage on its summer journey to Kashmir.[33]

Islamic India and Pakistan
Babur (1483–1530), a descendant of Genghis Khan and Timur Tamerlane, established a Mughal Empire in India. This family of empire-builders became a dynasty of garden-

makers. Babur was a poet, a naturalist and the author of one of the first Islamic auto-biographies.[34] He was born in the province of Fergana on the Jaxartes River. This province is part of modern Kazakhstan, north of Afghanistan and east of Samarkand, which Babur twice conquered and twice lost. He saw himself as Turkish and wrote in a Turkish dialect (Chaghatay) which takes its name from Genghis Kahn's second son. Commanders from the Himalayan region were taking control of India, as they had done in Persia. Babur employed Turkish and Mongolian tribesmen in the army and Persians as civilian administrators. Persian remained the language of government in India until replaced by English and Hindi.

The greater part of Babur's memoir is taken up with details of military campaigns and family histories. But he also finds space to record leisure activities. In the foothills of Kabul he counted 32 unique varieties of tulip.[35] He enjoyed hunting, particularly large and rare beasts, and loved natural scenery. Wherever he settled, Babur made gardens. His design records, though short, are fuller than those of any contemporary garden-maker. One of his gardens was in Kabul:

4.29 A cascade at Nishat Bagh

> In 1508–09, I had constructed a chahar bagh garden called Bagh-i-Wafa on a rise to the south of the Adianapur fortress. It overlooks the river, which flows between the fortress and the garden. It yields many oranges, citrons and pomegranates.[36]

Babur found India too hot, too flat and too little suited to chahar bagh gardens. He describes how he made a garden on the River Jumna at Agra. Thought to be the Ram Bagh, this garden survives but is much altered since Babur's time.

> I always thought one of the chief faults of Hindustan was that there was no running water. Everywhere that was habitable it should be possible to construct waterwheels, create running water, and make planned, geometric spaces. A few days after coming to Agra, I crossed the Jumna with this plan in mind and scouted around for places to build gardens, but everywhere I looked was so unpleasant and desolate that I crossed back in great disgust. Because the place was so ugly and disagreeable I abandoned my dream of making a chahar bagh.

> Although there was no really suitable place near Agra, there was nothing to do but work with the space we had. The foundation was the large well from which the water for the bathhouse came. Next, the patch of ground with tamarind trees and octagonal pond became the great pool and courtyard. Then came the pool in front of the stone building and the hall. After that came the private garden and its outbuildings, and after that the bathhouse. Thus, in unpleasant and inharmonious India, marvellously regular and geometric

4.30 Humayun's tomb was built in the middle of a perfect chahar bagh. The modern planting is unrelated to the original conception

4.31 Jahangir's tomb at Shahdara was planned – by his wife, who was a Persian princess – as a garden. It is outside the old walled city of Lahore

gardens were introduced. In every corner were beautiful plots, and in every plot were regularly laid out arrangements of roses and narcissus.[37]

Babur's descendents came to appreciate the hot plains of north India. Some married local princesses. Many became garden-makers, as did their wives. The Mongol tradition of celebrating one's ancestors fused with the Persian tradition of garden design. This created a variant on the paradise garden: a place of resort during the owner's life and a resting place after his death. As a garden type, this has a kinship with the mortuary temples of Ancient Egypt. Moghul emperors also retained their founder's love of the Himalayas. The court journeyed to Kashmir in summer and made a group of gardens which have received adulation: 'Magnificently sited and within a total landscape of superb quality, the impact made by the gardens of Kashmir is without parallel.'[38]

Humayun (1530–1556), Babur's son, was less interested in gardens than his father but was buried in the first imperial tomb garden, the oldest Mughal garden to survive in its original form. Humayun's mortuary temple was set in the middle of a chahar bagh. It is symmetrical, square and ornamented by a grid of shallow water channels.

Akbar (1556–1605), Babur's grandson, laid out Fatehpur Sikri and the Fort at Agra. He also conquered Kashmir and regarded the province as his private garden. Akbar's mortuary temple, at Sikandra near Agra, is larger than his father's but shares its square plan and disciplined symmetry with the tomb at the centre of the garden.

Jahangir (1605–1627), Babur's great-grandson, appreciated the potential of Kashmir as a place to make gardens. He married a Persian princess from Kandahar. She was exceptionally capable and is thought to have been the leading force in the gardens made during their delightful Kashmir summers. Shalamar Bagh ('Abode of Love') is a chahar bagh with a central canal flowing to Lake Dal. Achabal has a similar plan and the canal is fed by an abundant spring. At Vernag, the central canal runs

4.32 Shalamar Bagh, Kashmir. Susan Jellicoe, who took the photograph, considered it 'one of the noblest gardens in the world, with delicate ground modelling and the tranquillity of geometry'

300 m from an octagonal pond to the river. At Nishat Bagh, which may have been made by Jahangir's brother-in-law, there is a central canal and terraces stepping up the hillside. At Shardara, outside Lahore, the garden was planned by Jahangir's wife as a setting for her husband's tomb.

Shah Jehan (1628–1658), Babur's great-great-grandson, made the most famous of all Mughal gardens: the Taj Mahal. It was built (1632–1654) as a tomb garden for his favourite wife, Mumtaz Mahal. This 'matchless exemplar of the classical Persian style'[39] is a perfect chahar bagh. The mortuary temple, instead of being at the centre, stands on the edge of the garden beside the Jumna River. The composition was intended 'to drive home the message implicit in the building's form and location that the tomb was an allegorical representation of the Throne of God above the gardens of Paradise on the Day of Judgement'.[40] In Lahore, Shah Jehan made gardens within the old city, now known as Lahore Fort. Outside its walls, he made the Shalamar Bagh, inspired by his father's garden of the same name in Kashmir. It is on a vast scale with a chahar bagh plan, a canal and a great tank. Shahjehanabad in Delhi, now called the Red Fort, was a palace-fortress-town with numerous internal courts.[41]

4.33 Achabal, Kashmir. Susan Jellicoe, who took the photograph, wrote that 'water gushes out of the hillside with great vigour all the year round, feeding a tremendous waterfall, the highlight of the garden, that crashes down between the two small pavilions into a large basin'

4.34 Unlike earlier tomb gardens, the Taj Mahal has a garden, not a tomb, as its centrepiece

4.35 (centre left) Nishat Bagh has a central canal, flowing from the mountains to the lake

4.36 (centre right) Shalamar Bagh, Lahore, 'the most grandiose of the Mughal gardens'

4.37 (left) Shalamar Bagh, Lahore

Aurangzib (1658–1707), Babur's great-great-great-grandson, was less interested in making gardens than his forebears but became a zealous mosque-builder, integrating designs with their surroundings. The Badshahi ('Imperial') Mosque in Lahore illustrates this principle. It has a great court from which a flight of steps opens onto a nineteenth-century (public) paradise garden. The Mughal empire survived until 1857 but in garden design, as in much else, the great days were those of six emperors who ruled between 1526 and 1707. Sylvia Crowe remarks that this period 'coincides with great epochs of garden-making in other parts of the world'. As evidence, she cites the making of the Villa Lante (c. 1566), Vaux-le-Vicomte (1656) and 'the greatest period of the Japanese tradition, which culminated in the perfection of the Katsura Imperial Villa at Kyoto' [42] In all these countries it was a time when none could challenge a monarch's power. Royal courts believed in what the English called 'the divine right of kings'. The age of democracy was yet to dawn.

4.38 (left) Shah Jehan laid out gardens in the old city of Lahore, now known as the Fort

4.39 (below) Shahjehanabad (the Red Fort) in Delhi was a city planned like a garden

Types and examples

Hunting park

4.40
Hunting park

Use: Kings enjoyed hunting animals and seeking unusual plants. It seems likely that reserves were made for this purpose when so much land had been taken into cultivation that wild places were in short supply, in Babylonia, Assyria, Persia and elsewhere. Parks could also be used to teach young men the arts of war. Modern national parks and nature reserves are lineal descendents of the ancient hunting parks. We visit them to admire the scenery, exercise our bodies and 'shoot' photographs of plants and animals.

Form: No physical examples or plans survive from the ancient world, but there are written records and relief sculptures showing exotic plants and animals. A varied topography of woods, water, grassland and hills was desirable. Boundaries are likely to have been made with mud brick, rubble stone or timber, depending on local circumstances and availability of building materials. One can obtain an impression of the character of ancient hunting parks from later examples, like Khirbat al Mafjar (Figure 4.37) and Richmond Park (Figure 4.8). The plan shows a palace on the edge of a hunting park. Evidence for this arrangement having been used in ancient times is lacking.

Palace court

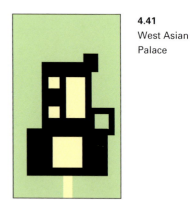

4.41
West Asian Palace

Use: Early palaces, like the settlements from which they evolved, were planned to integrate roofed and unroofed space. Large palaces had outdoor courts for specialised uses: entrance areas, parade grounds, living rooms for the family, workshops and places for the king to receive companies of visitors (the use of 'court' to describe a king's entourage arose from this function). Like the cities of which they formed part, ancient palaces have either been destroyed or have become archaeological sites.

Form: Large palaces had internal courts of different sizes, sometimes square, sometimes rectangular, sometimes irregular. No details of the internal layouts of Mesopotamian, Sassanian or early Islamic courts survive. Some later Islamic courts were designed with a chahar bagh pattern of canals. Arcades were built round courts for shelter and for shade.

Khorsabad 700 BC

The city of Khorsabad was built by King Sargon II (r. 722–705 BC) and abandoned when he was killed. His palace (dur Sharrukin) is an immediate predecessor of Sennasherib's Palace, at Nineveh. The outer wall of Sargon's fortress covered an area of 3 sq km and had seven fortified gates. In times of siege, it became an armed encampment. The buildings had thick mud-brick walls without windows but with doors opening onto internal courts of various sizes. The Throne Room was built into the wall between the State Court and a smaller domestic court used by women and children. Smaller courts near the Grand Entrance were part of the service wing. A group of temples had a ziggurat. Some of the courts were planted but the arrangement is unknown. One can speculate that the large ceremonial courts were unplanted but that the smaller residential courts had shade plants and pools like Egyptian gardens. The enclosure with a temple to the god of vegetation, Nabu, is likely to have contained plants.

Khirbat al Mafjar ('Hisham's Palace') 750 AD

The estate belonged to a mid-eighth century Umayyad caliph, either Hisham or Walid II (the latter was renowned for his love of hunting and his libertinism). It comprised a palace with a paved court, a bathing house, a mosque, a fountain court and a 60-hectare *hayr* (walled enclosure) containing, like a Persian paradise, plants and animals. Mosaics and other ornamentation are of a very high standard. The peristyle court was paved. The fountain court may have been a garden.

> It is clear from the plan that the courtyard was the centre of life and communication in the palace.[43]

> We can therefore say that the structure and what belonged to the floor [of the bath house] were Western, more specifically Byzantine, whereas the wall decorations and most of the iconography were Iranian.[44]

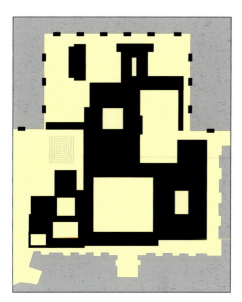

4.42 Khorsabad

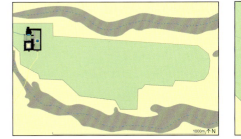 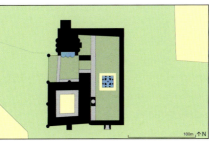

4.43 Khirbat al Mafjar

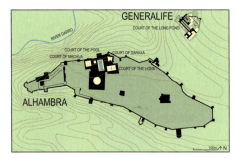

4.44 The Alhambra

The Alhambra and The Generalife 1350 AD

In Arabic, *Alhambra* means 'red castle'. The overall plan of the plateau resembles that of Hadrian's Villa but the individual courts were inspired by the palace courts and paradise gardens of West Asia. Muhammad ibn-Yusuf ibn-Nash (1333–1354) commissioned its famous garden. The Court of the Lions is one of the earliest examples of a regular chahar bagh. The Court of the Pool is ordered, beautifully proportioned and richly detailed. The palace windows frame views of the surrounding landscape as though they were oriental miniatures. The Court of the Long Pond (Patio de la Acequia) in the Generalife has pavilions at both ends, an arched gallery on the third side and a high wall on the fourth side. With echoes of a Roman peristyle garden, it has jets of water arching over the Long Pond. Today's ground level is 0.5 m above the Arab level of *c.* 1250, which was temporarily uncovered in 1959. The Arab garden had a central canal and a chahar bagh division into four parts.

> The great palace gardens of Granada are divided into small walled enclosures, for the private enjoyment of one man and his wives; the precious water is led down from a tiny source through court after court, in slender fountains and rivulets which sing of coolness – these immensely subtle and delicious gardens are paradises, oases in an arid land.[45]

Mosque courts

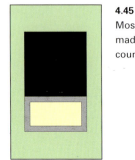

4.45
Mosque and madrasah courts

Use: 'Mosque' refers to the whole space designated for prayer, including both the roofed and unroofed parts. Mosques had other public functions: educational, social, political and even military. Provision for the ceremonial washing which takes place before prayer was often an ornate fountain in the outdoor court, which would also serve as a water supply for town dwellers without private supplies. Courts were occasionally used for planting and are gardens only in the sense of being enclosed outdoor spaces. Theological colleges (madrasahs) are often attached to mosques, and have garden courts.

Form: The first mosque, Muhammad's own garden, was a four-sided outdoor space enclosed by a mud-brick wall. Many early courts were not right-angled. Later courts were more often rectangular or square in plan, enclosing a space that was geometrically perfect. In the planning of large and sophisticated mosques, the covered and uncovered parts took on separate identities. Courts were beautifully paved and surrounded with arcades, not unlike Roman peristyles and medieval cloisters. Large mosque courts had pools and tended towards the design of paradise gardens.

Damascus 706 AD

Built in 706 AD, the Great Mosque in Damascus is one of the earliest to survive in near-original condition. It was built under the administration of the great Muslim leader Caliph al-Walid on the foundations of a Roman temple. There are entrances on each of the four sides. The central feature of the mosque is a large courtyard with arcades on three sides. On the fourth side, facing Mecca, is the covered part of the mosque known as the sanctuary. It has three aisles running parallel to the *qibla* wall and a nave which led to the caliph's palace. The columns which support the roof came from Roman buildings and two of the three minarets are based on Roman corner towers. A treasury building stands on Corinthian columns at the east end of the courtyard. This mosque, an architectural interpretation of Muhammad's house in Medina, drew on Greek and Roman precedents to formalise the place of courtyards in mosque planning.

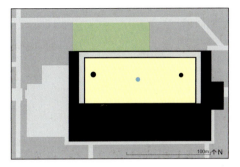

4.46 The Great Mosque, Damascus

Cordoba 785 AD

The Great Mosque in Cordoba, started in 785 by Abd al-Rahman II, is larger than the Great Mosque in Damascus and was built over a longer period. The Gothic cathedral now at its centre secured its survival. The sanctuary is famed for a 'forest' of columns, borrowed from older buildings, supporting the roof on double arches. The court, always an integral part of the design, originally had a freestanding treasury building. Around 990, the court was planted and became the Patio of Orange Trees. The original lines of trees are said to have been aligned with the internal columns of the mosque. Today, they are set in a grid of irrigation channels.

> This mosque has a great patio with a pond in its centre. All around this patio a hundred and seventeen orange trees are planted.[46]

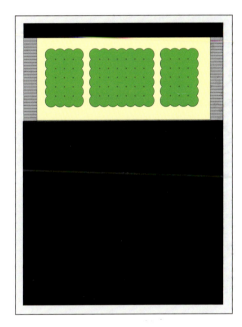

4.47 The Great Mosque, Cordoba

Süleymaniye Mosque 1550 AD

The Süleymaniye Mosque in Istanbul was designed by the greatest Ottoman architect, Sinan, for Süleyman The Magnificent. It stands on a slope overlooking the Golden Horn and was built in the garden of a Byzantine palace. The mosque forms part of a complex which included schools, mausoleums, a hospital and a hostel. It is an enclosure within an enclosure. The outdoor court and the domed mosque are separate but joined; each with its own identity. The court has colonnades on all four sides.

> Alberti learnt from Vitruvius; Sinan from the direct study of Hagia Sophia in the light of his training in the Ottoman tradition. The two men also share a puritanical approach to decoration, seeking the idea of pure philosophy. For both, the laws of harmonic numbers commanded universal conformity so that the concept of God as the perfect geometrical figure, the circle, was as easy for Sinan to grasp as it was for Alberti.[47]

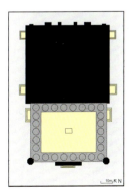

4.48 Süleymaniye Mosque, Istanbul

4.49
Paradise
garden

Paradise garden

Use: The ancient Persian word *pairidaeza* was later applied to walled gardens of the type shown in the diagram. Order was their leading characteristic. Outside towns, paradise gardens could be large encampment gardens with pavilions. Inside towns, they were secluded courts, set apart from the noise and dust of the outside world. Water, in channels, pools, fountains or cascades was an essential component of the paradise garden. Paradise gardens were used for cool relaxation, entertaining friends, sleeping and enjoyment of scents, sounds, fruits, flowers and decorative animals.

Form: The classic form of a paradise garden is a rectangle divided into parts by water channels. The plan evolved slowly, under the influence of Persians from the sixth century BC, Arabs from the eighth century AD, and Mongols from the sixteenth century to the eighteenth century. The Koran[48] describes paradise as a garden of eternity (*jannat al-khuld*) with four rivers: of water, milk, wine and honey. This concept lies behind the evolution of the chahar bagh, or quadripartite garden, with the four parts separated by water channels and symbolising the four elements: earth, water, fire and air. When made on slopes, paradise gardens were terraced. What is now known as a chahar bagh plan was also used for small outdoor courts within buildings. The diagram is a compromise between palace courts, enclosed by buildings and encampment gardens with pavilions and orchards enclosed by walls.

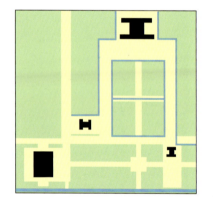

4.50 Pasargadae

Pasargadae 550 BC

David Stronach, who excavated Pasargadae, described its layout as one of the oldest examples of a classical Persian chahar bagh. The drawing is based on his work.[49] Remnants of shallow stone water channels defining the space between the two palaces survive. The paths were made of beaten earth or gravel. Two small pavilions are shown on the plan. The garden is likely to have been set within woodland planted with cypress, pomegranate, cherry trees and flowering plants.

Humayun's Tomb 1570 AD

Near the bank of the Yamuna River in Delhi lies the tomb garden of Humayun, whose father, Babur, is credited with having introduced the chahar bagh to India. Humayun's garden (*c.* 1573) is a geometrically perfect chahar bagh but differs from Babur's gardens in having a building at the centre. It is divided into 36 squares by a grid of paths and water channels. Humayun's mausoleum, in red sandstone and white

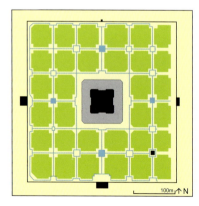

4.51 Humayun's Tomb, Delhi

marble, stands at the centre of the grid, symbolising the emperor's palace in paradise. Thus, this garden is a setting for a building, rather than a place to be viewed from a pavilion. Humayun's tomb garden was not the first example of the type but it is the oldest to survive in good condition.

Humayun's tomb fits squarely into the Iranian tradition of imperial mausoleums.[50]

Shalamar Bagh in Lahore 1633 AD

The garden was planned by Shah Jahen (c. 1633) to mark the completion of a canal bringing water from the River Ravi to Lahore. It was designed in an opulent manner with terracing, pavilions, a wide canal, fountains and a great tank with a marble platform in its midst. The original buildings were demolished in the eighteenth century to provide building materials for the Golden Temple at Amritsar, and were subsequently reconstructed. The plan has a chahar bagh pattern of canals.

> The upper terrace at Lahore was known as the *Farah Baksh* (The Bestower of Pleasure), while the middle and lower terraces, forming the more public part of the garden, were known together as the *Faiz Baksh* (The Bestower of Plenty).[53]

Shalamar Bagh, Kashmir 1620 AD

Shalamar, 'one of the noblest gardens in the world, with delicate ground modelling and the tranquillity of geometry',[51] is on the shore of Lake Dal in Kashmir. The garden was made by the Emperor Jahangir and his wife, Nur Jahan (c. 1620). Its name means 'Abode of Love'. Additions were made by Shah Jehan and, in later ownership, parts of the garden were altered and parts allowed to decay. The garden was approached from the lake by a long canal (which has been bisected by a modern road). There was a private garden for the emperor and another for the court ladies, for whom Shah Jehan built a black marble pavilion. It has a throne and a waterfall. The overall garden plan is a traditional chahar bagh with a central pavilion in a rectangular pool at the crossing-point of the canals. The structure planting was of poplars and plane trees.

> Shalamar is near the lake. It has a pleasant stream which comes from the hills and flows into the Dal Lake. I bade my son Khurram [Shah Jehan] dam it up and make a waterfall, which it would be a pleasure to behold. This place is one of the sights of Kashmir.[52]

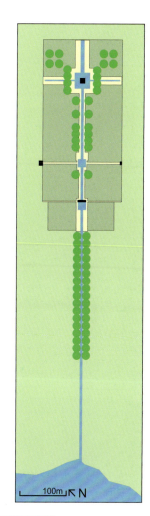

4.52 Shalamar Bagh, Kashmir

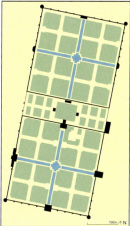

4.53 Shalamar Bagh, Lahore

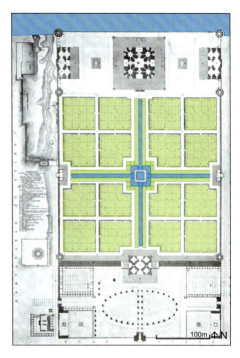

4.54 The Taj Mahal (based on the 1828 plan)

Taj Mahal 1632 AD

The mausoleum and garden were made between 1632 and 1654 as a memorial to Mumtaz Mahal, favourite wife of the Mughal emperor Shah Jahan. The plan of the gardens was recorded in 1828 by the British Surveyor-General of India: it is a classical four-fold paradise garden but with a tomb on its edge, overlooking the River Jumna. The gatehouse is at the end of the main axis and there are pavilions at the ends of the cross-axes. The original plan for the Taj Mahal, by Ustad Ahmad, was probably drawn on a grid base-plan. Its symbolism was inspired by 'the then well-known cosmological diagrams depicting the garden of paradise on the Day of Judgement'.[54] During the nineteenth century the garden was regrettably Europeanised, with informal tree-planting.

> What a garden! . . . the great centre of the picture being ever the vast glittering ivory-white Taj Mahal, and the accompaniment and contrast of the dark green of the cypresses, with the rich yellow green trees of all sorts! And then the effect of the innumerable flights of bright green parrots flitting across like live emeralds.[55]

Notes

1 The dates and the evolutionary path remain matters of debate but there is wide agreement that *Homo erectus* migrated from Africa between one and two million years ago and that only *Homo sapiens* remained by 30,000 BC: Johanson, D.C. and Edgar, B., *From Lucy to Language*, Simon & Schuster, 1996.

2 Gothein, M-L., *A History of Garden Art*, London: J. M. Dent, 1928, Vol. 1, p. 29.

3 ——, op. cit., Vol. 1, p. 29.

4 ——, op. cit., Vol. 1, p. 30.

5 Chardin, Sir J., *Travels in Persia*, London: Argonaut Press, 1927.

6 Carroll, Maureen, *Earthly Paradises: Ancient gardens in history and archaeology*, London: British Museum Press, 2003, p. 65.

7 Diodorus Siculus, *The Library of History*, II 7, 3 and II 10, 1.

8 Strabo, *Geography*, XVI, I, 5.

9 Dalley, S., 'Ancient Mesopotamian gardens and the identification of the Hanging Gardens of Babylon resolved', in *Garden History*, Summer 1993, Vol. 21, No. 1, pp. 1–13; and 'Nineveh, Babylon and the Hanging Gardens: cuneiform and classical sources reconciled', in *Iraq*, Vol. LVI, 1994, pp. 45–58.

10 British Museum London (Room 89) WA124939. The caption, in 2002, read: 'An Assyrian park, with aqueduct, columned pavilion, and royal stella with altar in front. Assyrian about 645–635 BC, from Nineveh, North Palace'.

11 Smart, N., *The Religious Experience of Mankind*, London: Fontana, 1971, p. 307.

12 Dickie, J., 'The Islamic garden in Spain', in Macdougall, E. B. and Ettinghausen, R. (eds), *Dumbarton Oaks Colloquium on the History of Landscape Architecture*, Dumbarton Oaks, 1976, pp. 89–105.

13 The Koran, Surah XLVII, 2 ff.

14 D. N. Wilber, *Persian Gardens and Garden Pavilions*, Dumbarton Oaks, 1979, p. 3.

15 It is known as the St Gall plan – see Chapter 5.

16 Pindar-Wilson, R., 'The Persian garden: bagh and charhar bagh', in Macdougall, E. B, Ettinghausen, R. (eds), op. cit. (Ref. 12), pp. 71–85.

17 Harvey, J., 'The square garden of Henry the Poet', in *Garden History*, Vol. 15, No. 1, Spring 1987, pp. 1–12.

18 Gothein, M-L., op. cit., Vol. 1, p. 41.

19 ——, op. cit., Vol. 1, p. 145.

20 Stark, F., *Baghdad Sketches*, London: Guild Books, 1937, p. 176.

21 Ettinghausen, R. and Grabar, O., *The Art and Architecture of Islam 650–1250*, New Haven: Yale University Press, 1987, p. 20.

22 Clavijo, *Embassy to Tamerlane 1403–6*, London: Routledge, 1928, p. 206.

23 Khansari, M., Moghtader, M. R. and Yavari, M., *The Persian Garden – Echoes of Paradise*, Washington, DC: Mage Publishers, 1998, p. 91.

24 ——, op. cit., p. 11.

25 Chardin, Sir J., op. cit., p. 77.

26 Sackville-West, V., 'Persian Gardens', in Arberry, *The Legacy of Persia*, 1953, pp. 267–8.

27 ——, op. cit., p. 269.

28 Blair, S. S. and Blom, J. M., *The Art and Architecture of Islam 1250–1800*, New Haven, Yale University Press, 1994, p. 124.

29 Clarijo, op. cit , p. 230.

30 The Roman emperor Hadrian also used parts of his garden to remind him of conquered territories.

31 Lenz, T. W., 'Memory and Ideology in the Timurid Garden', in Westcoat, J. L. and Wolschke-Bulmahn, J., *Mughal Gardens: Sources, places, representations and prospects*, Washington, DC: Dumbarton Oaks Research Library and Collection, 1996, pp. 31–59.

32 le Strange, G., *Clavijo Embassy to Tamerlane 1403–1406*, London: Routledge, 1928, p. 233.

33 Westcoat, J. L., 'Gardens, Urbanisation, and Urbanism in Mughal Lahore 1526–1657', in Westcoat, J. L. and Wolschke-Bulmahn, J., op. cit. (Ref. 31), pp. 139–69.

34 *Memoirs of Babur,* 2 vols, 1921–2, and Thackston, W. M. (transl. and ed.), *The Baburnama: Memoirs of Babur, Prince and Emperor*, London and New York: Oxford University Press, 1996.

35 Thackston, W. M, op. cit., p. 177.

36 ——, op. cit., p. 173.

37 ——, op. cit., p. 359.

38 Crowe, S., Haywood. S., Jellicoe, S. and Patterson, G., *The Gardens of Mughul India: A history and guide*, London: Thames & Hudson, 1972, p. 50.

39 Khansari, M., *et al.*, op. cit., p. 67.

40 Blair, S. S. and Blom, J. M., op. cit., p. 280.

41 Blake, S. P., 'The Khanah Bagh in Mughal India: houses and gardens in the palaces and mansions of the great men of Shahjehanabad', in Westcoat, J. L. and Wolschke-Bulmahn, J., op. cit. (Ref. 31), pp. 171–87.

42 Crowe, S. *et al.*, op. cit., p. 54 (I attribute the comment to Crowe).

43 Hamilton, R. W., *Khirbat al Mafjar: An Arabian mansion in the Jordan valley*, Oxford: Oxford University Press, 1959, p. 27.

44 Ettinghausen, R., 'The throne and banqueting hall at Al-Mafjar', in Blom, J. M. (ed.), *Early Islamic Art and Architecture*, Aldershot: Ashgate, 2000, p. 27.

45 Shepheard, P., *Gardens*, London: Macdonald & Co., 1969, p. 16.

46 The Moroccan Ambassador, 1690, quoted in Casa Valdes, Marquesa de, *Spanish Gardens*, Woodbridge: Antique Collectors Club, 1987, p. 28.

47 Goodwin, G., *A History of Ottoman Architecture*, London: Thames & Hudson, 1971, p. 216.

48 The Koran, Surah XXV, 15.

49 Stronach, D., *Pasargadae: A report on the excavations*, Oxford, 1978.

50   Blair, S. S. and Bloom, J. M., op. cit., p. 270.

51   Jellicoe, S., op. cit., p. 115.

52   *Memoirs of Jahangir*, 1620. Trans., A. Rogers, Ed. H. Beveridge, London 1909, Part 2.

53   Crowe, S. and Haywood, S., *The Gardens of Mughal India*, London: Thames & Hudson, 1972, p. 150.

54   Begley, W. E., 'The garden of the Taj Mahal: a case study of Mughal architectural planning and symbolism', in Westcoat, J. L. and Wolschke-Bulmahn, J., op. cit., pp. 213–31.

55   Lear, E., *Indian Journal*, 15–16 February 1874.

Chapter 5

Medieval gardens
600 AD–1500 AD

The medieval period is one of the most interesting in garden history, but frustrates the scholar on several counts. First, 'The present sum of all our fragments of knowledge does not reveal the configuration of an actual medieval garden, other than a few Hispano-Arab ones'.[1] Second, the re-creations which might contribute to our understanding of medieval gardens lack the excellence of medieval art and architecture. Third, most historical illustrations of medieval gardens date from the Renaissance period. We must therefore turn to general history, art history, texts and archaeology for information, never forgetting that symbolism lay at the heart of medieval culture.[2]

'Middle Ages' began as a pejorative label for the millennium covered by this chapter, signifying its inferiority to the old glory of classical times and the new glory of the Renaissance. Scholars subsequently identified an Early Middle Age, or Dark Age (500–1000 AD), a High Middle Age (1000–1300) and a Late Middle Age (1300–1500). Although the adjective 'medieval' derives from 'middle age', it seems less pejorative. The relationship between Ambras Castle and Innsbruck, in Austria (5.1 and 5.2) represents conditions north of the Alps at the close of the period.

After the collapse of Roman power in the West, Europe became a continent of warring tribes. Lack of records made the age 'dark' for historians, though research is lightening their gloom. The five centuries after 476 AD can be seen as an Age of Faith in which religion provided the test of truth and reason was demoted to the status of an argument for faith. Individual opinion was discouraged and 'innovation was a sin'.[3] Christianity had spread from West Asia, through Rome, to the cities and then the country districts of North Europe. The Roman Catholic Church was the only institution from the ancient world to survive into the modern world and the only international organisation, the arbiter even of trivial land disputes in Scotland. The rawness of medieval life made it easy to believe that paradise, which had not been on offer in pagan times, would be superior to life on earth. Hell, for sure, would be worse. Preachers informed their congregations in plain terms about the conditions in hell: 'The horrible cold, the loathsome worms, the stench, hunger and thirst, the darkness, the

5.1 Innsbruck *c.* 1600. The Braun and Hogernberg drawing shows a compact town overlooked by Ambras Castle (left, above town) with houses and gardens developing outside the medieval defences (right, below town)

5.2 Ambras Castle: a 1649 drawing of the old garden

5.3 A plan of the restored garden in 2001 (part renaissance and part medieval). See also Figures 5.4 and 5.5

5.4 Ambras Castle, a recreated herber nestling between the castle and the castle walls

5.5 Mugano (Italy): the densely-populated hill-towns of medieval Europe lacked space for gardens and, when suffering hunger or plague, gave a foretaste of hell

chains, the unspeakable filth, the endless cries, the sight of demons'.[4] Densely populated cities gave residents some experience of these conditions.

Gardens symbolised heaven. Islam, as discussed in the previous chapter, had banned human imagery, favoured the use of geometry and treated gardens as symbols of paradise. The early Church Fathers had an ambivalent attitude, fearing that beauty, like luxury, would imperil the soul. But sacred painting, sculpture, literature and, to a lesser extent, gardens, were valued as aids to private contemplation and doctrinal exegesis. Plotinus, a pagan philosopher, and Augustine of Hippo, a Christian saint, were the thinkers who did most to promote a symbolic art, glorying in the unseen order of an awesome universe.

Plotinus (205–270) was born at Assiut in Upper Egypt, a capital city during the Middle Kingdom and famous for the worship of Osiris in Hellenistic times. Plotinus moved to Rome and became the key figure in developing a Neoplatonic theory of art. He equated the Form of The Good (see Chapter 1) with a supreme being who could be mystically sensed but not directly known. Plotinus believed the Forms to be 'fully organized into a coherent general scheme of things', a scheme that became known as 'the great chain of being'.[5] It had a hierarchical structure: from God at its head, through angels, saints and mankind to the animal kingdom. Everything in the visible world was believed to be formed in the image of an eternal Form. Each rose, for example, was thought to be shaped from the universal 'Rose Form', which must have existed before any particular rose could be made and which would continue to exist if all roses became extinct.

Medieval enthusiasm for symbols derived from philosophy: 'nature appeared to the symbolical imagination to be a kind of alphabet through which God spoke to men and revealed the order of things'.[6] Herbs were seen as beautiful, because they are green. A vase of red and white roses with thorns could be viewed as martyrs and virgins surrounded by their persecutors.[7] The five petals of the rose symbolised the five books of Moses (the Pentateuch), the five wounds of Christ and other pentads. In colours, white symbolised virginity, red symbolised the blood of Christ, blue, as in ancient Egypt, symbolised truth and justice.[8] A rose could symbolise life on earth. It 'flowers in early morning' and fades 'in the evening of our age'.[9] The tortured flesh of a Christian martyr could symbolise his 'brilliant interior beauty'.[10]

In his tract, *On Intellectual Beauty*,[11] Plotinus explained how the Forms inspire the work of designers. When a block of stone is 'wrought by a craftsman's hands into some statue of god or man', its beauty results from 'the Form or Idea introduced by the art', which 'is in the designer before ever it enters the stone'. Likewise, 'music does not derive from an unmusical source': it comes from the eternal and mathematical Forms of Rhythm and Harmony. Therefore beauty derives from the Platonic Forms and art should imitate the forms. Imitation should not be disparaged, despite Plato's critical remarks on the subject.

> The arts are not to be slighted on the ground that they create by imitation of natural objects; for, to begin with, these natural objects are themselves imitations; then, we must recognise that they give no bare reproduction of the thing seen but go back to the Ideas from which Nature itself derives . . . Thus Pheidias wrought [his famous statue of] Zeus upon no model among things seen but by apprehending what Form Zeus must take if he chose to become manifest to sight.[12]

To the Emperor Gallienus, Plotinus proposed a city constituted on Plato's *Laws* 'to be called Platonopolis'.[13] It was a hint that Neoplatonic ideas could be applied to physical design projects, and indeed, such ideas later influenced architecture and gardens. Neoplatonism was transmitted to Medieval and Renaissance art by St Augustine (396–430), another son of Graeco-Roman Africa and the greatest Christian thinker of antiquity. Augustine was bishop of Hippo Regius (the modern city of Annaba in Algeria). His father was a passionate pagan and his mother a passionate Christian. The son reconciled his parents' beliefs, showing that pagan philosophy could illuminate Christian thought: first, by using reason to reveal the unseen order of God's Creation and second, by infusing order into works of art.

St Augustine thus became the steersman for medieval aesthetics and, as will be explained below, for a Christian approach to gardens. His key aesthetic concepts were order, unity, equality, number and proportion. 'Examine the beauty of bodily form', he wrote, 'and you will find that everything is in its place by number'.[14] Number gives rise to order, which in turn gives rise to symmetry. Design, when orderly and symmetrical,

5.6 White and red roses symbolised the blood of Christ and the purity of the Virgin Mary

5.7 The five petals of the rose symbolised the five wounds of Christ, the Pentateuch and other pentads

5.8 Leonardo's diagram (*c.* 1492), inspired by the writings of Vitruvius, shows the relationship between the forms of the square, the circle and the human body

5.9 Medieval and Renaissance thinkers were fascinated by the relationship between microcosm and macrocosm (Robert Fludd, 1617)

shares formal characteristics with the universal Forms. The principle that a good design is a microcosm of the macrocosm underlies the sacred geometry of Christian and Islamic architecture. 'Vitruvius taught that four was the number of man, because the distance between his extended arms was the same as his height – thus giving the base and height of a square'.[15] Squares manifest the relationship between Man and God. Cathedral design is based on mathematical symbolism. A thousand years after Augustine, mathematical order provided the basis for 'formal' gardens, in the sense of gardens embodying the Platonic Forms. Wittkower explains the geometrical ideas of Pythagoras and Plato, commenting that 'Generally speaking, equilateral triangle, square and pentagon formed the basis of medieval aesthetics'.[16] Though documentary evidence is lacking, mathematical symbolism can also explain the use of square plans for Islamic courts and Christian cloister garths.

> Medieval symbolism found a particularly large field of application in the very rich Christian liturgy, chiefly in fact in interpreting religious architecture . . . It is easy to understand that the round church was the image of the perfection of the circle, but it must be realised that the cross-shaped plan did not only represent Christ's crucifixion, but rather was the *ad quadratum* form, based on the square, designating the four points of the compass and epitomizing the universe. In both cases the church was a microcosm.[17]

The Dark Ages were a period of migration for peoples, as well as ideas, and geometrical perfection became characteristic of religious space from India to Europe. Latin, Persian and Arabic became the languages of scholarship and diplomacy, as Greek had been in Hellenistic and Roman times. Much that the Romans created in Western Europe had fallen into decay, and learning Latin helped scholars to understand the old civilisation.

North Europeans were not uncultured, either before or after Roman times. The structure of the medieval household was directly descended from 'the classical Roman empire, and the peoples, whom the Romans called barbarians'.[18] Medieval gardens share these parents, as classical ideas were adopted by tribal societies and Christianity modernised ancient belief systems. The end of slavery and the Church's insistence on monogamy[19] diminished the classical role of gardens as places for social opulence: compared to their Roman precursors, Frankish gardens were simpler and more spiritual.

Charlemagne, King of the Franks, became Holy Roman Emperor in 800 AD. When not on campaign, he lived at Aachen in North Germany. He introduced the tithe, whereby one–tenth of a peasant's income went to the church. His concern for religion was matched by his passion for gardens: his court compiled a list of plants, issued as the *Capitulare de Villis*, for use in royal gardens. A few years after the king's death, his court sent instructions for an exemplary monastery to be designed in Switzerland, at Reichenau. The design, described below as the St Gall plan, is Europe's oldest drawn

plan for a building project. It is of interest that the text of Vitruvius found in 1415 was also in the St Gall library.[20]

Charlemagne's empire scarcely outlived its founder. Power became local and nation states in the modern sense were slow to develop (Britain one of the first). France became a great feudal power but not until after the Renaissance did it become a unitary power. Power in Italy and the German-speaking lands remained regional until the nineteenth century. An un-Roman chasm yawned between the eastern and western worlds, the worlds of Christ and of Muhammad. For all these reasons, monasteries, castles and walled towns became the social organisations which exercised power in medieval Europe.

5.10 Geometrical perfection was a goal of medieval art: Durham cloister in England (left) Monasterio de Pedralbes cloister in Spain (right)

Medieval gardens

Lasting for a thousand years, Europe's Middle Age had intervals of peace and prosperity which could have been used to make great gardens. The leaders of the

5.11 St. Augustine in a garden

ninth-century 'renaissance' associated with Charlemagne, and of the twelfth-century 'renaissance' associated with cathedral-building, had all the necessary skills and resources. Castles and towns lacked internal space, but extensive gardens could have been made outside fortifications, as the gymnasiums and groves of Ancient Greece had been. Religion favoured gardens: Eden had been a garden; the Jewish *Song of Solomon* laid the foundation for Christian gardens of love:

> Awake, O north wind; and come, thou south; blow upon my garden, that the spices thereof may flow out. Let my beloved come into his garden, and eat his pleasant fruits.[21]

Christ spent the night before his arrest in the Garden of Gethsemane; the first mosque was a garden; the scene of St Augustine's conversion in Milan took place in a garden. Yet medieval gardens were small, because a different attitude to faith produced a different attitude to gardens. Cathedrals satisfied the ritual and ceremonial aspect of religion, as temples had done in Egypt, Greece and Rome. Christian gardens therefore became places for meditation, even if, despite the prevailing asceticism, people dreamed of romance.

St Augustine wrote of his wanton youth: 'I could not discern the clear brightness of love from the fog of lustfulness. Both did confusedly boil in me, and hurried my youth, unfastened, over the precipice of unholy desire'. He therefore cherished the calm sanctuary where, with tumult in his breast, he renounced sexual passion:

> A little garden there was to our lodging, which we had the use of, as of the whole house; for the master of the house, our host, was not living there. Thither had the tumult of my breast hurried me, where no man might hinder the hot contention wherein I had engaged with myself, until it should end as Thou knewest, I knew not. Only I was healthfully distracted and dying, to live; knowing what evil thing I was, and not knowing what good thing I was shortly to become. I retired then into the garden.[22]

Augustine also turned against the pagan gods he identified as 'malignant and deceitful demons'.[23] Had he read Suetonius' account of Tiberius' dealings with pagan gods in groves and grottos, his revulsion from this aspect of his father's religion would be all the more comprehensible:

> A number of small rooms were furnished with the most indecent pictures and statuary obtainable, also certain erotic manuals from Elephantine in Egypt . . . [Tiberius] furthermore devised little nooks of lechery in the woods and glades of the island, and had boys and girls dressed up as Pans and nymphs posted in front of caverns or grottoes; so that the island was now openly and generally called 'Caprineum', because of his goatish antics. Some aspects of

his criminal obscenity are almost too vile to discuss, much less believe. Imagine training little boys, whom he called his 'minnows', to chase him while he went swimming and get between his legs to lick and nibble him.[24]

The cavern of Eros and Cupid is identified with the Blue Grotto, under Capri, though it is said that Suetonius exaggerated Tiberius' evil. Augustine was by no means the first to condemn pagan statues and sacred trees. The Life of St Martin, who died in 397, records him speaking of 'a moral necessity why the tree should be cut down, because it had been dedicated to a demon' and of 'the crowds of heathens [who] looked on in perfect quiet as he razed the pagan temple even to the foundations, he also reduced all the altars and images to dust'.[25] St Martin nearly perished on both occasions but was saved by divine intervention. Everything connected with paganism was anathematised and destroyed.

Architecture and gardens, however, could be designed in perfect accord with St Augustine's *City of God*. The book opens as follows:

> The glorious City of God is my theme in this work . . . a city surpassingly glorious, whether we view it as it still lives by faith in this fleeting course of time, and sojourns as a stranger in the midst of the ungodly, or as it shall dwell in the fixed stability of its eternal seat, which it now with patience waits for, expecting until 'righteousness shall return unto judgment,' and it obtain, by virtue of its excellence, final victory and perfect peace . . . the King and Founder of this city of which we speak, has in Scripture uttered to His people a dictum of the divine law in these words: 'God resisteth the proud, but giveth grace unto the humble'.[26]

Augustine inspired medieval garden-makers to abjure earthiness and look upward for devine inspiration. A perfect square with a round pool and a pentagonal fountain became a microcosm, illuminating the mathematical order and divine grace of the macrocosm (the universe). Numbers were symbolic. Quadrads (designs based on the number four) might represent the four winds, the four seasons or other sets of four. 'The very regularity of the Gothic garden defies the romantic notion of Gothic irregularity and mystery'.[27] Religion and romance were intertwined. Flowers communed with the soul. Even in pagan times, the rose had been sacred (to Venus). Roses and lilies had grown on the tomb of the Virgin Mary after she went to heaven.

> These two famous flowers should call to our mind
> The two greatest gifts of the Church to mankind.
> In the blood of her martyrs she plucks a red Rose,
> And in sign of her faith a white Lily she shows.
> O virginal mother! O store of ripe seed!
> Inviolate maid, wed to Heaven indeed.[28]

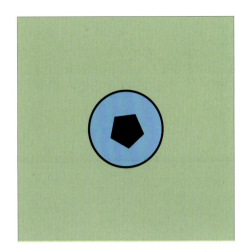

5.12 A square plot with a pentagonal fountain in a circular basin

5.13 Christianity supported the making of ideal places. The illustration is from an 1868 edition of Bunyan's *Pilgrim's Progress*

CHRISTIAN MEETS EVANGELIST.

5.14 The rose was an adored theme in Islamic art

The Madonna lily, *Lilium candidum*, seen by crusaders in the Holy Land, produced the epithet 'lily-white'. In 1213, the Abbot of Cirencester wrote that 'The stalk of the lily, when it is green, produces a most splendid flower, which changes from green to white. So must we persevere in the best of behaviour so that, immature plants as we are, we may attain to the whiteness of innocence'.[29] The rose was an adored theme of Islamic and Christian art. Edward I took 'England's rose' as his insignia, and countless medieval love poems took the rose as their theme. Most famed was the *Roman de la Rose*, expressing the inextricable bonds between faith, chivalry, gardens and eroticism, of which Huizinga wrote: 'Few books have exercised a more profound and enduring influence on the life of any period'.[30]

The *Roman de la Rose* stimulated the imagination of medieval Europe concerning the treasures within castle and garden walls. Readers could learn how to court a lady and, through a thinly veiled subtext, how to seduce her. The *Roman* opens with the Lover approaching the wall of the garden of love. It climaxes with 'plucking the rose'.

Dame Leisure opens the gate for him, Gaiety conducts the dance, Amor holds by the hand Beauty, who is accompanied by Wealth, Liberality, Frankness, Courtesy, and Youth. After having locked the heart of his vassal, Amor enumerates to him the blessings of love, called Hope, Sweet Thought, Sweet Speech, Sweet Look. Then, when Bel-Accueil, the son of Courtesy, invites him to come and see the roses, Danger, Malebouche, Fear, and Shame come to chase him away . . . Virginity is condemned, hell is reserved for those who do not observe the commandments of nature and of love. For the others the flowered field, where the white sheep, led by Jesus, the lamb born of the Virgin, crop the incorruptible grass in endless daylight. At the close Genius throws the taper into the besieged fortress; its flame sets the universe on fire. Venus also throws her torch; then Shame and Fear flee, the castle is taken, and Bel-Accueil allows the lover to pluck the rose.[31]

Medieval society could provide the necessary level of security for gardens of love. They could be in or near castles, fortified towns and monasteries.

Castle gardens

The art of organised warfare was amongst the skills which inhabitants of northern forests learned from the Romans. This led to a need for residential castles. Forts, on the Roman model, had been occupied only by soldiers enforcing the will of a distant power and using roads to summon reinforcements. When power became local, residential castles replaced army forts and domesticated warfare. Castles became crowded homes for a lord, his wife, his family, armed retainers and, in times of danger, the entire local populace.

For us, castles symbolise the society of the High Middle Ages (1000–1300). When called, a knight rode forth in his lord's or lady's service, clad in armour and mounted on a warhorse. Making boasts and taking vows, he lived and died by a code of chivalry. A rich wife, or a prisoner worth a ransom, were his chief means of advancement, trade being un-chivalrous. Marriage was no love affair: it was a serious business with dynastic implications. Though fair maids might dream of love, chatelaines had to breed families and run great estates in their lords' absence. In peacetime a young wife might have leisure to sew, make a garden, listen to minstrels or conduct an illicit romance. Sitting on a flowery mead to make daisy chains was an approved pastime. As adults, medieval women became domestic stalwarts with more knowledge of medicine herbs, horticulture and gardens than other castle residents.

5.15 Details from the *Très Riches Heures*: a castle garden (top, Paris), a burgher's garden (middle, Dourdan) and a peasants' garden, at the close of the Middle Ages

Castle-building developed rapidly in Europe after the ninth century, particularly in France. Castles, like Helmsley Castle in Yorkshire, often began as a stockade on a conical mound (motte) with a ditch at the foot of the slope. Later castles were built in stone, often with a nearby garden and orchard. When outer curtain walls and moats were added, garden plants could be tended within the fortified zone. In times of siege villagers would take refuge within the bailey, trampling everything, and ladies could

5.16 (top left) Helmsley Castle, Yorkshire, is typical of the motte-and-bailey arrangement which provided some protected space for peacetime gardening

5.17 (top right) An orchard at Penshurst, Kent

5.18 (above) A perfect herber (*c.* 1465) from the Mystical Marriage of St Catherine

5.19 (right) Land within the fortifications of Werfen Castle in Austria is used as a garden

take exercise only on the ramparts. Symbolic illustrations, like those in the *Très Riches Heures du Duc de Berry* (c. 1410) allow, in what arc 'virtually colour-photographs',[32] glimpses of ornamental gardens occupying land within curtain-walled enclosures. They correlate with the garden descriptions in the *Roman de la Rose* and with the numerous illustrations from the late-medieval period, drawn to accompany the poem and reproduced in books on medieval gardens. We see flowery lawns, basins, turf seats, summer houses, flowers, neat trees, trellis-work and rose arbours in which maidens could steal a forbidden kiss from a 'veray parfit gentil knight'.[33] Who would not seek relief from the stench, noise and lack of privacy within the keep, or from the excrement-strewn mud of the bailey and barnyard?

St Albertus Magnus explained how to make a 'pleasure garden', in 1206 – although it unlikely that he ever made such a garden for the Dominican monastic order to which he belonged. He was the son of a wealthy German lord and was probably describing the type of garden he had known as a boy. His teacher, St Thomas Aquinas, had developed St Augustine's ideas on aesthetics, stressing the role of cognition in perceiving transcendental beauty. Albertus referred to Aristotle as his chief authority on science, and would have understood the significance of. geometry in Christian design. He, and his English contemporary Henry the Poet,[34] wrote about 'square' gardens. Here are Albertus' instructions for a perfect 'green cloth' framed by 'a bench of turf' and 'every sweet-smelling herb':

> The whole plot is to be covered with rich turf of flourishing grass, the turves beaten down with broad wooden mallets and the plants of grass trodden into the ground until they cannot be seen or scarcely anything of them perceived. For then little by little they may spring forth closely and cover the surface like a green cloth. Care must be taken that the lawn is of such a size that about it in a square may be planted every sweet-smelling herb such as rue, and

5.20 Castle ramparts and yards could be used as garden space in peaceful times: Salzburg Castle

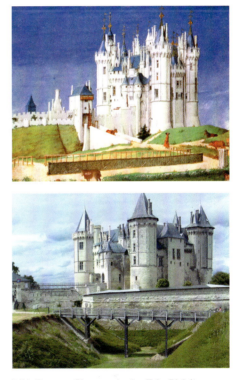

5.21 Saumur Chateau, in the *Très Riches Heures* and today, showing the accuracy of the Limbourg's painting

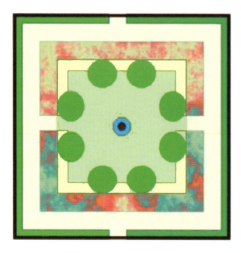

5.22 A reconstruction, based on St Albertus Magnus' account of how to make a pleasure garden

sage and basil, and likewise all sorts of flowers, as the violet, columbine, lily, rose, iris and the like. So that between these herbs and the turf, at the edge of the lawn set square, let there be a higher bench of turf flowering and lovely; and somewhere in the middle provide seats so that men may sit down there to take their repose pleasurably when their senses need refreshment. Upon the lawn too, against the heat of the sun, trees should be planted or vines trained, so that the lawn may have a delightful and cooling shade, sheltered by their leaves.

Figure 5.22 shows a reconstruction, based on Albertus' text and on symbolic paintings in medieval manuscripts. The following points should be noted:

- medieval garden illustrations were as diagrammatic as those of buildings
- despite their simplicity, medieval gardens surely had the high quality we find in medieval buildings
- Albertus' mention of a square plan implies a wider use of geometry, as in religious architecture
- Albertus' delight in flowers and scents implies the riches of a millefleurs tapestry, which is difficult to show on a diagram.

Gardens were also made outside curtain walls. Areas of woodland were fenced for country pleasures, as in ancient Mesopotamia. Wooded pleasure parks can be distinguished from hunting parks but the roles overlap: a *pleasance* (pleasure-ground) might have a *gloriette* (pavilion) where the ladies could eat while watching the men hunt, fish or joust. The word *gloriette* comes, via Spain, from West Asia.[35] A pleasance was a place of resort. In *Mai and Beaflore* the prince banquets in 'a little garden of trees full of white-rose bowers under the castle. Many were sitting there on seats; poor and rich ate together'.[36] Nobles maintained extensive hunting parks, subject to forest laws:

A forest is a certain territory of woody grounds and fruitful pastures, privileged for wild beasts and fowls of forest, chase, and warren, to rest and abide there in the safe protection of the king . . . And therefore a forest doth chiefly consist of these four things: of vert and venison; of particular laws and proper officers.[37]

5.23 A re-created medieval seat, in Sissinghurst Castle Garden

The rights of peasants to exploit the resources of a hunting park were carefully defined: they might graze livestock and collect fallen wood, but were subject to mutilation or execution if caught poaching game or felling trees.

Some information about castle gardens can be gleaned from Renaissance plans, such as De Cerceau's drawing of Montargis, in *Les Plus Excellents Bastiments de France* (1576). It shows a herber within the castle walls and extensive orchard and vegetable gardens outside the curtain wall. De Cerceau was a Protestant refugee who lived at Montargis for a time (see p. 130).

Royal palaces had grander gardens than those of the nobles but were similar in kind. Because his empire was secure, Charlemagne did not need to build his palaces and gardens behind fortifications. His palace at Aachen (*c.* 780) was near a hot spa and had a courtyard like a Roman villa. His successors had less security and found it necessary to live behind fortifications and to make their gardens in the woods – or, if space allowed, within the bailey. Massive castles were built in Northern France; Vincennes and St Germain had space for gardens, but these are likely to have been small.[38] Henry III of England had gardens outside the fortifications of Windsor Castle and created the post of Royal Gardener in 1268.[39] Edward I made a garden for the Palace of Westminster on his return from the Crusades in 1272. It was fortified and the herber occupied 'about half-an-acre of the Palace precinct'.[40] The King's Knot and the parterre beneath Stirling Castle 'occupy the site of a great garden which was probably laid out by James I of Scotland soon after 1424, in imitation of the King's Garden below Windsor Castle where he had first seen his queen'. At the Louvre 'the great garden of the palace was connected to the Petit Jardin on the other side of the street by a private arched bridge',[41] which is reminiscent of Amarna (see p. 44). Sundials are one of the few surviving features of medieval castle gardens.

With the deployment of canon in the fifteenth century, it became easier to smash castle walls. It was then necessary to have an army for defence and a centralised government to organise the army. Many castle owners developed their gun platforms, ramparts and bailies into Renaissance gardens of the kind discussed in the next chapter. Prague has a royal garden north of Hradschin Castle and aristocratic gardens on its southern ramparts.

5.24 The land east of Amboise Castle is still a garden (see plan p. 131)

5.25 A sundial at Penshurst Castle in a re-created garden

5.26 The King's knot, viewed from the battlements of Stirling Castle

5.27 Prague and its castle *c.* 1512

5.28 Gardens below the ramparts of Prague Castle

Monastery gardens

Though a life of retreat offers various joys,
None I think will compare with the time one employs
In the study of herbs, or in striving to gain
Some practical knowledge of nature's domain.[42]

Monasteries can be compared with the temples of the ancient world. Regularity lay at their heart and members of the public were excluded unless the monastery had a public church, an infirmary or a school. But monastic gardens were contemplative and functional, never ceremonial. While knights devoted themselves to war, the arts of civilisation were kept alive by the clergy, mostly from the upper classes. The Knights Templar had both monastic and military roles. Taking their name from Jerusalem's ancient Temple, they fought to protect Christian pilgrims visiting shrines in the Holy Land.

Monasticism originated in Egypt. Early monks (from *monos*, meaning single) lived in self-denial and poverty, following Christ's example. St Anthony of the Desert, an early monk, was an Egyptian who lived from 251–356 AD. He gave his father's estate to the poor and 'shut himself up in a remote cell upon a mountain' where he 'cultivated and pruned a little garden', his heart 'filled with inward peace, simplicity, goodness'.[43] Monastic communities developed and the movement spread round the shores of the Mediterranean in the fourth and fifth centuries. The Roman Empire supported Christianity after 313 AD and when Roman society collapsed, three centuries later, the church became reliant on monasticism. Pope Gregory, himself a monk, sent his brethren on evangelical missions to former outposts of empire. Monasteries became repositories of classical civilisation, like pools in the bed of a dried-up river. By Charlemagne's time, some of these pools had become enviably deep and well-stocked, thereby sowing the seeds of their eventual destruction.

Manual labour was regarded as devotional and work in a garden especially so, for 'the Lord God took the man, and put him into the Garden of Eden to dress it and to keep it'.[44] The Rule of St Benedict (*c.* 540) stated that 'Whenever possible the monastery should be so laid out that everything essential, that is to say water, mills, garden and workshops for the plying of the various crafts, is found within the monastery walls'.[45] Brothers were reminded that 'idleness is an enemy of the soul.' The Carthusians, founded as a solitary order, gave each monk a cell, a workspace and a private garden. Vegetables were grown for the table, herbs for the hospital. Flowers were cherished like religious icons. Cultivation of choice fruits was a favoured pastime. The day was divided into 'hours' for prayer, reading, work, eating, meditation and sleep.

Cloisters were intrinsic to monasticism. The word 'cloister' means 'enclosed' and describes that part of the monastery from which the public is excluded. In communal orders, the cloistered area had a colonnaded court which became known as *the* cloister. Its form derived from Roman peristyle courts which, as noted in Chapter 3, frequently contained shrines. The cloister lawn was known as a 'garth'. Later authors wrote of cloister 'gardens'. 'Garden' is cognate with 'garth', but now implies the presence of ornamental plants, which were rare in medieval cloisters. The garth often had a roofed fountain to supply water for washing, either in the centre or at the edge (Monasterio de Pedralbes, Figure 5.10). Arcades were busy places, used as covered paths, for reading, for teaching, for exercise in bad weather and for work. Adjoining the arcade were rooms in which to eat, cook, sleep, read and store provisions. Umberto Eco explained the importance of a garth:

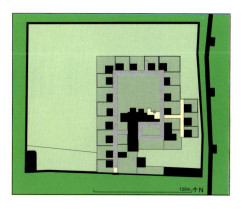

5.30 Diagram of a Carthusian monastery. Each cell has its own garden. The monastery was in Nurenberg but does not survive

5.31 Cloister arcades have always been busy places. Westminster Cathedral cloister in London is now used as a café

5.32 Many cloister garths, like this one at Salisbury Cathedral, Wiltshire, have been planted as gardens

5.33 San Giovanni in Rome has a beautifully calm cloister marred by thoughtless planting

The green turf which is in the middle of the material cloister refreshes encloistered eyes and their desire to study returns.[46]

Some monasteries, especially in England, were also cathedrals (i.e. they had a church with a bishop's throne) and many cathedrals had cloisters even if there was no resident community. Alec Clifton-Taylor offers a reason:

For monastic cathedrals [cloisters] were indispensable, and they were felt to be such an agreeable accessory that several of the non-monastic cathedrals added them, for the sheer pleasure they provide: and what better reason can be imagined?[47]

The earliest document to mention the building of a European cloister is the Life of St Philibert, Abbot of Jumièges (c. 655). He studied the design of 'all monasteries in the bosom of France and Italy' but does not name their designers. Works of art were unattributed for the reason given in Chapter 57 of St Benedict's Rule: 'If any (craftsman) be puffed up by his skill in his craft, and think the monastery indebted to him for it, such a one shall be shifted from his handicraft, and not attempt it again till such time as, having learnt a low opinion of himself, the abbot shall bid him resume.' St Philibert's biographer therefore wrote that 'Divine Providence built battlemented ramparts rising up in a massive square . . . The cell of God's Saint himself looks out from the south, adorned with an edging of stone. Arcades accompany the laboriously stone-built cloister; the soul is delighted by varied decoration and girt about with bubbling waters.' This is in line with St Augustine's beliefs: the monastery was viewed as a creation of Divine Providence, working through the hand of St Philibert and using the square as a symbol of God's perfection. Mention of the cloister being 'girt about with bubbling waters' is of great interest: 'bubbling' implies moving water and 'girt about' suggests a greater extent of water than in a fountain basin, either in channels of the type used in West Asian paradise gardens or outside the garth.

The oldest cloister plan was drawn some 175 years later, by Abbot Haito of Reichenau for Abbot Gozbert of St Gall. Haito had been to Constantinople and had supervised the design of a church. He asked Gozbert to dwell upon the plan 'in spirit', reminding him that 'we drew it through the love of God out of fraternal affection, for you to study only'. It was thus presented as an Augustinian (Platonic) Form – not a plan for a real place – and it was mathematically composed. Medieval schoolmen liked Plato's argument that reason implies the existence of a perfect world. Columns, arcades and buttresses are planned according to the proportion of the Golden Section.[48] The cloister has a quadripartite plan with crossing paths, the oldest representation of a four-square plan of the type discussed in the previous chapter. There are two semi-circular spaces labelled 'paradise', at the east and west ends of the church, confirming the influence of West Asia on the St Gall plan. The word 'paradise' 'entered Christian church history as the name for the porticoes adjoining the oldest

Byzantine basilicas, planted as gardens'.[49] In Europe, the quadripartite plan symbolised both the tips of the Holy Cross and the Four Rivers of Eden. The cloister garth is marked with the words *semitae* (footpaths) and *savina* (juniper) in the centre. Juniper, which symbolised the Tree of Life and therefore paradise,[50] had a liturgical role: its branches were used to sprinkle holy water. The only other monastery plan to have survived, for Christ Church, Canterbury, was drawn in 1160 and, like the St Gall plan, shows domestic accommodation and a church adjoining the cloister, together with a fountain, a fishpond, a cemetery, a herbarium, an orchard and a vineyard.

One of Haito's pupils, Walafrid Strabo, reveals an expert knowledge of plants in the poem from which the quotation at the start of this section is taken. *Hortulus* ('The Little Garden') was 'a bestseller throughout the Middle Ages'.[51]

> Of heroical deeds, do not scorn my desire,
> But this my poor vegetable epic inspire!
> Though the stem of the Chervil be straggly and weak,
> And its seed mean and paltry, not easy to seek
> In the thick of the leaves, it is green all the year
> And freely bestows of its comfort and cheer
> On the poor.

Landsberg distinguishes the following monastic horticultural types:[52]

- Cemetery orchard: the St Gall cemetery orchard would have contained tombs and fruit trees – it symbolised paradise
- Infirmary garden: used to grow medicinal plants
- Green court: an area of grass and trees, used for grazing horses and for other incidental functions
- Obedientiary gardens: obedientiaries (the Prior and other office holders – who were 'obedient') might have their own private gardens
- Cellarer's garden: for growing vegetables, culinary herbs and other utilitarian plants (e.g. Covent Garden in London, which later became a vegetable market)
- Herber: a small enclosed garden containing a lawn and herbaceous plants
- Vineyard: the Domesday Book (1086) records 38 vineyards England
- Kitchen garden: used to grow both food and medicinal plants.

Monastic foundations became repositories of wealth. This was virtually unavoidable, since knowledge, education and skill made monks the best gardeners, the best farmers and the best manufacturers of their day. Benefiting also from gifts and legacies, monasteries became opulent. Their churches came to rival cathedral churches and the old virtues of self-denial and manual work vanished. Architectural historians

5.34 This Templars' monastery (founded 1172, Coulommiers, France) has a re-created medieval cellarer's garden, probably in its original position. Wattle fencing protected the crops from animals

5.35 An obedientiary garden at Klosterneuberg in Austria

classify the style of the Early Middle Ages as Romanesque and that of the Late Middle Ages as Gothic, with sub-divisions to suit different countries.

Garden historians, having less evidence, can distinguish usefully only the symbolic purity of the Early Middle Ages and the comparative luxury of monastic gardens during the Renaissance. The employment of professional gardeners led to the replacement of herbers, orchards and cloister garths with elaborate parterres, clipped hedges and ornate fountains. At the abbey of St Bénigne, the rose and the lily were used as patterns for parterres. Envy replaced admiration. Tales of vice spread abroad, Charlemagne himself noting that monks are too often 'found to be sodomites'.[53] The scene was set for a tragedy. Braunfels describes: 'the great onslaught on the monasteries, prepared by the Enlightenment and released by the French Revolution' in which 'the idealism of the monks was impugned, their treasures were barbarously scattered and destroyed, their monasteries sold, their churches deconsecrated, and many of the

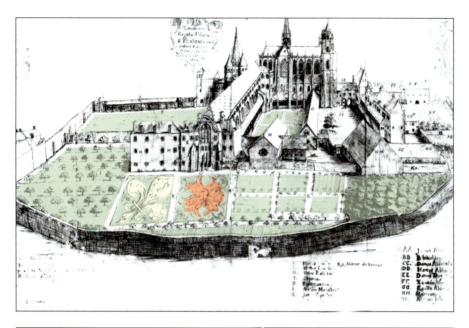

5.36 (top left) A seventeenth-century drawing of St Bénigne shows lily and rose decoration in the *hortus superior*

5.37 (top right) A drawing of Clairvaux (1708) shows a profusion of parterres

5.38 (left) Westminster Abbey, London: the Little Cloister was an infirmary garden before it became an ornamental space

5.39 Monasteries and cloister garths became places of luxury: Santa Chiara, Naples (left) and Mosteiro dos Jeronimos, Lisbon (right)

5.40 The twelfth century fortified farm at Bois Richeux, France, has a re-created medieval garden with a dovecot, a vine arbour, raised beds and plants from the *Capitulare de Villis*

finest of them torn down'.[54] It parallels the ruthless vigour with which St Martin and his contemporaries had destroyed the sacred trees, statues and sanctuaries of the detested pagans.

Town gardens

The only generalisation that can be made about medieval cities is that it is impossible to generalise about their form, since 'medieval towns and cities came in all shapes and sizes, adapting themselves freely to every geographical and economic circumstance.'[55]

Settlements were large and small, bonded and free, chartered and unchartered, walled and unwalled, on hilltops and in valleys. Some had space for gardens, others did not.

North Europe had many unwalled settlements belonging to feudal lords or monastic foundations. The tenant's oath of loyalty was a contract between free men. He then became a bondsman holding land in return for services – military, agricultural and domestic – owed to his lord. Village houses were placed beside roads. Farmland was ploughed in long thin strips by ox-drawn ploughs. Smaller areas were cultivated by gardening techniques or ploughs without wheels. Plants were cultivated for their usefulness, although some were also valued for their beauty. Even the lily and rose had medicinal uses. Legal reports provide the information that house doors were frequently open so that 'while the baby of the family slept in its cradle by the open hearth, chickens, pigs and the family cat rooted in the straw'.[56]

Every feature of a medieval village was multi-functional. No plans survive but archaeology has yielded some information and will surely yield more. Village gardens were enclosed by earth banks, hedges, ditches, walls and fences. The house and its surrounding land were known as a close, a toft, a croft or a messuage. Rectangular plant beds, of a size which could be reached from paths without trampling on plants, were used primarily for vegetables but also for growing some decorative herbs and flowers. The commonest vegetables were kale, leeks, parsley, parsnips, peas and beans, all of which could provide food in winter. Homes with only one room had another use for gardens. Mumford writes that late medieval astrological calendars 'show lovers having intercourse in the open . . . erotic passion was more attractive in the garden and the wood, or under a hedge, despite stubble or insects, than it was in the house'.[57]

Towns were constituted on a different basis. Typically, house-owners were freemen: merchants, craftsmen and professionals who needed the protection of town walls because they had no lord. Burghers made features resembling those in castle gardens:

- Covered walks: pergolas were used to create shady walks. Vines and roses were the favoured plants
- Arbours: semicircular arbours were used to shelter seating areas
- Seats: these were often covered in turf, herbs, stone or timber, and usually lacked a back support
- Plant beds: these might be raised or sunken
- Turf and flowery meads: both pure grass and flowery lawns were valued
- Boundaries and fences: hedges were used to keep out cattle and other animals. Walls and fences made from wattle and boards were also used
- Fountains: many medieval illustrations show fountains, which are often set in pools
- Moats, rivers and pools: used for fish and as boundaries
- Baths: ladies would refresh themselves before a meal by washing their feet
- Fishponds: known as 'stews', fishponds were popular and useful features of the medieval garden
- Dovecots: ornamental, as well as an important source of food.

The walled towns of North Europe were often better suited to garden-making than those of South Europe: they had more water and were less likely to be on rocky hills. However, not all Mediterranean settlements were densely-built hill-towns; some had space for both functional and ornamental gardens. Renaissance maps and drawings show these gardens to have been surprisingly similar to those of Northern Europe.

The Middle Ages did not, of course, come to a sudden end in 1500. Adoption of Renaissance urban patterns, if rapid in the great commercial cities, took centuries to reach the backward regions of backward countries. When armies, instead of fortifications, became the means of protecting towns, living in country villas became sufficiently safe to make the great villa gardens which will be discussed in the next chapter.

5.41 Medieval towns sometimes had space for gardens just inside or outside the city walls: Segovia

Types and examples

Castle gardens

5.42
Castle gardens

Use: Forts had been occupied only by soldiers. A castle was a place for a lord to live with his family, dependents and retainers. Castle gardens were sometimes within the fortifications and sometimes outside. In both cases they were primarily for the use of ladies, children, swains and troubadours. In times of siege, an army, or the whole population of the surrounding area, might occupy the space inside the outer fortifications and trample the garden to mud.

Form: A garden could be a small hexagonal, rectangular, or irregular enclosure, within or near the fortified area. No examples survive but a good idea of their appearance can be gained from the symbolic illustrations in medieval books, which show flowery lawns, trellis fencing, turf seats, tunnel-arbours and a profusion of sweet-scented flowers. Castles also had orchards, pleasure parks and hunting parks outside the fortified zone. There are many surviving castles where one can imagine castle gardens within the inner or outer bailey, and there are some sixteenth-century plans and records of castles with knot gardens.

Montargis 1560

Louis XII of France (1462–1515) invaded Italy and arranged for his daughter, Renée, to marry Hercules d'Este of Ferrara. Following d'Este's death in 1560, Renée returned to France and lived in the hilltop castle of Montargis. As a Protestant princess, she had been unhappy in Italy, but despite this had come to love Italian gardens. The hilltop castle to which she returned had a donjon (keep), protected by a turreted outer wall.

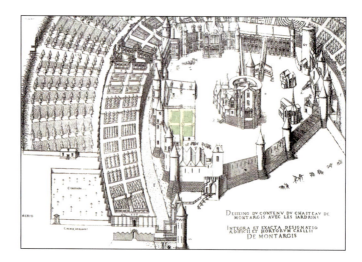

5.43 Montargis

Du Cerceau was employed to rebuild the castle and lay out a garden on the slope beyond the walls. His drawing also shows a small herber in just the place where one would expect to find a medieval garden: within the fortifications. It may well have been a survival from the castle's medieval period. The old castle was demolished after the French Revolution but has been partly rebuilt.

> Most gardens were divided into enclosed rectangular pleasaunces . . . Almost the only exception is in the semicircular gardens of Montargis, planned by du Cerceau in a radiating scheme, with the castle as centre, and trellis arbours as rays.[58]

Amboise 1576

The early Renaissance castle garden as it exists today is similar to the garden shown in the du Cerceau drawing of 1576. Before that, Amboise probably had a small enclosed herber containing a lawn and herbaceous plants. The castle is on a rocky plateau with spectacular views of the River Loire.

> The platforms, the bastions, the terraces, the high-niched windows and balconies, the hanging gardens and dizzy crenellations, of this complicated structure, keep you in perpetual intercourse with an immense horizon.[59]

Ambras Schlosspark 1570

Ambras was converted from a fortress to a palace when it was acquired by Archduke Ferdinand II in 1564. It now has re-created medieval and Renaissance gardens. The castle is now surrounded by a large landscape park in the English style, and woods hide the castle in a way which would not have been allowed when the defences were functional. But when the castle is floodlit, and one looks across Innsbruck from the northern side of the valley, it is still possible to see how Ambras commanded the heights above Innsbruck.

> The castle at Ambras was built on the hill, 'in magnificence excelling the finest villas of the ancients.' In the women's part the visitor first saw hanging gardens and wired aviaries, but it is not clear whether by this is meant real roof-gardens or high terraces, for the gardens proper are at the foot of the hill.[60]

Cloister gardens

Use: Cloister courtyards, used for walking, reading and working, were at the heart of monastic communities. They gave access to the adjacent buildings: the refectory, dormitory and cellar, where food was stored. Another door led to the church. The garth (lawn) was an aid to contemplation.

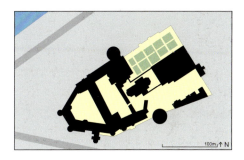

5.44 Amboise

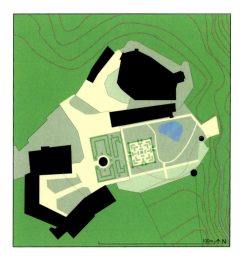

5.45 Ambras

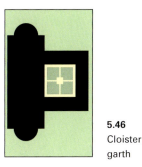

5.46 Cloister garth

Form: The typical cloister is a square courtyard surrounded by a covered walk, similar in plan to the Greek and Roman peristyle courts from which they derive. Early cloisters may have contained herbs and shrubs but there are no medieval records of their having contained vegetation other than close-scythed grass. During the Renaissance, princes of the church became leaders in the art of garden design and many simple plats of grass were transformed into ornamental gardens. In the nineteenth century some became gardenesque, with herbaceous plants and shrubs. Monastries also had flower, vegetable and orchard gardens, but no medieval examples of these survive.

St Gall 820

The famous St Gall plan was drawn by Abbot Haito of Reichenau (763–836), who resigned as abbot, at the age of 56, to live in simple conformity with St Benedict's rule. A love of regularity pervades his plan: the cloister is exactly 100 feet square and the placing of elements is symmetrical. The plan includes an infirmary garden, a cemetery garden and a gardener's house.

The most astonishing document of early medieval Benedictine monastic architecture is the plan of an ideal Carolingian monastery preserved in the library of St Gall. It represents the only architectural drawing antedating the thirteenth century in Europe to reveal the exercise of powers of planning.[61]

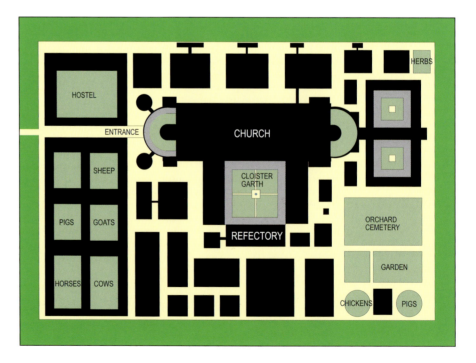

5.47 St Gall

San Lorenzo fuori le Mura, Rome 1200

The north part of the church was built in the sixth century, above a catacomb that houses the tomb of San Lorenzo (St Lawrence). The south section of the church, on a different alignment, was built in the twelfth century. The two parts were joined in 1216. The 'simple, very austere'[62] cloister, of *c.* 1190, has an unusually intimate scale. An illustration from 1924 shows it with a Renaissance pattern of gravel and low box hedging. The pattern has been retained and the cloister is now stocked with flowering herbaceous plants, creating a fresh and sweet atmosphere.

> In the garden the peace of past centuries still fills its surrounding arcades while shafts of sunlight stream down between the classical and medieval columns, which are so appropriately mingled in this place where memories of pagan, early Christian and medieval Rome are fused together.[63]

Salisbury 1260

Salisbury Cathedral is a prime example of the Early English Gothic style, splendidly placed in an open landscape. It was built 1220–58. The graceful, arcaded cloister contains what would have been a plain square of grass in the Middle Ages but now has a great tree and is managed like a suburban garden. Clifton-Taylor admires the cedars but does not mention the scruffy foundation planting.

> These are the largest and, with the exception of Gloucester, the finest cloisters in England, as well as being the earliest to survive in their present form. Four spacious walks, all with simple quadripartite vaults, open upon a garth in which today grow magnificent cedars.[64]

5.48 San Lorenzo fuori le Mura, Rome

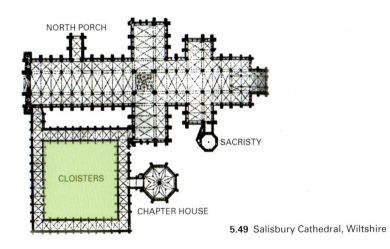

NORTH PORCH

SACRISTY

CLOISTERS

CHAPTER HOUSE

5.49 Salisbury Cathedral, Wiltshire

5.50
Medieval
town
garden

Town gardens

Use: Lack of evidence besets the study of every aspect of medieval gardens but it seems fair to surmise that the gardens of wealthy burghers near town centres were used like castle gardens while the poor used what land they had for culinary and medicinal plants, some of them decorative. The gardens of the middle classes must have ranged between those of the rich and the poor, with much depending on the availability of space within the walls of a particular town at a particular time.

Form: Evidence from archaeology and from Renaissance maps of medieval towns shows that many gardens were irregular in shape, with boundaries made by buildings, walls, fences, hedges and ditches. Beaten-earth and gravel paths were used to demarcate planting beds. Such gardens are unlikely to have had lawns, as these would have wasted space, fostered weeds and required laborious care.

Bruges 1500

Bruges became the largest trading city in North Europe. Its walls enclosed 3 hectares in the ninth century, 86 hectares in the eleventh century and 400 hectares in the fourteenth century. Space was scarce before each expansion and relatively abundant afterwards. The wealthy lived near the market square, in tall terraced houses with small courts and yards. Poorer folk, who lived near the town walls, had vineyards, small fields and what we would call market gardens. There was a vast uncovered area on the western fringe of Bruges, used for the traditional Friday market fair. It was partly planted with trees and flanked by a navigable canal.[65] Wealthy burghers also owned orchards and vineyards in the suburbs, as did their Ancient Greek predecessors.

5.51 Town gardens inside the gates of Bruges (from the 1562 plan by Marcus Gerards)

Notes

1   Landsberg, S., *The Medieval Garden*, London: British Museum Press, 1995, p. 4.
2   Eco, U., *Art and Beauty in the Middle Ages*, Yale University Press, 1986, p. 52.
3   Le Goff, J., *Medieval Civilisation*, Oxford: Basil Blackwell, 1988, p. 325.
4   Huizinga, J., *The Waning of the Middle Ages*, London: Penguin, 1965 edn, p. 209.
5   Lovejoy, A. O., *The Great Chain of Being: A study of the history of an idea*, New York: Harper & Row, 1960, p. 61.
6   Huizinga, J., op. cit., p. 255.
7   Eco, U., op. cit., p. 55.
8   Hope, A. and Walsh, M., *The Colour Compendium*, New York: Van Nostrand Rheinhold, 1990, p, 281.
9   Alan of Lille, quoted in Eco, U., op. cit., p. 59.
10 Eco, U., op. cit., p. 9.
11 Plotinus, *The Enneads*, transl. MacKenna, S., London: Penguin, 1991, V.8.
12 Ibid. (Note that MacKenna's original translation uses 'reason-principles' in place of 'ideas' in this quotation.)
13 Porphyry, 'On the life of Plotinus and his work' in Plotinus, op. cit., p. cxii.
14 St Augustine, *De Libero Arbitrio*, transl. Burleigh, II, xv1, 42.
15 Eco, U., op. cit., p. 35.
16 Wittkower, R., *Architectural Principles in the Age of Humanism,* London: Academy Editions, 1988 edn, p. 150.
17 Le Goff, J., op. cit., p. 333.
18 Herlihy, D., *Medieval Households*, Harvard University Press, 1985, p. 1.
19 Herlihy, D., op. cit., p. 157.
20 Stierlin, H., *The Roman Empire*, Cologne: Taschen, 2002, p. 56.
21 *The Song of Solomon*, Ch 4, v. 16.
22 St Augustine, *Confessions*, Book 8.
23 ——, *The City of God*, Book IV.
24 Suetonius, *The Twelve Caesars*, Penguin, 1957, pp. 131.
25 Sulpitius Severus, *On the Life of St Martin*, transl. Roberts, A., New York, 1894.
26 St Augustine, op. cit., Book I.
27 Stokstad, M. and Stannard, J., *Gardens of the Middle Ages*, Kansas: Spencer Museum of Art, 1983, p. 31.
28 Walafrid Strabo, *Hortulus*, transl. Lambert, R. S., The Stanton Press, 1924, p. 37.
29 Alexander Neckham, quoted in McLean, T., *Medieval Gardens*, London: Collins, 1981, p. 162.
30 Huizinga, J., op. cit., p. 105.
31 Huizinga, J., op. cit., p. 109.
32 Harvey, J., *Medieval Gardens*, London: Batsford, 1981, p. 98.
33 Chaucer, G., *Canterbury Tales*, Prologue, Line 72.
34 Harvey, J., 'The square garden of Henry the Poet', in *Garden History*, Vol. 15, No. 1, Spring 1987, pp. 1–12.
35 Harvey, J., op. cit., p. 44.
36 Gothein, M-L., *A History of Garden Art*, London: J. M. Dent, 1928, Vol. 1, p. 189.
37 Manwood, 1717, p. 143.
38 Gothein, M-L., op. cit., Vol. 1, p. 183.
39 Harvey, J., op. cit., p. 78.
40 ——, op. cit., p. 82.
41 ——, op. cit., p. 75.
42 Walafridus Strabo, *Hortulus; or, the little garden, etc.*, transl. Lambert, S. R., Wembley Hill: Stanton Press, 1924, pp. 11, 38.

43 St Athanasius, *Life of St Anthony*.

44 *Genesis*, Ch. 2, v. 15.

45 *Regula Sancti Benedicti*, Ch 66.

46 Eco, U., op. cit., quoted in Landsberg, S., op. cit., p. 36.

47 Clifton-Taylor, A., *The Cathedrals of England*, London: Thames & Hudson, 1967, p. 136.

48 Braunfels, W., *Monasteries of Western Europe: The architecture of the orders*, London: Thames & Hudson, 1972, p. 45.

49 McLean, T., op. cit. (Ref. 29), p. 16.

50 *Genesis* ch. 2, v. 8. I am grateful to Bettina v. Greyerz at Sankt Gallen for this information. See Sennhauser, H. R., in *St Gallen, Klosterplan und Gozbertbau*, pp. 23–28.

51 T. McLean, op. cit. (Ref. 29), p. 18.

52 Landsberg, S., op. cit., Ch. 1, 'Types of medieval garden', pp. 11–48.

53 *Capitulare de Villis*, in Henderson, E. F., *Select Historical Documents of the Middle Ages*, London: George Bell & Sons, 1896.

54 Braunfels, W., op. cit., p. 221.

55 Benevolo, L., *The History of the City,* London: Scolar Press, 1980, p. 308.

56 Hanawalt, B. A., *The Ties that Bound*. Oxford: Oxford University Press, 1986, p. 43.

57 Mumford, L., *The City in History*, Penguin, 1961, p. 330.

58 Ward, H., *The Architecture of the Renaissance in France*, Vol. 1, 1911, p. 180.

59 James, H., *A Little Tour of France*, London: Heinemann, 1900, p. 47.

60 Gothein, M-L., op. cit., Vol. 2, p. 12.

61 Braunfels, W., op. cit., p. 36.

62 Conant, K. J., *Carolingian and Romanesque Architecture 800–1200*, Penguin, 1959, p. 229.

63 Mason, G., *Rome*, Woodbridge: Companion Guides, 1965, p. 244.

64 Clifton-Taylor, A., op. cit., p. 136.

65 Benevolo, L., op. cit., p. 369.

Chapter 6

Renaissance gardens
1350–1650

History and philosophy

The political landscape of Italy in the fourteenth century was very different from that of today. There was no national government and scarcely a national language. Settlements, subject to attack from neighbours and foreigners, had to be defended. Great cities, like Rome, Naples, Venice, Milan and Florence could hold their own against each another but fell to invading armies. Wealthy nobles therefore lived behind high walls. Some built castles on isolated peaks; others integrated their defences with the towns they controlled. On hilltops, space was limited and water scarce. Rather than live in isolated farmsteads, farmers made daily journeys from the safety of town to cultivate their fields. Such conditions did not favour garden-making.[1]

Yet the roots of an old dream, that of an earthly paradise, were stirring anew. Boccaccio's *Decameron* tells of a party of young men and women sojourning in the countryside while their city endures an infestation of the plague. They tell each other saucy tales and relish the health-giving air of a delightful garden on a forested hill looking over Florence.

In the midst of the garden was a plot of very fine grass, so green that it seemed well nigh black. It was embellished with perhaps a thousand kinds of flowers and enclosed with the greenest and lustiest of orange and lemon trees. The trees bore at once old fruits and new flowers. They not only afforded the eyes a pleasant shade, but were no less pleasingly scented. In the midst of the grass was a fountain of the whitest marble, enchased with wonder-goodly sculptures. A great jet of water sprang from a statue, that stood on a column in its midst. The water which overflowed the full basin issued forth from the lawn by a hidden pipe. It came to light encompassed by very goodly and curiously made channels. But before reaching the plain it turned two mills with exceeding power, to the no small advantage of the lord.

6.1 Boccaccio's *Decameron* tells of a party of young men and women playing in a garden

The sight of this garden, its fair order, the plants and the fountain and the rivulets, pleased the ladies and the three young men. They all of one accord said that if a Paradise might be created upon earth, they could not conceive any form, other than that of this garden, which it might have. Nor what further beauty might possibly be added.[2]

The young men and women of *The Decameron* were leaving castle life behind. Their joy, freedom and optimism infused the *quattrocento*; Boccaccio and other scholars knew that their country had been home to a heroic civilisation which had declined and fallen into a Dark Age; they dreamed that the darkness would lighten and that the civilised glories of ancient Rome would be rewon. Signs of progress were abundant: trade had revived and new ideas were reaching Italy from all directions. Merchant sailors told of Spain's Islamic gardens. Christian scholars, fleeing Constantinople as the Turkish conquerors drew nigh, carried knowledge of ancient and classical civilisations. In Italy, they found a culture already interested in its origins. Renaissance leaders were shifting the focus of their curiosity from Ancient Rome to Ancient Greece and the Bible lands. They were fascinated by the culture of Constantinople – Roman, but Greek-speaking. A rebirth of classical learning contributed to a new interest in gardens as places of luxury and works of art.

One family, the Medici, and one city, Florence, can be used to illustrate the times. The Medici became successful bankers but were of peasant stock from a village north of the city. Giovanni (1360–1429) was famed for his immense riches and simple tastes. His son, Cosimo the Elder (1389–1464), died at Careggi, the wealthiest man of his age. Money brought political power to the family and in 1469 Lorenzo, aged 20, became head of the family. His patronage of the arts earned him the sobriquet Lorenzo the Magnificent. Later members of the family included grand dukes, popes and a queen. The family died out in the mid-eighteenth century, having dominated the arts and culture of Florence for four centuries. Their legacy included not only scholarship, the fine arts and building, but also garden-making. Their interest in the latter, it has been suggested, derived from their never-forgotten rural background.

The Medici created country retreats on the wooded hills around Florence, for their own use and so that fashionable society might call to admire the family art collection and garden statuary. The association of Renaissance gardens with art, scholarship, health and nature was a key factor in their development. Medieval gardens had been ladies' work and monks' work, with individual plants cherished for their medicinal and symbolic values. Renaissance gardens became works of art, scholarship and male pride, integrating architecture, landscape and society.

Symbolically, the key event in the development of Renaissance gardens took place on a summer's day in 1439, in a hilltop garden at Careggi, 5 km from the centre of Florence, where Cosimo de Medici assembled a group of scholars. Conferring on the art and philosophy of the ancient world, they re-forged the link between garden design, the humanities and architecture. Medieval philosophy had been dominated by

6.2 Cosimo de Medici's loggia looks over his garden at Careggi and the Florentine landscape

religion, as had monastic gardens. Renaissance philosophy set reason on a course to recover its classical position as the ultimate criterion of truth, rather than a support for faith. Humanism, as an educational programme, affected every branch of art and knowledge:

> It is credited with the concept of human personality, created by the emphasis on the uniqueness and worth of individuals. It is credited with the birth of history, as the study of the processes of change, and hence of the notion of progress; and it is connected with the stirrings of science.[3]

The most honoured guest at Cosimo's garden party was Marsilio Ficino, founder of the new Platonic academy, translator of Plato and Plotinus, author of the *Theologica Platonica*. The grand master of western philosophy, Plato, began to emerge from Aristotle's shadow. The Neoplatonic theory that 'art should imitate nature' (see p. 15) took on a new life, though it had not slept through the Middle Ages. Ficino believed the soul could engage in rational contemplation of the Platonic forms and that this was the condition in which artistic creation takes place. Experiencing beauty demands reflection as well as observation. Animals, for example, may observe more than humans but are unable to appreciate art because they cannot engage in rational contemplation of the forms. Artist-scholars therefore applied reason to the fine arts, resulting in a series of books: Leonardo wrote on painting, Alberti on architecture, Dürer on geometry, perspective and human proportions.

Mathematics was seen as fundamental to perception and representation. It was basic to the theory of linear perspective, as discovered during the Renaissance and used to unify both paintings and construction projects. Nature was conceived of as mathematically ordered, as though God had himself been a mathematician. Vitruvius, rediscovered in 1415, was studied for his remarks on the mathematics of proportion. A translation of Euclid from Arabic to Latin, in 1482, gave designers a geometrical understanding of the Golden Section.[4] Circles, squares, proportions and geometrical patterns were used in design and perspective was used to integrate buildings with gardens.

The essential nature of the world was also interpreted culturally. Homer and Ovid, neglected by medieval thinkers on account of their paganism, re-entered the curriculum. Greek myths became a source of inspiration for painting and garden sculpture. The story of Diana and Actaeon from Book III of Ovid's *Metamorphoses* provides an example.[5] The writing is graphic, the scene delightful, and the incident thought-provoking: should girls be pleased that men are attracted to their nudity, or should they be affronted by the threat to their virginity? Actaeon's metamorphosis from a man into a stag, exemplifies truths about nature and gardens: seeds become flowers; flowers decay; boys become men; men decay; mould becomes soil; life is renewed. Ovid's *Metamorphoses* regained the position it holds to this day as one of the most popular works by a Latin author.

6.3 Diana the huntress, at Fontainebleau

Alberti applied these ideas to the design of villas. His *Ten Books on Architecture*, written in 1452 and published in 1485, had a profound influence on both architecture and gardens.[6] Though modelled on Vitruvius, 'Alberti's ultimate model is neither contemporary nor ancient architecture, but nature itself'.[7] The art of villa design, lost after the death of Charlemagne, was rediscovered. Pliny's famous letter on his Laurentine Villa (No XXIII, see p. 67) praised 'the beauty of the villa, the advantages of its situation, and the extensive view of the sea-coast'. Italy was rich in such sites and, it now being safe to build outside town walls, Alberti recommended sites that 'overlook the city, the owner's land, the sea or a great plain and familiar hills and mountains', adding that 'in the foreground there should be a delicacy of gardens'. Alberti also wrote about Ovid and about the desirability of building urban squares.

It was thus that garden design rejoined the circle of the fine arts. Dwellings were located in estates, as they had been in the suburbs outside Rome. Hunting parks were formed. Pagan statues were put back on their pedestals. Roman gardens were excavated and surveyed. Plant collections linked artistic and scientific interests. The study of Euclid fostered an enthusiasm for geometry and the first accurate drawings of European towns date from this period. The use of terraces and topiary, which Pliny loved, was re-explored. These interests in gardens came together in a beautifully illustrated book, *The Dream of Polyphilus*.[8] Although it is thought to have been written by a monk, it seems un-monkish in its association of passionate love with gardens and pagan imagery. *The Dream of Polyphilus* contains the oldest drawings of knot gardens, and, two centuries later, it influenced the making of sacred groves in England; William Kent is known to have owned several copies.[9]

The origin of knot gardens remains a matter of conjecture. Gothein comments as follows: 'We know how widespread the fashion for tree-clipping had become in the days of later Roman antiquity, but still the art had been so perfected (as we see it in the Quaracchi gardens) that it is impossible to think it is derived from faint indications in Pliny and other ancient writers; rather it must be due to long practice in the Middle Ages, and never since abandoned, although the threads are hard to follow'.[10] Illustrations of medieval gardens do not show knot gardens before the late fifteenth century. A possible source is Islamic carpets and gardens. No Islamic carpets survive from the period but patterns made by knotting rope had first appeared in Sumerian art and were used as a decorative motif in both Roman and Islamic designs. By the seventeenth century 'knot garden' had become a general term for square gardens with clipped box, sand, gravel, pebbles and flowers. They are equally at home in tight castle gardens and expansive villa gardens.

The physical divide between the inward-looking medieval enclosed garden (*hortus conclusus*) and the outward-looking Albertian villa symbolises the social and intellectual chasm between the two eras. Instead of making sequestered gardens for their womenfolk, noblemen began making palace gardens in the style of their Roman ancestors. Old castles, like Careggi itself, grew into proud villas. In the early years, gardens were sited in and near towns. Another Medici villa, on the edge of Fiesole,

6.4 One of the oldest drawings of a knot garden, from *The Dream of Polyphilus*, 1499

has outward-looking terraces that resemble castle ramparts. Later, it became safe to build villas in hilly locations, away from towns and the diseases associated with them, where the air was fresh, cool and healthy. Visitors to Florence can experience the change by journeying from the city centre, with its hard narrow streets, small courts and high façades, to a villa made by a later Medici prince, Cosimo I, at Castello. From the rear terrace one looks down to the Renaissance garden, still-enclosed but with very open views, or up and over the palace roof, to Florence and its southern hills. A typical Renaissance garden in the closing years of the fifteenth century had:

- clipped hedges
- a rectangular shape
- a geometrical relationship with the house to which it belonged.

As the Renaissance gathered momentum, other aspects of humanism influenced gardens:

- excavation of ancient Roman gardens
- restoration of pagan stories and pagan images to their classical place in the fine arts
- a resurgent challenge from reason to faith as the ultimate criterion of truth.

The first stage of the Renaissance is closely associated with the arts and architecture of Florence. By 1500 Renaissance practice was spreading, at various speeds, to other

6.5 (left) The Medici villa at Fiesole looks outward with the Renaissance

6.6 (right) An Albertian view of Florence from La Petraia, with the Duomo left of the fountain

arts, other parts of Italy and other countries. Dates and categorisations can only be arbitrary, but the following are typical:

- Early Renaissance (1300–1480)
- High Renaissance (1480–1520)
- Mannerism (1520–1580)
- Baroque (1580–1750).

As for Western civilisation as a whole, the period was formative. Shortly after 1500, Renaissance leadership passed from Florence to Rome and patronage from princes to popes.

Italy

On his deathbed in 1455, Pope Nicholas V urged his cardinals to re-establish Rome as the world's greatest city. Remembering his predecessor's wish when he became Pope in 1503, Julius II commissioned Bramante to design a new Basilica of St Peter, Michelangelo to paint frescoes on the Sistine Chapel and Raphael to decorate his private apartments. To outshine Florence, Julius assembled the noblest display of antique sculpture since Rome's fall a thousand years earlier. Though pagan, the statuary was made acceptable to the clergy by treating classical myths as moral allegories: Venus, for example, could stand for the sensuous life in contrast with the contemplative life.[11] As in St Augustine's time (see Chapter 3) Neoplatonism assisted the fusion of pagan and Christian ideas.[12] The sculpture displayed in the Vatican attracted visitors from all over Europe. To house it, Bramante designed the Belvedere Court (c. 1505). The design for this space 'dictated the basis of European garden design for more than two centuries to come'.[13] Gombrich has suggested that Bramante conceived the court as a sacred grove inspired by the *Hypnerotomachia Poliphili*.[14] On a sloping site, the

6.7 Bramante's Belvedere Court 'dictated the basis of European garden design' for 200 years, but fell to the austerity of the counter-reformation: it was bisected by a library. One part of the court survives; another is used as a car park, awaiting restoration

garden court joined the main Vatican Palace to the Villa Belvedere. The characteristics of Bramante's design were:

- a dominant central axis
- full integration of garden and architecture
- terraces linked by great flights of steps
- a garden theatre
- the use of classical (pagan) statuary
- niches for fountains (they had been central elements on medieval lawns).

6.8 Plan of the Vatican, showing Bramante's design for the Belvedere garden

Sadly, the progenitor of High Renaissance garden design fell victim to the counter-reformation. After Pius V ascended the papal throne, in 1565, a stern reforming spirit guided the Church of Rome. Catholicism, challenged by Protestantism, became austere. The free spirit of the Roman republic, and Boccaccio, was cast into the shade. Theatrical displays in gardens were discontinued; pagan statues were banished once more; a theological library was built in the Belvedere Court, Destroying Bramante's composition. Other Roman gardens inspired by Bramante were also destroyed. Fragments, such as the loggia of the Villa Madama, survive in Rome, but one must look further afield to see any of Bramante's principles preserved on a large scale.

Examples of integrated architecture and landscape can be seen at Villa Castello and Villa Lante. At the Villa Pia, in the Vatican Gardens, one cannot say whether the building was made as a setting for the building or the building as an ornament to the garden. At the Villa Lante, instead of one large palace, two small palaces were built, which had the character of garden pavilions. At the Palazzo Farnese, a summer-garden was laid out on one flank of the pentagonal palace and a winter-garden on the other. From the summer-garden, a path leads to a *casino* (little house) in the woods, which

6.9 (left) The Villa Lante demonstrates a perfect integration of architecture and landscape on a central axis

6.10 (right) The Medici villa at Castello is aligned with the garden, though the axis does not point to a significant feature of the building

6.11 (top left) The Villa Madama has sculpture, niches and porticoes on an architectural scale

6.12 (top right) The Villa Medici in Rome used to be enclosed by walls but is now open to Rome, treating St Peter's almost as a garden ornament

6.13 (left and below) Padua's Botanical Garden had scientific objectives and an intricate geometrical plan based on circles within squares within circles

is fully integrated, with the surrounding landscape. Most Renaissance garden designers followed Bramante in their dramatic use of geometrically integrated terraces, steps, water, and sculpture. The study of perspective and optics nurtured the taste for vistas. Plant collections for scientific and medical purposes were geometrically planned, as in the Orto Botanico (Botanical Garden) in Padua.

Spain

Arab culture was a strong influence on Spain during the Middle Ages, allowing a fusion of Islamic and Christian ideas; Moorish features retained or adapted in post-Islamic Spain, were described as *mudejar*. Both cultures made enclosed rectangular gardens, but Renaissance fountains, parterres and other features were grafted onto Islamic gardens, as at the Alcazar in Seville. It had been a great Moorish garden, and in the sixteenth century Charles V added Renaissance ornament to the enclosing wall and made a labyrinth on the lower terrace. He also built a Renaissance villa on the Alhambra plateau (his troops having inspected the architecture and gardens of Rome when they sacked the city in 1527).

Charles V's son, Philip II, implemented his father's will by building a vast Renaissance palace and monastery: the Escorial. Its gardens, like its architecture and its owner, have been judged gloomily morbid, a judgement perhaps influenced by Philip's association with the Spanish Inquisition and the Armada and other offensives. Yet he had a softer side and loved gardens. The garden he commissioned as a summer retreat, at Aranjuez, was almost cheerful, making good use of the River Tagus and the Ria Canal. Having been reared in the Spanish Netherlands, his tastes were more Dutch than Italian. Philip's successors introduced baroque avenues and fountains to Aranjuez.

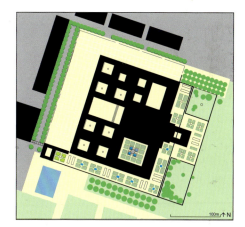

6.14 (above) The Escorial lies below the Guadarrama mountains like a galleon before a storm. The richness of the garden, controlled by geometry, contrasts with the barren hills

6.15 (left) The parterre garden at Aranjuez is separated from the palace by a river, more in the style of the early Renaissance than the High Renaissance. The trees are a sensible response to the local climate

6.16 Despite having been made in the 1660s, the Palacio de Fronteira has a Renaissance layout, well adapted to Portugal by the inclusion of a tank garden with ceramic tiles

Portugal

In Portugal, Italian ideas were adapted to suit the Moorish tradition of water tanks and brightly coloured tiles. Alfonso d'Albuquerque visited Italy as a young man and, remembering its charms, made the first Italian-influenced garden in Portugal, the Quinta da Bacalhoa. It has rectangular courts and a large water tank overlooked by three small pavilions. The garden of the Palacio de Fronteira, made over a century later, is famed for a great rectangular water tank flanked by a pavilioned wall. The latter is decorated with beautiful panels of glazed tiles. They depict the medieval knights who fought for Christendom, though the use of tiles was inspired by Islamic gardens.

France

Charles VIII of France invaded Italy in 1494, claiming the Kingdom of Naples as his inheritance. Whilst there, he and his generals saw the expansive glory of Italian Renaissance gardens and compared them with the cautious medieval gardens of France. Like other conquerors, Charles returned home with his head full of dreams and his wagons full of statues. He also took a garden designer and 21 other artists back to France. The designer worked first at Amboise and then at Blois. Neither garden survives in its original form. They were castle gardens, containing geometrical knots, surrounded by high walls. At Villandry, a garden of this type was made in the twentieth century, beside an old moated castle. The garden at Fontainebleau, commissioned by Francis I, had walled knot gardens around the château. It was the greatest Renaissance garden north of the Alps.

Other castle grounds were adapted to suit Renaissance principles, creating a series of romantic water castles in the lowlands of Northern Europe. Old moats were used in garden designs. New moats were made as garden features. The château at Chantilly, though substantially rebuilt, remains surrounded by a moat. At Chenonceaux, the parterre garden is itself moated. Books with plans showing how to design parterres were published by Mollet and Boyceau.

6.17 A Renaissance building in a medieval moat: Chantilly

6.18 The Renaissance water feature survives in a much-changed garden at Fontainebleau

A further step in the introduction of Renaissance ideas to France was taken by Marie de Medici, Queen of France, at the Luxembourg Gardens in Paris. A Medici by birth, she asked the architect Salomon de Brosse to reflect the spirit of the Boboli Gardens, which she had known as a child in Florence. Boyceau designed the parterre, which was aligned with the axis of the queen's palace. As at the Boboli, there are two axes at right angles. At one stage in his career, André le Nôtre, who became Europe's most famous garden designer, was the head gardener at the Luxembourg Gardens.

Holland

Erasmus, a Renaissance scholar born in Rotterdam in 1466, gave a description of an ideal garden in *The Godly Feast* (1522).[15] It was influenced by his stay in Italy but retained a strongly Christian spirit, mentioning religious instead of pagan statuary. The garden was a medieval square, enclosed by galleries and trelliswork. Verdeman de Vries interpreted and illustrated gardens of this type in the first pattern book to treat garden design as a fine art. The *Horturum viridariorumque elegantes et multiplicis formae* was published in 1583. His last book, *On Perspective*, showed how lines of perspective could be used to integrate the composition of architecture with gardens.

After 1609, when Holland won its independence from Spain, a distinctively Dutch type of classical garden emerged, based on Neoplatonic principles. Canals and trees defined a strict rectilinear framework. Within the enclosure were square and circular spaces bounded by clipped hedges, trees and trelliswork. The designers were interested in Renaissance botany, geometry and science. No examples survive but the growth-point of European garden design was shifting, with that of European trade and culture, from the Mediterranean Sea to the North Sea and the Atlantic Ocean.

6.19 A moated parterre, at Chenonceaux

6.20 (left) Verdeman de Vries showed how perspective could be used to compose gardens with architecture

6.21 (right) The Dutch classical garden was designed with circles and squares: Honslaarsdyjk

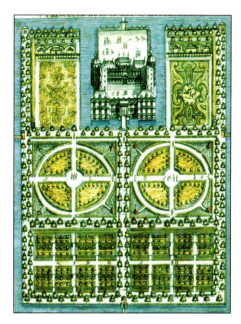

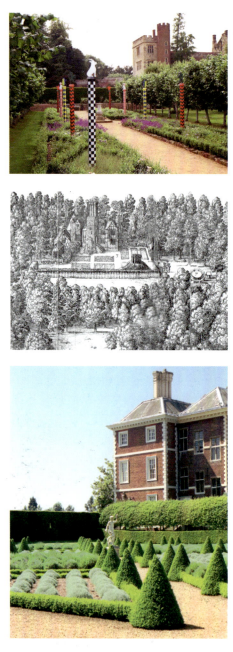

6.22 A modern interpretation of Henry VIII's heraldic beasts, at Penshurst Place, Kent

6.23 The drawing of Boscobel, Shropshire, done because Charles II hid here, was used to restore a modest, northern Renaissance garden

6.24 The garden at Ham House, Richmond, was restored according to an old drawing

England

Compared with the countries discussed above, few records, and even fewer examples survive of the gardens made in England during the Renaissance. One civil war opened the period; another closed it and since then, Britain's zest for garden-making has laid change upon change. Yet England did have Renaissance gardens. At Hampton Court, Henry VIII sought to outshine Francis I's Fontainebleau estate. He made rectangular gardens and ornamented them with knots and heraldic beasts set high on coloured poles.

At Nonsuch, Henry made a palace intended – as the name implies – to exceed all others. It was loved by his daughter, Elizabeth I, but no trace of it now remains. Theobalds, another great palace, was made by William Cecil, Lord Burghley, Elizabeth's first minister. Bounded by a canal, it had two large square gardens: a Privy Garden to the west and a Great Garden to the south. It too has gone.

When James VI of Scotland became James I of England, after the death of Elizabeth in 1603, there was more intercourse with continental Europe. Salomon de Caus, a French architect-engineer, was invited to work in England. His designs for Anne of Denmark, James I's queen, at Somerset House and Greenwich, were influenced by his travels in Italy: house and garden were aligned with one another, and fountains in Renaissance style were made. Advantage was taken of another continental skill, copperplate engraving, to illustrate de Caus' design for Wilton House. The garden has been changed, but the book survives as the fullest record of a Renaissance garden in England. It had *parterres de broderie*, and the statuary included copies of the Borghese *Gladiator* and other cultural icons of the Renaissance.

In 1642 a civil war ended the domestic peace which had prevailed since the Wars of the Roses. Boscobel House in Shropshire is the most interesting survival from the pre-1642 period. The design of the garden was unremarkable and the site would never have been remembered or maintained, but for a dramatic incident in 1644. Charles Stuart, the future Charles II of England, having been defeated by Cromwell, hid in a tree outside the enclosed garden at Boscobel. This incident led to full records being made of the garden, which made possible a reconstruction in the twentieth century. It is a modest, rural, north European interpretation of the Italian Renaissance style. The garden is enclosed by a fence, divided into compartments and aligned with the geometry of the house. An artificial mount allowed the wide views, sun and air which Alberti considered essential in the making of good gardens.

Scotland

The influence of the Renaissance upon Scotland's gardens was somewhat delayed, but its effects, once it did arrive, were sharp and clear. Scotland's climate is colder than Italy's, but its rugged terrain and unsettled social conditions had some similarities with the country in which the Renaissance was born. Two fascinating examples of Scottish Renaissance gardens survive from the seventeenth century, though both were imaginatively restored by Scotland's Department of Antiquities in the twentieth: Edzell in

6.25 Though the planting dates from *c.* 1960, Edzell is a prime northern example of an enclosed castle garden in the early Renaissance style

Angus and Pitmedden in Aberdeenshire have rectangular enclosures protected by sandstone walls.

Germany

After the Peace of Augsburg established a religious truce, in 1555, the German Lands were set fair to become the leading region of Europe. Noblemen, artists, doctors and scientists travelled to Italy, spent time there, and returned home with a desire to make new gardens. German was spoken in much of Central and North Europe, though there was no unitary state with a royal court to promote the art of garden design, as in Spain, France and England.

Wealthy burghers made gardens within city walls. Often, they were sober versions of Italian Renaissance gardens, with collections of medicinal plants. The nobility made gardens beside their castles. Ferdinand I's wife made a Renaissance parterre at the medieval castle of Ambras in the Austrian Tyrol (see Chapter 5, Figures 5.2 and 5.3). Ferdinand's brother, Maximilian II, employed Italian craftsmen and designers to help make the Neugebaude palace and gardens in Vienna. An Italian gardener was employed to lay out the gardens of the Belvedere Palace outside Prague castle.

Germany's greatest Renaissance garden, in Heidelberg, was the Hortus Palatinus, 'the Garden of the Palatinate', which took its name from the Palatine Hill in Rome (see p. 65). The garden was planned for the Protestant Frederick V, after his marriage to Elizabeth, daughter of James I of England. She invited her former tutor, Salomon de Caus, to design and supervise the work. It was a magnificent garden in a dramatic situation, rich in parterres, grottoes and waterworks. The designer has been criticised for not learning more from Alberti about the use of an axis and beautifully proportioned flights of steps to integrate garden enclosures, and it is true that the garden has an early Renaissance plan, despite its large size and late date. Work on the garden stopped when Frederick V became a Protestant commander at the outbreak of the Thirty Years War, in 1618. Today, it is a romantic ruin and one of Germany's leading tourist attractions.

6.26 Even in its ruined state, the Hortus Palatinus (Heidelberg) remains the foremost Renaissance garden in Germany

6.27 (left) Prague's Royal Garden and singing fountain were made outside the old fortress of Hradschin

6.28 (right) The Wallenstein garden in Prague has medieval seclusion with a Renaissance layout

6.29 Pratolino in 1570 and 2000. It had a great Mannerist garden, tending towards the Baroque

Czech Republic

Wallenstein, a Catholic commander during the Thirty Years War, began to make a garden in Prague in 1623. The Wallenstein Garden was dominated by a loggia, reminiscent of the Villa Madama in Rome, facing onto a parterre with a fountain. Much of the garden survives. Though clearly inspired by Italian villas, it lacks their informal charm – a consequence perhaps of its more northerly location, or of its owner's military preoccupations. Wallenstein was defeated by Gustavus Adolphus and murdered by his own officers in 1634.

Mannerism

'Mannerist' began as a derogatory term for artists who, lacking personal greatness, could be derided for working 'in the manner' of greater masters. Medieval designers would have taken this as a compliment but the individualism of the Renaissance led to a different attitude. 'Mannerist' is now used as a term of praise to describe art and design of the six decades between High Renaissance and Early Baroque, when artists, showing more personal vision, drifted away from the classical ideals of stasis and perfection. The distinction between High Renaissance and Mannerism can be seen by comparing two paintings of the same subject. Leonardo's *Last Supper* (1495) is calm, symmetrical and balanced. Tintoretto's *Last Supper* (1592) bustles with energy and directional thrust. A comparison of the gardens of the Villa Medici at Fiesole (c. 1458) and the Villa d'Este at Tivoli (c. 1560) reveals a serenity in the former and a restless energy in the latter. The Flemish sculptor, Jean de Boulogne, known in Italy as Giambologna, was famous for his mannerist statuary, including *The Rape of the Sabines*. There are examples of his work at Pratolino, the Boboli and other gardens. The most famous Mannerist architects were Palladio and Vignola. Palladio used the natural landscape as a setting for his villas. Vignola worked on the Palazzo Farnese at Caprarola and the Villa Lante at Bagnaia.

6.30 (top left) Giambologna's statue of Appenina, at Pratolino, is the most dramatic extant feature in what was once a great Mannerist garden

6.31 (top right) At Hellbrunn, the Mannerist parterre is surrounded by water and is not aligned with the house

6.32 (centre left) Palazzo Farnese, Caprarola, has a Mannerist pleasure garden in the woods behind its fortified palace

6.33 (centre right) Gamberaia brings the surrounding landscape into composition with the garden

6.34 (left) The Villa d'Este has one of the most popular gardens ever made

6.35 The Sacro Bosco ('Sacred Wood'), at the Villa Orsini outside Bomarzo, is a mannered departure from ideal perfection

6.36 Hellbrunn has the best mannerist garden north of the Alps, and the best hydraulic marvels anywhere. The water-powered models featured below, are inside one of the grass-covered boxes (left)

6.37 Bomorzo and Hellbrunn represent, in different ways, a departure from the static perfection of the high renaissance

The creation of Cardinal Ippolito d'Este, The Villa d'Este (1550) is one of the most popular gardens ever made, despite a lack of solidity in its construction. Controlled by powerful intersecting axes, the garden sparkles with drama. It has myriad fountains, a water theatre, statues and other icons, all telling the glorious history of the Este family and its Herculean ancestry. The transition between Renaissance and baroque gardens is evident in the plan: the avenues, though still confined within the garden enclosure, are gaining strength and pushing against the boundaries. Yet it remains a mannered and light-hearted place, always bubbling, like the Villa Lante, with entertainment, novelty and invention.

The Sacro Bosco at Bomarzo (1552) was started just after the Villa d'Este. Its owner and designer, Duke Vincino Orsini, shared an interest in Ovid, Ariosto and classical mythology with Ippolito d'Este but made an utterly different garden. The first explanation of Bomarzo's unique character comes from its name: Sacro Bosco. 'Sacred wood' is a literal translation but 'sacred grove' conveys the meaning with greater precision in English. The idea of the sacred grove comes from the ancient world (see Chapter 3); this example was inspired by Homer's *Odyssey*, Virgil's *Aeneid*, and Ariosto's romantic epic *Orlando Furioso*. If the early Christians had not been so efficient in destroying pagan sanctuaries, the Sacro Bosco would not be quite such a startling place, though it would remain bizarre. The second explanation of its character may be found in Ariosto's concern with the struggle between Christians and pagans. Duke Orsini had been a soldier and, seeing a new and dangerous world opening before him, used mythology to explore the paradoxical relationships between life, death, man, religion and nature. The garden is a mannered departure from classical perfection.

The Bishop of Salzburg made a garden at Hellbrunn in 1613–1615. His family had close links with Italy and the garden drew inspiration from that country. The garden was sited near the hills, outside the town, like a Medici villa. It had two water parterres, one of which survives, and a range of typically Italian automata and water devices, which survive today in good condition. Hellbrunn also has a dramatic outdoor theatre in a quarry.

Styles and examples

Early Renaissance

Use: Renaissance gardens developed by stages from their medieval precursors. Noblewomen continued to use gardens to take the air in safety, but men resumed their involvement with gardens – and more resources became available. The principles of ancient garden design were rediscovered and combined with new artistic and scientific ideas about the 'nature of the world'. As in Roman times, Renaissance gardens were used for social gatherings and great occasions.

Form: As castles evolved into fortified manor houses, more space became available for gardens. Square and rectangular planting beds were laid out like carpets, so that their unity, order and regularity could be viewed from upper windows. Crusaders may have seen eastern paradise gardens designed in this way, or traders may have seen examples in Muslim Spain. Patterns, taking their name from carpet patterns, were used in the design of what became known as 'knot gardens'.

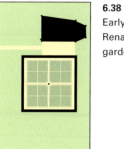

6.38
Early Renaissance garden

Careggi 1450

'Two miles from Florence [Michelozzo Michelozzi] made the palace of the Villa di Careggi, which was a rich and magnificent structure. Michelozzo brought water to it in the fountain which may be seen there at the present time.'[16] Vasari describes how Michelozzi was employed to transform a medieval fortified manor house into a comfortable residence with elegant loggias. The garden nestles behind a high wall and is famed as the place where Cosimo de Medici assembled his Platonic academy. The garden was laid out in imitation of a Roman villa with space for outdoor living, of the type described by Pliny. A drawing of 1636 shows the house and garden much as they are today, though without the circular pool. The original planting was more botanical, with 'countless specimens of trees and shrubs'.[17] Cosimo also employed Michelozzi to work on the Villa Medici at Fiesole. Careggi looks inward, with the Middle Ages. Fiesole looks outward, with the Renaissance.

> Yesterday I came to the villa of Careggi, not to cultivate my fields but my soul. Come to us, Marsilio [Ficino], as soon as possible. Bring with you our Plato's book *De Summo Bono*, which I presume you have now translated into Latin according to your promise; for there is no employment to which I so ardently devote myself as to discover the true road to happiness.[18]

Villa Medici, Fiesole 1450

The villa has a hillside site and gracious terraces, as Alberti recommended in his treatise of 1452. There are panoramic views of the River Arno and Florence. Giovanni de

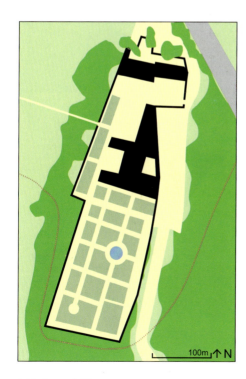

6.39 Careggi, Florence

6.40 Villa Medici, Fiesole

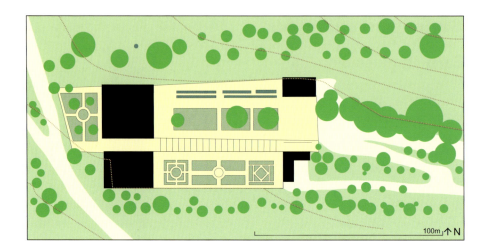

Medici, Cosimo's overweight, libidinous favourite son was a child of the Renaissance, who loved art, music and beauty. After Giovanni's early death, the villa was inherited by Cosimo's grandson, Lorenzo the Magnificent. Had it been built 50 years earlier, the garden would surely have been walled in the medieval manner. Had it been made 50 years later, the terraces would surely have been joined with great flights of steps in the style of Bramante. It is likely that the upper terrace was originally used as an extension of the house and the lower terrace as a vegetable garden. Today, they have tree-shaded walks, lawns and parterres. Cosimo's Platonic academy was moved from Careggi to Fiesole.

> Such a villa, designed solely to provide luxurious mental refreshment, and placed in the most beautiful situation of any round Florence, could not fail to attract scholars for the interchange and acquisition of knowledge . . . As a work of garden architecture, it was a thoroughly sound conception, and one of the most important foundations of future garden design.[19]

Edzell Castle 1604

The plan shows a castellated house integrated with a Renaissance castle-garden, in the foothills of the Scottish highlands. The layout was probably the work of its owner, Sir David Lindsey, Lord Edzell. The square garden is enclosed by massive but well-proportioned red sandstone walls with astrological carvings of the planetary deities. Alternating niches may have been used for flowers and nesting birds. Nothing is known of the original planting but a parterre was made here in the 1960s. The castle and garden gave protection in the medieval manner while encouraging the family to take an interest in Renaissance art and science.

> It is ane excellent dwelling, a great house, delicat gardine, with wall sumptuously built of hewen stone, polisht, with pictures and coats of armes in the

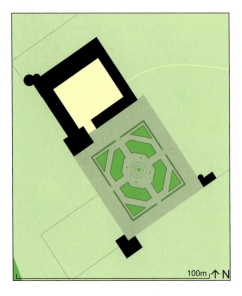

6.41 Edzell Castle, Perthshire

walls, with a fine summer house with a hous for a bath on the south corners thereof, far exceeding any new work of our times'.[20]

Heidelberg 1614

Only the bones survive, once famed as 'the eighth wonder of the world'. It was made by Frederick V and his wife Elizabeth, daughter of King James I of England. A devoted couple with a shared love of the arts, they fled to exile in Holland in 1620, after the Battle of the White Mountain. The *Hortus Palatinus* (Garden of the Palatinate) was designed by Elizabeth's drawing master, Salomon de Caus. A famous garden designer, author and hydraulic engineer, he also wrote a book (*Hortus Palatinus*) on the garden. The surviving terraces allow one to see the structure of the Renaissance garden but the Mannerist water tricks, games, musical devices and parterres were destroyed during the Thirty Years War (1618–1648). It did not have a High Renaissance central axis.

> The ascent is long and steep, the way plain, and no guide needed . . . and there, among treasures of art, decaying and decayed, and the magnificent bounties of nature, the stranger may wander the day through.[21]

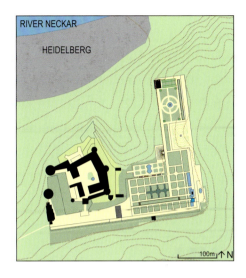

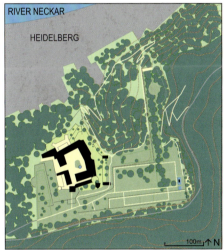

6.42 Hortus Palatinus, Heidelberg

High Renaissance

Use: Alberti advised making 'open places for walking, swimming, and other diversions, court-yards, grass-plots and porticoes, where old men may chat together in the kindly warmth of the sun in winter, and where the family may divert themselves and enjoy the shade in summer . . . and have a view of some city, towns, the sea, an open plain'. Medieval gardens had been inward-looking places, physically and spiritually. High Renaissance gardens began to reach outward, physically and intellectually. Displaying a collection of antique statuary became an important garden use – a way of connecting with history, the fine arts and the landscape.

Form: The organising principles of High Renaissance gardens were developed by Bramante, following a suggestion from Alberti. Bramante used a central axis to integrate house and garden. A series of rectangular enclosures with terraces at different levels was thus fused into a single composition. Flights of steps, alcoves, niches and fountains were disposed in relation to the axis and embellished with statues, fountains and terracotta pots containing flowers and fruit trees.

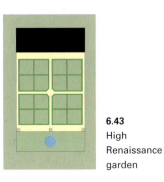

6.43 High Renaissance garden

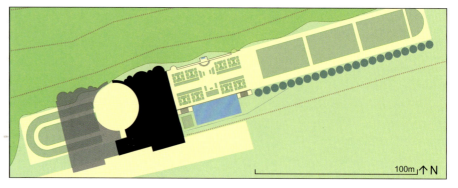

6.44 Villa Madama, Rome

Villa Madama 1518

The Villa Madama became influential because of its superb quality and because it was designed by Raphael, whose painting was seen as the pinnacle of Renaissance perfection, before its 'descent' into mannerism and baroque. Madama was one of the first High Renaissance villas to be built outside Rome. Like the Medici villas outside Florence, it was conceived as a villa of the type described by Pliny the Younger in his garden letters. The distinction between inside and outside was blurred and there is an outward view from the terrace to the Tiber. The original plan included a courtyard, a monumental flight of steps, a circular court, an open-air theatre, a hippodrome, and a terrace. In the woods there is a grotto. The famous Elephant Fountain by Giovanni da Udine survives in an alcove. The villa was conceived more as a place to entertain than a place to live. Its scale is monumental but there is a perfect balance between architecture, garden and landscape.

> If fate had allowed the building to proceed, a jewel comparable with anything the Renaissance can offer would be now before our eyes, but changes of fortune have left only the ruins of a fragment.[22]

> The existing fragment is, however, well worthy of study, for the purity of its architecture and the broad simplicity of its plan are in marked contrast to the complicated design and overcharged details of some of the later Roman gardens.[23]

Villa Medici at Castello 1537

Though cold, secretive, moody and despotic, Cosimo I, Grand Duke of the Medicis, was a generous patron of the arts. He employed a sculptor, Niccolò Tribolo, to design the garden of his villa at Castello. The plan shows spacious terraces on several levels, arranged around a central axis. There is a fine grotto, set into the garden wall, inspired by Cosimo I's love of hunting. Tribolo's sculpture follows an iconographical theme, drawn from Ovid's *Metamorphoses*, celebrating the greatness of the Medici family. Much of the original garden decoration described by Vasari has gone. A lunette of the garden, painted in 1599, shows the garden layout much as it is today, but the planting has been thinned and the garden does not have as much charm as one feels it could

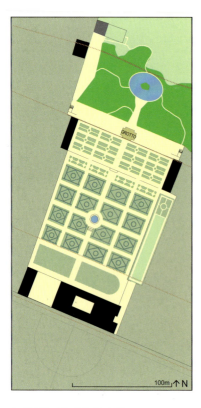

6.45 Villa Medici, Castello

have. After a visit he made in 1580, Montaigne described the garden with his customary freedom from prejudice:

> The house itself is not worth looking at; but there are several gardens admirably laid out, all of them on the slope of a hill, so that all the straight walks are upon a descent, but a very gentle and easy one; the cross walks are level and terraced. In every direction, you see a variety of arbours, thickly formed of every description of odoriferous trees, cedars, cypresses, orange trees, lemon trees and olive trees . . . We went to look at the principal fountain, which discharges its contents through two large figures in bronze [*Hercules and Antaeus*], the lower of which has taken the other in his arms, and is squeezing him with all his might; the latter, almost senseless, has his head thrown back, and discharges the water from his mouth; and the machinery is so powerful that the fountain rises to a height of 222 feet above the figures, which themselves are 20 feet high . . . There is also a very handsome grotto, in which are to be seen all sorts of animals, sculptured the size of life, which are sprouting out water, some by the beak, others by the mouth, or the nails, or the nostrils.[24]

Palazzo Farnese at Caprarola 1550

The plan shows a Renaissance castle garden to the south and a mannerist pleasure garden to the north, separated by woods. The Renaissance parterres flank a great pentagonal fortress at the head of the town. Their layout has changed but they remain impressive, if somewhat formalistic. The garden retreat in the woods, designed by Vignola, is a richly integrated mannerist composition. Known as the *Casino del Piacere* (House of Pleasure), it hides in a glade at the end of a long path. There is a water staircase, fountains, terraces, a *casino* and loggia used as a private retreat by Cardinal Odorado Farnese.

> It is like a fortress, with a winding staircase outside and a moat and drawbridge, in a new style and fine invention. The gardens are filled with rich and varied fountains, graceful shrubberies and lawns, and every requisite for such a royal villa.[25]

Valdstejn (Wallenstein) Garden 1614

One of Europe's greatest military commanders had a sector of medieval Prague destroyed to make his palace and garden. Wallenstein was cold, egotistical, avaricious and autocratic, though he had studied in Padua and admired the Italian Renaissance. The scale and character of his garden compare with the Villa Madama, but it is shut off from the town in the medieval style – one senses the hard defensiveness of a man whose life was spent in war. A monumental loggia overlooks a disciplined parterre. Hercules, symbolising power, stands in a large tank of water. Other bronze statues, lining the main axis, are copies of originals taken as war booty to Drottningholm by the Swedish general, Gustavus Adolphus, who led the Protestant forces against Wallenstein in the Thirty Years War.

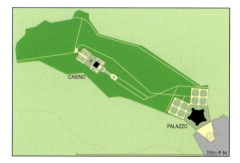

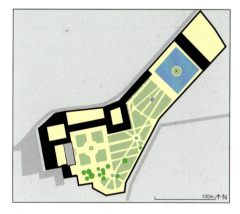

6.46 (top) Palazzo Farnese, Caprarola
6.47 (bottom) Valdstejn Garden, Prague

The house was no ordinary nobleman's mansion, a slice of autonomous territory rather, amidst the patchwork of the city, a miniature realm enclosed by outbuildings and a park wall like a circumvallation. When Wallenstein's coach had rolled into the courtyard to the left of the front, he had all that he needed – a chapel, a riding-ground at the lower end of the park, and (the absolute essential) a bathing pool, in a grotto bedizened with crystals, shells, and stalactites, as well as walks between statues and fountains.[26]

Palacio de Fronteira 1660

This garden is distinguished by its great stairways, water tanks, *azulejos* (coloured glazed tiles) and decorative parterres. From the plan, one might think it a Renaissance garden inspired by du Cerceau and dating from the 1550s. In fact, as the exuberant detailing reveals, the garden was made in the 1660s. The water tanks have panels decorated with glazed tiles, plaques and busts, adding brilliant hues to the garden: terracotta, indigo, cerulean, turquoise, lemon-yellow. The Chapel Walk is an outdoor gallery with tiled panels showing allegories of the arts and sciences. Fronteira exemplifies a uniquely Portuguese approach to garden design: comfortable, grand, lush, intimate and brilliantly coloured.

The eye is arrested by something new and strange, a basin lying at the side, which occupies nearly the whole length of the garden. In the water stand two statues, and there are two little flowery islands in it, while the high wall that supports a narrow terrace is articulated with three doors, between which are twelve panels with the figures of knights made in faience. The wall of the narrow upper terrace has no plants, but is decorated with plaques and also has five niches containing the portrait busts of Portuguese kings.[27]

6.48 Palacio de Frontiera, Lisbon

Mannerist

Use: When Renaissance art was thought to have reached its peak of perfection, designers and their clients became attracted by surprise, novelty and allusion. Gardens were furnished with dramatic features for outdoor masques and parties. Virtuoso water displays were admired and the creation of garden features to impress one's friends became a design objective.

Form: The characteristics of mannerist painting and sculpture – movement and drama – became important in gardens. Hydraulic marvels and elaborate water features were driven by streams flowing through gardens. Streams also had an allegorical role. It was as though designers had taken heed of Leonardo's remark that 'it is a wretched pupil who does not surpass his master'. Dramatic sites were chosen and embellished with exotic sculpture. There was a new interest in classical literature and, with Palladio, a Neoplatonic respect accorded to circles and squares. Houses became ornaments in great outdoor compositions.

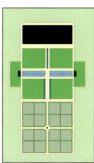

6.49
Mannerist garden

Villa d'Este 1550

The plan shows a highly developed Renaissance plan with a central axis stepping down a terraced hill. The Ville d'Este is an important mannerist garden, verging on the baroque. 'If we drew up a list of the seven wonders of the gardening world, this villa might well rank as the first', declared Jellicoe in 1937.[28] Cardinal Ippolito d'Este, as proud as he was rich, ensured that no other garden has such spectacular waterworks. Visitors entered at the lowest point of the garden. As they ascended the hill, the water marvels revealing the story of the family's illustrious ancestors (including Hercules himself) unfold. The garden contains many references to Ovid's *Metamorphoses*. Detours were necessary to see the garden's different sections but if everything went according to plan one arrived at the top believing the Estes to be the most brilliant family in history. The Aniene River supported the story by supplying the fountains and, with the aid of a water organ, a musical accompaniment. Many of the statues were obtained from Roman sites. Pirro Ligorio supervised the excavations and supplied the erudition and imagination behind the conception of the garden. The Rometta Fountain is a miniature representation of Rome, topped by a statue of Romulus and Remus.

> There are such depths of mystery in the infinite green distances and in the cypress-shaded pools of the lower garden, that one has a sense of awe rather than of pleasure in descending from one level to another of darkly rustling green.[29]

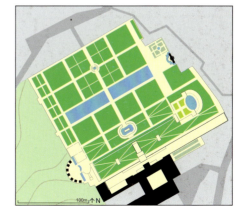

6.50 Villa d'Este, Tivoli

Villa Lante 1573

'A place not of grandeur or tragedy but of enchanting loveliness',[30] the garden of the Villa Lante is 'a perfect thing of the imagination.[31] It has a perfectly balanced plan with rich embellishment. In the eyes of many, it is the best example of the best period in garden design – the mannerist phase of the Italian Renaissance.

It was conceived by Cardinal Gambara, who had a modern taste for outdoor living, and the overall design is attributed to Vignola. Buildings are treated as garden ornaments, illustrating a good principle – that of making architecture subservient to the garden layout. The circle and square are prominent in the layout: a square terrace is subdivided into smaller squares, and there are circular and semi-circular pools. The water parterre has a central fountain. The design was inspired by earlier projects: the geometry of the plan by Bramante's Belvedere; the use of water by the Villa d'Este; the circular island either by Hadrian's 'marine theatre' at Tivoli or the isolette in the Boboli Gardens. The echo of the Temple of Queen Hatshepsut in the terraces that command views down a sloping hillside, however, appears to be coincidental.

A river of delight flows from a grotto at the summit of the hill but does not stick to the central axis. Symbolically, the garden represents the tale of humanity's descent from the Golden Age described in Ovid's *Metamorphoses*. Paths lead to an outdoor dining area with a fountain table and to other enclosures. The Water Chain is the best and earliest example of a stepped cascade. The Villa also has a park with the character of a hunting park, but too small for a real hunt.

> A gentle and pretty maiden, well adorned with varied and sumptuous clothes and also with jewels on her fine head, pearls in her ears, and many rings on her well-kept hands.[32]

6.51 Plan of the Villa Lante, Bagnaia

Notes

1   Manzoni, A., *The Betrothed Lovers*, transl. Charles Swan, 3 vols., Pisa: Niccolo Capurro, 1828. Italy's most celebrated nineteenth-century author, Manzoni paints a vivid picture of late-medieval life in this historical novel.

2   Boccaccio, G., *Decamerone*, London: Bibliophilist Society, 1918.

3   Davies, N., *Europe: a History*, Oxford: Oxford University Press, 1996, p. 479.

4   Padovan, R., *Proportion: Science, philosophy, architecture,* London: Spon, 1999, p. 137ff.

5   Ovid, *Metamorphoses*, London: Penguin, 1955, pp. 77–80.

6   Alberti, L. B., *Ten Books on Architecture*, London: Tiranti, 1955.

7   Padovan, R., op. cit., p. 220ff.

8   The book was published as *Hypnerotomachia Poliphili* and is attributed to Colonna, Francesco. It was written in 1467 and published in 1499. An English interpretation is Fierz-David, L., *The dream of Poliphilo*, Bollingen NY, 1950, with an introduction by C. G. Jung.

9   Goode, P. (ed.), *Oxford Companion to Gardens*, Oxford, 1986, p. 268.

10 Gothein, M-L., *A History of Garden Art*, London: J. M. Dent, 1928, Vol. 1, p. 211.

11 Hall, James, *A History of Ideas and Images in Italian Art*, London: John Murray, 1983, p. 228.

12 Wind, E., *Pagan Mysteries in the Renaissance*, London: Faber & Faber, 1958.

13 Masson, G., *Italian Gardens*, London: Thames & Hudson, 1966, p. 123.

14 Gombrich, E. H., *Symbolic Images*, London: Phaidon, 1975, pp. 102–8.

15 Erasmus, *The Godly Feast*, 1522.

16 Vasari, G., *The Lives of the Painters, Sculptors and Architects*, 1550, London: Dent, 1963, Vol. 1, p. 321.

17 Burckhardt, J., *Civilisation of the Renaissance*, 1860, p. 176.

18 Letter from Cosimo de Medici to Marsilio Ficino, 1462.

19 Jellicoe, G. A., *Italian Gardens of the Renaissance*, London: Ernest Benn, 1925, p. 4.

20 Ouchterlong of Guinde, *c.* 1722, quoted in Little, G. A., *Scotland's Gardens*, Edinburgh: Spurbooks, 1981, p. 184.

21 Mary Wollstonecraft Shelley, *Rambles in Germany and Italy in 1840, 1842 and 1843*, London, 1844.

22 Gothein, M-L., op. cit., Vol. 2, p. 231.

23 Wharton, E., *Italian Villas and their Gardens*, New York: The Century Co., 1904, p. 84.

24 M de Montaigne, 1580. From his *Travel Journal*, Frame, D. M. transl., North Point Press, 1983.

25 Vasari, G., op. cit., Vol 4, p. 95.

26 Mann, G., *Wallenstein*, London: Deutsch, 1976, p. 237.

27 Gothein, M-L., op. cit., Vol. 1, p. 383.

28 Jellicoe, G. A., *Gardens of Europe*, London: Blackie & Son, 1937, p. 125.

29 Wharton, E., op. cit., p. 144.

30 Sitwell, Sir G., *An Essay on the Making of Gardens*, London: John Murray, 1909.

31 Jellicoe, G. A., *Italian Gardens*, London: Ernest Benn, 1925, p. 27.

32 Riccio, 1595, quoted by: Lazzaro, C., *The Italian Renaissance Garden*, New Haven and London: Yale University Press, 1990.

Chapter 7

Baroque gardens
1600–1750

7.1 The greatest Baroque garden, Versailles, was designed for drama

History and philosophy

'Baroque', like many of the labels used by art historians, began as a term of abuse. Baroque art was regarded as imperfect in comparison with the perfection of the High Renaissance. Bazin suggests that the word derives from *barocco*, meaning an 'irregular pearl'.[1] But he admires baroque art and sees the years from 1600 to 1750 as 'the period of Western civilisation that is richest in expressive variety'. Bazin distinguishes baroque from classical as follows:

> Classical compositions are simple and clear, each constituent part retaining its independence; they have a static quality and are enclosed within boundaries. The Baroque artist, in contrast, longs to enter into the multiplicity of phenomena, into the flux of things in their perpetual becoming – his compositions are dynamic and open and tend to expand outside their boundaries.[2]

Bazin's main interests were painting, sculpture and architecture but his comment fits baroque gardens exceptionally well. They integrate a 'multiplicity of phenomena' (landform, water, vegetation, sculpture, fountains, terracing, roads, paths, steps, bridges and architecture); they are 'dynamic and open', with avenues piercing garden boundaries as effectively as canon broke city walls in the baroque era; their dramatic water features create a 'flux of things' in 'perpetual becoming'. Drama was the essence.

Baroque art is associated with the Counter-Reformation and the rise of science in the seventeenth century. The forces of attack gained over those of defence: after the deployment of canon there was less point living in a walled city, and it became necessary to have regional powers, with all their associated symbols of power, instead of city-states. It became necessary to train, equip and organise armies, to protect large villas outside the towns. Baroque art is also associated with absolutist government. Louis XIV was the leading patron of the arts but, as the favoured style of kings and

nobles, baroque art affected all Europe, including the Protestant countries. The speed with which the new style was adopted varied according to political, economic and religious circumstances, but where- and whenever they emerged, baroque gardens shared many common features.

Should one seek a prime cause for the changes which affected Europe during the Baroque Age, the best candidate is the weakening of church authority. The arguments of Copernicus (1473–1543), Kepler (1571–1630), Bacon (1561–1626), Galileo (1564–1642) and Newton (1642–1727) were, slowly and reluctantly, accepted by the church. The most notable example of this was Galileo, whose use of the telescope to study the organisation of the solar system led him to conclusions that could only conflict with religious teaching. Catholics and Protestants fought each other but accepted the use of reason, as did armies, philosophers, politicians, industrialists and artists. The resultant changes are known collectively as The Enlightenment because the 'light of reason' illuminated, and thus undermined, the dogma of earlier times. Mathematics helped to explain the universe and, following the key influence of the philosopher, Descartes (1596–1650), was linked ever more closely with natural philosophy and the fine arts.

Though Descartes did not write on aesthetics or gardens, the term 'Cartesian garden' is often applied. It points to the rationalist philosophy on which the Baroque Age was founded and reminds us of Descartes' personal contribution to geometry. In philosophy, Descartes' *Discourse on Method* proposed the application of 'systematic doubt'.[3] It would, he argued, tell us what knowledge men can have which is certain beyond any possibility of doubt. His conclusion was that we cannot doubt either the truths of mathematics or the existence of God. Descartes' *Discourse* inspired artists and authors to emphasise certainty in human affairs. Scientists looked for 'laws of Nature', a phrase invented by Descartes, and critics looked for 'rules of taste' to

7.2 The baroque period gave Europe its most dramatic sculpture (the Boboli Gardens, left) and fountains (Schleissheim, right)

7.3 Astronomy became a royal enthusiasm in the baroque period. The Observatory at Greenwich Park, London, is seen here, with the remains of the giant steps that once carried the axis up the hill from Le Nôtre's grass parterre

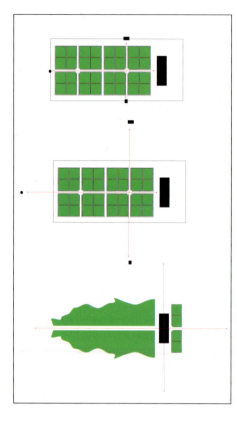

7.4 Development of the baroque: (1) axes within gardens (2) axes aimed on landmarks outside gardens (3) axes projecting beyond gardens

distinguish good art from bad art. The rules appealed to long-accepted standards, such as formal poetic structures. Even the greatest scientist of his age, Newton, believed himself to be rediscovering truths known to the ancients.[4] Rules of taste were examined for their antiquity and their mathematics. The Golden Section passed both tests, having been explained by Euclid.[5] Alexander Pope equated the 'rules of old' with a Newtonian conception of Nature.[6]

Geometry was the branch of mathematics with the most obvious application in garden design. Axes, as introduced to gardens by Bramante, became their dominant feature. The stages in the advance of axes were as follows:

- Single axis, within boundaries (Belvedere Court, Vatican, 1505)
- Transverse axes, using focal points within boundaries (Villa Castello, 1538; Villa d'Este, 1560; Villa Lante, 1566)
- Transverse axes, projecting to remote focal points (Villa Mattei, 1582; Villa Montalto, 1585)
- Long axes projecting through the landscape to churches and distant focal points (Villa Aldobrandini, 1589; Villa Torlonia, 1621)
- Radiating and cross axes, within boundaries (Boboli Gardens, 1549–1620; Luxembourg Gardens, 1612)
- Radiating axes, projecting beyond boundaries (Vaux-le-Vicomte, 1656; Versailles and Paris, after 1665)
- Radiating axes, projecting through cities (Karlsruhe, Germany, 1715; Washington, DC, USA, 1791; New Delhi, India, 1911; Brazilia, Brazil, 1956).

Axes could weld garden, architecture and landscape into unified geometrical compositions. The principal features of baroque gardens were:

- avenues
- canals
- parterres
- green walls
- buildings on axes
- focal points within gardens (e.g. fountains)
- focal points outside gardens (e.g. churches)
- axially coordinated steps, water features and statues, as pioneered by Bramante
- integration with the surrounding landscape.

Baroque ideas influenced the planning of avenues in the princely suburbs of capital cities: at Frascati outside Rome; at Versailles outside Paris; at Potsdam outside Berlin; at Hampton Court outside London; at the Peterhof outside St Petersburg. Although the Reign of Terror in France after 1793 cooled Europe's enthusiasm for this avowedly aristocratic style, similar principles were applied to the layout of Paris itself after the failed revolution of 1848 (the military idea behind this – which proved successful in the 1871 Paris Commune – was that revolutionaries could be chased down the broad boulevards and shot like the beasts in a nobleman's park).

The characteristics of baroque parks and gardens varied with the circumstances of the countries in which they were made. As Bazin remarks, it was 'the moment at which each of the peoples of Europe invented the artistic forms best fitted to its own genius'.[7] One can distinguish an Early Baroque period in Italy, when the tendency began, a High Baroque period in France, when a climax was reached, and a Late Baroque period when the style was adopted, with different accents, throughout Europe. A distinction can also be made between gardens, with a domestic space related to the dwelling, and parks, integrated with the surrounding landscape. A few baroque projects, including Isola Bella and Drottningholm, achieved both objectives. Mirabelle in Salzburg and Quelez in Portugal are gardens. Versailles, near Paris and Caserta in Italy are parks. The style also had a powerful influence on town planning in capital cities (Rome, Paris, Berlin, Washington, DC) and elegant resorts (Versailles, Potsdam, St Petersburg, Aranjuez).

Early Baroque in Italy

Italy was dominated by Spanish influence during the reign of the Hapsburgs (1525–1700), although some areas, including Venice, the Papal States, Tuscany and Genoa, retained nominal independence. It was a period of relative economic decline as the focus of world trade and industry shifted from the Mediterranean to the Atlantic. But it was also the period when Rome recovered its ancient role as the hub of western civilisation: the place which every artist and every tourist felt compelled to visit. Visitors were interested both in ancient remains and new projects. Leading baroque projects were initiated by the church; the greatest of all was the completion of St Peter's, by Madero and Bernini (1605–1666). This included a giant oval piazza, inspired by the peristyle court of Old St Peter's.

The use of focal points in garden design was first seen at two proto-baroque villas in Rome: Montalto (c. 1570; demolished) and Mattei (c. 1582).[8] The Villa Montalto belonged to Sixtus V before he became Pope. It was designed, with Domenico Fontana's help, to have a network of avenues, some projecting beyond the garden boundary towards Roman landmarks. The garden was 'adorned with choice works of ancient art, although at one time he [Sixtus] had scornfully opposed the cult of antiquity'. The most significant feature of the garden was that:

Here for the very first time the artist is working in a larger style with perspective. Long avenues are made with definite endings, architecture or sculpture . . . Villa Montalto had not only its own *points de vue* to rejoice in, but also the help of buildings outside.[9]

7.5 Plan of the Boboli garden

7.6 Fontainebleau has a renaissance core with Baroque additions

7.7 Bernini's piazza in front of St Peter's in Rome is bounded by a curved peristyle

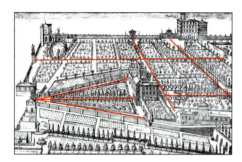

7.8 The Villa Montalto, which belonged to Pope Sixtus V, had avenues with focal points, as did his subsequent plan for the glorification of Rome

It was at Villa Montalto that Sixtus developed an enthusiasm for building which he later applied to the whole city of Rome. In 1588 he began to build baroque axes to run between focal points in the city. A number of other early baroque gardens were also made in Italy but the economy was in decline, partly because Sixtus preferred to hoard gold in the Castel Sant'Angelo, instead of permitting it to circulate. This cash starvation dealt a death blow to commerce and industry.[10]

Frascati has a group of baroque gardens which, as Steenbergen and Reh have shown, were aligned on the dome of St Peter's.[11] Many were damaged by allied bombing in the Second World War and have been restored. The Villa Ludovisi in (Torlonia) is now a public park and retains a quiet dignity. The Villa Mondragone is larger but less dramatic. Villa Aldobrandini dominates the small town of Frascati, with the palace as its focal point. On the town front, Frascati occupies the foreground and Rome the background. On the garden front, there is a water theatre, a cascade and a shaft of space projecting uphill into dark woods. Grandeur and drama surround the place.

The garden of the Villa Garzoni at Collodi, in Tuscany, does not use the house as a focal point but the garden is very much a place of show. Italian gardens were often open to visitors, and this is one that can be appreciated as a spectacle from outside the main entrance. From the entrance, a strong central axis draws the eye, and then the visitor, into the garden, up the cascade, through the woods. A colossal terracotta statue of Fame waves to the spectator from on high. The garden is a boastful stage, not a place of Renaissance seclusion. At Isola Bella on Lake Maggiore, the garden occupies a whole island: the waters of the lake, framed by the surrounding hills, become an immense garden feature. They provide a visual feast with 'the unceasing

7.9 The Villa Ludovisi (Torlonia) was bombed in 1944. Before the war, avenues 'slashed through the middle of the bosco, as if a giant had gouged into the mass of ilex, [and] a corridor of open space led back to the splash of the great Torlonia cascade' (N. T. Newton)

7.10 Isola Bella is an island garden, fully integrated with the landscape

change of the water's surface, shut in by towering hills'.[12] As at Collodi, the garden is a focal point in the landscape and the landscape is part of the garden. The 'beautiful isle' has dramatic hanging gardens, a harbour, grottoes, statues and a villa rising directly from the shore. The natural landscape had no place within Renaissance gardens. In baroque gardens, the demarcation lines between landscape and garden were blurred: gardens merged into forests, lakes and hills. Yet the landscape of Italy was not so well suited to the full development of this style as the rolling hills and forests of northern Europe. Nor was Italy as wealthy as France became during the seventeenth century.

High Baroque in France

France suffered from devastating religious wars in the sixteenth century but reached a settlement, embodied in the Edict of Nantes, in 1598. It laid the foundations for the most brilliant period in French history although it was subsequently revoked. With Germany in ruins, England kingless and Italy dominated by Spain, France assumed a position of political and cultural pre-eminence which continued until 1815. Under Louis XIV (1661–1715) the fine arts flourished as an instrument of state policy.

It was a high official in Louis' court who set the course of garden design. Nicolas Fouquet commissioned Le Vau, Le Brun and Le Nôtre to design his château and garden at Vaux-le-Vicomte. The first great work of the French baroque remains the example most admired by design critics. Historians write of 'the style of Louis XIV' but, in gardens, it could be more accurate to say 'the style of Nicholas Fouquet'. Grander in scale than any of its Italian predecessors, Vaux-le-Vicomte overtly expresses its artistic, political and geographical roots. Artistically, it is a product of the baroque enthusiasm for drama. Politically, it relates to the wealth and power of a unified state with global ambitions. Geographically, it fits the landscape of Northern France – gently rolling country, rich in billowing woods and flowing water, through which it is comparatively easy to cut avenues and route canals. Gothein sees Vaux as a balance between two tendencies: on the one hand, order, discipline and proportion, and on the other, variety and change.

Vaux-le-Vicomte is theatrical: a magnificent spectacle to be viewed from the house but with many surprises for the energetic visitor and proud owner. To inaugurate the garden, Fouquet held a famous party. Louis XIV loved the party, admired the design, imprisoned the owner and carried off the design team to create what became the most celebrated royal estate in the world: Versailles.

In 1668 Louis XIV came under the influence of a woman, who, like himself, was in the full tide of youth. 'His love for Madame de Montespan gave the inward stimulus to his being; she was the woman who supplied what in these years he wanted. She

7.11 (top left and top right) Vaux-le-Vicomte is admired by designers for the perfect composition of landscape and architectural forms

7.12 (lower left and right) Versailles, at its best when thronged with admirers, is lackadaisical on a sultry afternoon

was beautiful, proud, self-willed, and full of spirit and fun, a nature which wanted to rule and gave in to him alone.'[13] Louis XIV became known as the Sun King (*Roi Soleil*) and this metaphor provides the simplest way of interpreting the plan of the grounds at Versailles. Whereas Renaissance castles had been sited at the edge of their gardens, the palace of Louis XIV, like the Villa Aldobrandini, was at the heart of the realm. Axes radiate towards the furthest corners of France – and beyond. It was a sun plan for a Sun King, not so much a garden as we now understand the term, as a government centre. A century later, Versailles inspired Pierre L'Enfant's plan for another government centre, Washington, DC; two centuries later it inspired the axial planning of Delhi's government quarter; and three centuries later it influenced the axiality of Brazilia.

Versailles was immediately seen as the grandest, if not the most charming, of gardens – and it retains this status. The villas of the ancients and all Renaissance villas were cast into the shade by its audacious scale. First the French nobility, then the kings of Europe took their lead from Versailles. Le Nôtre undertook some commissions himself and passed others to assistants. Chantilly was one of Le Nôtre's favourite projects and one of his first for the nobility. The moated medieval château was given a breathtaking water garden. At Fontainebleau the Renaissance layout was remodelled in the baroque style. Le Nôtre also worked at Meudon, Saint-Cloud and Marly-le-Roi. The Grand Trianon at Versailles was designed as a retreat for Madame de Maintenon.

In keeping with the spirit of the age, baroque gardening dynasties branched outward. Jacques Mollet became head gardener to Henri IV in 1595. His son, Claude, and one of his grandsons, André, published books on garden design. Other grandsons, and some great-grandsons, became gardeners in their turn. André Le Nôtre's grandfather (Pierre, d. 1610) had worked for Catherine de Medici. André's father (Jean, d. 1655) lived and worked in the Tuileries Garden and in due course gave up his job to André (d. 1700), who worked in the Luxembourg Gardens and at Fontainebleau before joining the design team for Vaux-le-Vicomte. In 1657 André went to work for Louis XIV. Louis funded his dreams and, in 1693, awarded him the Order of Saint-Michel; but above all he gave him affection. André died in 1700, the most distinguished landscape architect since Senenmut.

High Baroque outside France

The glare of Versailles was brightest on the rolling hills and plains of North Europe, but its rays also shone across the Alps, the Baltic and the Atlantic. Many observers, especially those from England, found an excess of brilliance. Except when large fêtes were in progress, the gardens seemed too large, too empty, too grandiose. But it was simple to avoid this error. Later monarchs also found something excessive about Louis XIV's absolutism and imagined they could run 'enlightened' despotisms at home. If money were no object, it was in fact rather easier to make a Versailles than a Villa Lante. Not only were the principles clear and flexible, but also a professional staff, trained by Le Nôtre, was available for weekly hire. There was also a book, *The Theory*

7.13 André Le Nôtre, like his father, worked on the Tuileries Garden, here seen looking into the Louvre and out to the Arc de Triomphe and La Défense

7.14 Chantilly as a renaissance garden and as a baroque garden

7.15 (left) Hampton Court, Surrey, has both a privy garden and, glimpsed on the right, a baroque park

7.16 (right) The baroque avenue at Claremont, Surrey, has a domestic scale and character

and Practice of Gardening, by Dézallier d'Arganville, which set forth the principles on which Versailles was based.[14]

The first of d'Arganville's principles was that a single grand idea should unify the design, with sufficient variety to charm and surprise the visitor. Palatial buildings were sited on raised terraces overlooking parterres. Water features – simple, powerful and with balanced proportions – were set among great trees. Secret gardens were made in woodland compartments (*bosquets*), to surprise the visitor. Avenues ran through forests and projected beyond estate boundaries to increase their apparent size. Statues and water features were made by the best artists and technicians of the day.

Although the schema is simple, baroque gardens took different forms, influenced by social and physical geographies. The High Baroque worked best in those parts of North Europe with undulating land, copious water and deciduous forests. On flat land, it was difficult to achieve drama and variety. In mountainous country, there was likely to be too much variety and not enough unity. In hot, dry climates, it was difficult to make sufficiently large areas of wood and water to bring the composition into balance. The style also required lavish resources directed by royal and princely powers – on a scale unavailable in the first of the countries we shall consider.

English baroque

England was protected from Continental wars by her choppy seas and powerful navy, but experienced internal strife from the start of the Civil War in 1625 to the restoration of Charles II in 1660. The subsequent period of rapid economic and cultural change was associated with anti-baroque tendencies: liberalism, empiricism and the Industrial Revolution. A dalliance with baroque garden design lasted for a few decades and ended with a romantic passion for Dame Nature in the eighteenth century. London's palace gardens, including Greenwich Park and Kensington Gardens, were touched by the baroque but are not prime examples of the style.

Before ascending the English throne in 1660, Charles II had passed 16 years of exile in France. His memories of England, and of the enclosed garden at Boscobel (see page 148), were none too happy. Having some enthusiasm for Louis XIV's approach to autocratic government and absolutist design, Charles made England one of the first countries to follow the path of Le Nôtre. His mother Henrietta Maria, a French princess who had been present at the opening of Vaux-le-Vicomte, came to live at the Queen's House in Greenwich Park and Charles invited Le Nôtre to design a parterre for her. It was Le Nôtre's only English project – a baroque park to help the dowager queen feel at home in England. It did not work and she returned to France. Charles also employed André Mollet to design canals and avenues for St James's Park, perhaps to make himself feel more at home in England.

Outside London, avenues were the most popular aspect of the High Baroque style. Not only were they fashionable, and even useful, but they could also be attached to England's Renaissance gardens without undue expense. A close examination of Knyff and Kip's copperplate engravings of English estates in the early eighteenth century reveals a profusion of avenues tacked onto Renaissance layouts.[15] Perhaps 'Low Baroque' could serve as a name for this design approach but some of the avenues, such as that at Levens Hall, Cumbria, have an informal charm.

Dutch baroque

Holland experienced a Golden Age from 1609 to 1713, in which the country was wealthy, Protestant and independent. Despite wars with Spain, England and France, Holland took a leading role in the arts. William III, Stadholder of the United Provinces from 1672 and King of England 1688–1702, favoured a modified absolutism in government and a modified baroque style in garden design. The gardens he commissioned for Het Loo in Apeldoorn and Hampton Court in London reveal this taste.

As a nation, the Dutch had no reason to like Louis XIV. But the cultural influence of so powerful a neighbour could not be resisted: William and Mary's garden at Het Loo became known (unfairly, because it is more Dutch and less grandiose) as 'the Dutch Versailles'. At Honslaarsdyk, William made another garden, with a more interesting and distinctively Dutch design (Figure 6.21). The avenues outside the garden, not shown on the drawing, were lines of trees projecting into agricultural land. This garden, which no longer exists, would have been a much more interesting subject for a restoration project than Het Loo. Dutch baroque gardens were also made at Enghien and Neuberg. The country had a great deal of water but, especially in the polder lands, a shortage of forests.

German baroque

When the Thirty Years War ended in 1648, large sections of Germany were devastated, and theological and territorial disputes continued to make a political union impossible. For the art of garden design, this was an advantage: there were more court gardens to be made. Each state had a palace and most were touched by the rays which shone from Versailles. Germany was rebuilt, but it lacked experienced

7.17 The baroque garden at Het Loo has radiating avenues outside its wall

7.18 Nymphenburg, near Munich, has a great baroque garden, set in a forest with outward views

7.19 Herrenhausen, Hannover, has a highly disciplined baroque garden, bounded by a canal in the Dutch manner, with a serpentine park outside

designers; often, the princes and bishops employed an Italian architect and a French garden designer. Many of the places they made are original and eccentric. In time, the baroque developed into the rococo with graceful curves and rich decoration. Rococo is the name for a style that originated in Paris in the early eighteenth century, partly as a reaction to the ponderous grandeur of Versailles. It was popular in the courts of southern Germany and Austria.

Sophie, daughter of the king who made the Hortus Palatinus (see p. 149), commissioned a student of Le Nôtre to design the Grosser Garten at Herrenhausen, Hannover, in 1666. It was a textbook example of regularity in the relationship of house to garden. Sophie had spent her youth in Holland and remembered the geometrical discipline of Dutch gardens. Since Herrenhausen's avenues do not project beyond its canal, this regularity is even more pronounced than at Versailles. Another German prince, the, Elector Max Emanuel, returned from a period of exile in Paris with a liking for French gardens. At Nymphenburg, he made great flower parterres, canals and avenues around the focal point provided by the castle.

At Karlsruhe in south–west Germany, the idea of radiating avenues was developed in a way never before seen in France, or any other place. A hunting-tower was used as the node for a star of 32 avenues. Façades of buildings were planned to create unified frontages onto avenues with parterres behind. At a later date the garden plan was transformed into a town plan. Another distinctive design, made for the castle of Wilhelmshohe at Kassel, is more Italian than French in its use of rugged scenery. Only the upper part of the cascade was completed, but even this fragment is vast and dramatic.

In the mid-eighteenth century, confidence in enlightened despotism and enthusiasm for the High Baroque waned together, leading to rococo gardens and, as discussed in the next chapter, to landscape gardens. The formal garden at Schwetzingen, made after 1753, is less axial and more compartmentalised than high baroque designs. Other German gardens tended towards the rococo. Socially, their

function was for gay social events rather than displays of raw power. This translated into outdoor rooms with comparatively weak overall plans. The Ermitage at Bayreuth, made after 1735, has a theatre in the form of a Roman ruin, made for outdoor opera. Veitshöchheim, near Wurtzburg in Bavaria (*c.* 1763) has numerous hedged garden rooms with mischievous rococo statuary and other relaxed details – the bishops who made this garden must have been more inclined to aestheticism than asceticism.

Austrian baroque

Austria, though the centre of the Holy Roman Empire, could not undertake major building projects during most of the seventeenth century. It was restrained by the Thirty Years War in the first half of the century and by the Turkish menace until 1688. Following the return of peace, fine gardens were made. Gardens were made in and near Vienna, at Belvedere, Schwarzenberg, Liechtenstein, Schloss Hof and Schönbrunn. Hungary was part of the empire, and a great baroque garden was made at Esterhazy.

The Belvedere Garden, just outside the walls of Vienna, was inspired by the palace of Versailles and laid out by a French designer. Its scale is closer to that of an Italian garden than a French park, befitting its intended use for high society. There was no forest and the water features are too small for boats. Schönbrunn, made by the great Empress Maria Theresa, is the Versailles of Austria. In a reversal of the standard baroque plan, the palace stands at the foot of the hill and there is a *gloriette* where the palace 'should' be. Paintings and photographs showing the garden from the *gloriette* do not do justice to Fischer von Erlach's imperious design: the scale of the parterres needs the balance provided by the spectacular fountain and the *gloriette*-topped hill.

Hellbrunn (1615), the country retreat of a prince archbishop, falls into the same stylistic group as the Villa Aldobrandini (1598) and the Boboli (1620). It has two axes, it takes advantage of the landscape and it has an elaborate water feature. Salzburg, the city which gave birth to Mozart in 1756, has a garden with some of the character

7.20 The upper cascade of Wilhelmshohe at Kassel

7.21 Schönbrunn is a great court garden, almost on the scale of a hunting park

7.22 Mirabelle, with the gaiety of a Mozart opera, retains the air of a court garden better than any of its counterparts

of his music. Mirabelle is a court garden in the midst of a city. Its prime axis is aligned with Salzburg's castle. The garden is gay and has an outdoor theatre beautifully suited to a performance of *The Magic Flute* or *The Marriage of Figaro*. Today, the garden is understandably popular with young couples and wedding photographers.

Scandinavian baroque

Sweden enjoyed an Age of Greatness in the seventeenth century. Its king, Gustavus Adolphus II, was the leading Protestant commander in the Thirty Years War. After taking Prague he transported the statues from his opponent's garden to Drottningholm (1665–1700). But 'for fashion and etiquette, for architecture and art, the Court of Louis XIV provided the divine archetype'.[16] Gustavus' daughter, Queen Christina, summoned French designers to Sweden and the dowager Queen Hedvig Eleonora planned a full-blown baroque garden at Drottningholm. It is the best example of the baroque style in a cold climate. The garden itself may have been designed under by Le Nôtre's personal supervision, in France by Nicodemus Tessin.

A wise and loved Queen, Hedvig Eleonora tried to restrain her grandson, Charles XII, from the military campaign which ended Sweden's Age of Greatness. Her garden at Drottningholm has avenues and fine parterres, aligned with a frontage on Lake Mälaren and a focal point on a hill. It is a national symbol, drawing from Europe's history but fully adjusted to, and at home in, the Swedish landscape. In commemoration, Emanuel Swedenborg wrote a *Sapphic Ode*:

> Sweden, of ancient Goths thou parent land,
> Weep! Nurse of nations and of warriors brave,
> With locks and garments torn by frantic hand,
> Weep o'er yon grave![17]

King Frederick IV of Denmark visited Paris in 1700 and returned with a penchant for the baroque. This resulted in the parterre garden at Frederiksborg and the radiating

7.23 Drottningholm is proudly at home in a northern landscape, with statues taken from the Wallenstein Garden in Prague

avenues at Fredensborg. At Frederiksborg, it is a pleasure to find a baroque garden where the designer, instead of attempting yet another Versailles, drew upon Chantilly. Like medieval French lowland castles, Frederiksborg Castle is in the middle of a lake. It was used as a summer residence for the Danish royal family before becoming a national museum. The castle is arranged on three islands with its main axis projecting over a fourth island and across the moat-lake. A canal penetrates the lakeshore and the axis ascends a terraced hillside to an oval pond, defined by clipped box and pleached limes. A restoration programme was started in 1995. Departing from the axis to walk round the lakeshore gives one a different prospect: what looks like a baroque garden from within the castle becomes a romantic castle on an island in a lake in a park.

Russian baroque

Russia was a backward country from the Time of Troubles (1606–1613) until the reign of Peter the Great (1689–1725). Peter won great military victories and opened Russia to the art and technology of Europe. Baroque town planning and garden design were among his imports; St Petersburg and the Peterhof are the spectacular results. Peter was a marginally-enlightened despot with a savage streak of cruelty, but in his building projects, one sees the enlightened side of his character. The Peterhof was severely damaged in the Second World War and then rebuilt.

Iberian baroque

Spain was ruled by the Habsburgs from 1516 to 1700. This assisted the influx of artistic ideas to Spain but all the gold of South America was not enough to pay for the protracted European wars that ensued. Military overreach ended Spain's domination of Europe by 1630. Baroque art reassured the Habsburg dynasty that it was doing its duty for the Holy Roman Empire and the Catholic faith. After the House of Bourbon took the Spanish throne, in 1700, baroque gardens were made at Aranjuez and La Granja. The latter, benefiting from the un-Mediterranean climate of Central Spain, is an exceptionally fine example of the style. The glistening white of the sculpture coordinates with the snow-capped peaks, the marble cascade and the whitish bark of the trees.

Late Baroque in Italy

Having originated in Italy, developed in France, and spread throughout Europe, the baroque style returned to its homeland. It had some influence on the flat lands of Northern Italy (e.g. at Monza), to which it was not unsuited. The most significant 'Versailles of Italy' was attempted at Caserta in 1752, by a Bourbon prince, Charles III, who had spent his youth at La Granja. The longest cascade in Europe emerges from the palace and flows 3 km into a vast canal. It is awe-inspiring, as one would expect of the Late Baroque, but it lacks the sense of proportion which guided the best Italian and French designs of earlier periods.

7.24 Plan of La Reggia, Caserta

7.25 Quelez in Portugal is a baroque palace garden, with the richness of a southern landscape

7.26 La Granja is a southern garden with northern tints

7.27 (left and far right) The great baroque axis at Caserta has a scene from Ovid at the foot of its upper cascade

Styles and examples

Early Baroque

Use: Early Baroque art is associated with the Counter-Reformation and the quest to re-establish the power of prelates and princes. Garden layouts became a means of advertising power. Since physical security now rested more on guns and armies than city walls, rural life became as safe (or unsafe) as town life. The villas of Frascati were built with their lines of sight coordinated on the dome of St Peter's in Rome. Pope Sixtus V used baroque ideas, drawn from garden design, to glorify Rome. Vistas were fixed on obelisks and spires. Courtly gatherings took place in baroque gardens and the larger parks were used for hunting.

Form: The baroque style began with the projection of axes beyond the boundaries of enclosed Renaissance gardens. In towns, the avenues focused on church domes and other features. Outside towns, they pushed into the landscape, bringing mountains, lakes and forests into composition with gardens. The results were dramatic. Lines of view projected ever-outwards. Enthusiasm for the discoveries of geometry, optics and perspective influenced garden design. The avenue became the most characteristic feature of Baroque parks and gardens. It began life as a shady walk on the edge of a square medieval plat. Then:

- Bramante used an axis as the central feature in a garden layout
- Avenues projected towards garden features
- Avenues projected towards features outside the garden (e.g. the dome of St Peter's)
- Avenues began to radiate in all directions, to the greater glory of their owners.

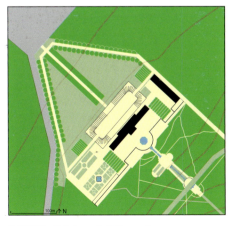

7.28 Early baroque garden

Villa Aldobrandini 1600

This is the best-known example of the early Italian baroque style. Instead of standing on the fringe of the garden, the palace is its centrepiece, theatrically set into a wooded hill and, like the other Frascati villas, casting an eye over the landscape towards the dome of St Peter's in Rome. Every aspect of the place is aristocratic. It was designed for a 'nephew' of a Pope (the euphemism for a papal child) in an imposing situation with a broad terrace dominating Frascati. To the rear, there is a water theatre with niches for statues and fountains. Atlas holds a globe in the central niche. Behind the theatre, an avenue with a central water cascade pushes upwards into the oak and chestnut woods.

7.29 Villa Aldobrandini, Frascati

There are garlanded Pillars of Hercules. Work on the garden began in 1598 and was finished in 1603. The Villa Aldobrandini was badly damaged during the Second World War and subsequently rebuilt. Many of the statues have gone and the fountains that used to soak and delight unsuspecting visitors were not working at the time of writing.

> In my opinion [one of] the most delicious places I ever beheld for its situation, elegance, plentiful water, groves, ascents, and prospects. Just behind the Palace (which is of excellent architecture) in the centre of the enclosure, rises a high hill, or mountain, all over clad with tall wood, and so formed by nature, as if it had been cut out by art, from the summit whereof falls a cascade, seeming rather a great river than a stream precipitating into a large theatre of water, representing an exact and perfect rainbow, when the sun shines out.[18]

A baroque villa without water is almost unthinkable ... At the Villa Aldobrandini the water appears high at the top in an untamed, natural setting as a *fontanone rustico*; it falls straight down between hemispherical boulders, gathers, falls again over a high wall into a pool, disappears and reappears, alternates again between falling and gathering in a pool. Now the structure becomes more definite: the water falls again over a wavy, sharply inclined ramp, and finally the cascade appears as the centrepiece of the teatro behind the villa.[19]

Villa Garzoni 1652

The villa provides an ornamented baroque spectacle in a bucolic valley, with its garden standing apart from the house and its medieval village. Guests reached the garden by walking through shady woods from the house. They burst into the glare of the mid-seventeenth century at the top of an axial cascade. False perspective on the cascade exaggerates its length when seen from above and its drama when seen from below: it narrows as it descends. A heroic terracotta statue of Fame waves gaily from the upper garden. Behind her is a bath-house which once had a music room and every kind of luxury for male and female bathers. They could chatter without, it is said, being able to see one another. The cascade flows down the terraces to a semicircular parterre. The garden design reveals itself to passers-by in the valley below, unlike a secluded Medici garden.

> Here ... is one of the most spectacular baroque gardens of Italy, whose layout makes the fullest use of a precipitous hillside site in a manner that is usually associated with Rome.[20]

Isola Bella 1630

A small rocky island in Lake Maggiore is wholly occupied by the Borromeo villa and its garden extravaganza. Local legend relates that the Borromeo ladies asked the Count to build the house on an island so that they would not have to listen to the screams of the prisoners in the dungeons of his mainland castle. Like a flower-strewn barge,

7.30 (above) Villa Garzoni, Lucca

7.31 (below) Isola Bella, Lake Maggiore

the island appears to drift amongst the snow-capped mountains of the lake, belying the gruesome motivation behind its creation, and the labour involved in transporting the soil and stone to the site. Isola Bella uses the lake and mountains as garden ornaments in a vast composition: axes join the house to the scenery. The stepped terraces remind one of painters' interpretations of the Hanging Gardens of Babylon.

> The whole island is a Mount, ascended by several Terraces and walks all set about with oranges and citron trees, the reflection from the water rendering the place very warm, at least during the summer and autumn.[21]

High Baroque style

Use: Gardens have always expressed their proprietors' status and attitudes, and baroque garden design reflected the increasingly haughty attitudes of owners and their guests. France led the development of High Baroque gardens, which were associated with an autocratic style of government. The palace and garden of Versailles were freely open to gentlemen, providing they carried swords, and the crowds would part admiringly when Louis XIV made a stately progression through his garden, perhaps accompanied by its designer, André Le Nôtre. The forest rides were used by hunting parties.

Form: Designers drew upon developments in mathematics and science, using 'Cartesian' geometry to lay out avenues that drew the surrounding landscape into the composition. The characteristic features of High Baroque gardens were: a centrally positioned building, extensive avenues, elaborate parterres, fountains, basins and canals. Lines of perspective integrated residential architecture, garden architecture, sculpture, fountains, cascades, planting and other features. Command of the waters was essential and in many gardens there were so many fountains that they could be operated only during a social event. These days, in gardens open to the public, they tend to operate on Sunday afternoons.

7.32 High Baroque garden

7.33 Vaux-le-Vicomte, France

Vaux-le-Vicomte 1656

The most elegant and geometrically harmonious of all High Baroque gardens was designed by Le Nôtre and Le Vau. Their composition is mathematically proportioned: its axial principle derives from Bramante and was recommended by André Mollet. At Vaux, the axis passes through parterres, over basins of water, and into forest compartments. Brilliant use of landform allows many surprises, yet the composition is balanced from every point of view. The estate belonged to Louis XIV's finance minister, Fouquet, and was a place of show; it was not designed, or ever used, for domestic pleasure. The king was impressed by Vaux, but appalled by its owner's presumption. He had Fouquet arrested, and confiscated the garden statuary. After this, Vaux fell into disrepair, until it was restored by Henri and Achille Duchêne, after 1875. It remains a showpiece, a splendid location for a day's promenade.

> In order to clear the ground for the castle, garden, and a proper open space round them, it was necessary for Fouquet to buy three villages, and to pull them down. The place grew with astonishing quickness over its foundations. The powerful financier had inexhaustible wealth at his disposal, so he pressed on the work eagerly. It is said that at times as many as eighteen thousand labourers were employed together, and the cost was computed at sixteen million livres.[22]

> Plans and aerial views of Vaux do little to advance our understanding; like all Le Nôtre's compositions it has to be seen on the ground. And it takes time; it cannot be seen at a glance; it grows in the mind.[23]

> In some of the great French gardens, at Vaux and Versailles for example, one is conscious, under all the beauty, of the immense effort expended, of the vast upheavals of earth, the forced creating of effects.[24]

Versailles 1661

Versailles was conceived as a palatial centre of government for an absolute monarch, Louis XIV: it is the prime example of the French baroque style, and has the most famous garden in the world. Andre Le Nôtre worked on the design from 1661 to 1700. Yet 'garden' is scarcely the right designation. The scale is monumental and there is no

7.34 Plan of Versailles

sense of enclosure. Nor is it a friendly place: 'overbearing' is a common English response to this site, and critics have often been disenchanted. Horace Walpole saw Versailles as 'the gardens of a great child'.[25] Avenues project ever-outward to distant horizons, integrating the royal palace with the town, the garden, the forest and the hoped-for empire. There are immaculate parterres, great basins, an orangery, a vast collection of outdoor sculpture and some of the best fountains ever made.

When Versailles became the official residence of the court, the gardens lost any privacy they may have had, and became an instrument of propaganda demonstrating to all Europe the superiority of French gardening. Louis himself wrote instructions on how tours should be conducted.[26]

Gray the poet was struck with their splendour when filled with company, and when the water-works were in full action. Lord Kaimes says only they would tempt one to believe that nature was below the notice of a great monarch, and therefore monsters must be created for him, as being more astonishing productions. Bradley says 'Versailles is the sum of every thing that has been done in gardening.' Agricola, a German author, declares that the sight of Versailles gave him a foretaste of Paradise. Our opinion coincides with Gray's: 'Such symmetry' as Lord Byron observes, 'is not for solitude'.[27]

The palace of Versailles . . . is not in the least striking: I view it without emotion: the impression it makes is nothing.[28]

Drottningholm 1680

The summer palace of Sweden's royal family stands on an island in Lake Mälaren, known as the Island of the Queen. Hedwig Eleonora was the wife of one warrior king, Charles X, and the grandmother of another, Charles XII. The garden is thought to have been designed in France under Le Nôtre's supervision but, like all the best baroque gardens, it exploits the surrounding landscape. The design 'embodied in stone the ideals of Sweden's Age of Greatness'. The prime axis runs from a harbour with a landing stage. Behind the palace lie elegant baroque parterres and an avenue pressing into the woods. The garden is ornamented with sculpture taken as booty from the Wallenstein garden in Prague and Frederiksborg in Denmark. A Chinese summer house was built in 1753, as a birthday present for another queen, Louisa Ulrika (1720–1782). Drottningholm has examples of baroque, rococo and Romantic taste.

Hedwig Eleonora . . . found a medieval castle on one of the islands in Lake Mälaren, and she began to make alterations in 1661. This castle also stood on a raised terrace, and its approach was by water from an oval-shaped harbour. The garden lay towards the south, and showed the influence of Versailles more than any other in Sweden; its fine parterre was laid out in

7.35 Drottningholm, Stockholm

patterns of box, with a border of clipped trees and flowers. In the centre, steps in the open mount up by a wide middle walk to a basin with a Hercules fountain.[29]

Peterhof 1716

Russia's most important baroque garden, attached to Peter the Great's summer palace, was inspired by Versailles and designed by Jean-Baptiste Le Blond, a pupil of Le Nôtre. There is a good water supply and the palace stands on a natural terrace over-looking the Baltic. A fabled marble cascade lined with gilded statues flows from the palace to the sea, along the Samson canal, symbolising Russia's conquest of the Baltic coast in the Great Northern War. One hundred and seventy-three fountains line the canal and ornament the woods. On the south front of the palace are parterres, allées, grass plots, basins, fountains and statues. Like St Petersburg itself, the Peterhof is a symbol of Peter's desire to make Russia into a sophisticated European power.

Peterhof, in respect to situation, is perhaps unrivalled. About five hundred fathoms from the sea-shore this region has a second cliff, almost perpendicular, near twelve fathoms high . . . The declivity from the back-front of the palace towards the sea has two magnificent cascades, rolling their streams over the terraces into large basins, and beneath which the visitor may walk as under a vault, without receiving wet, into a beautiful grotto.[30]

Every night during the festival the gardens of the palace were illuminated, Russians said that there were ten millions of lamps . . . rows of lamps were placed, over which the fluid rushed from the cascade like a shower of

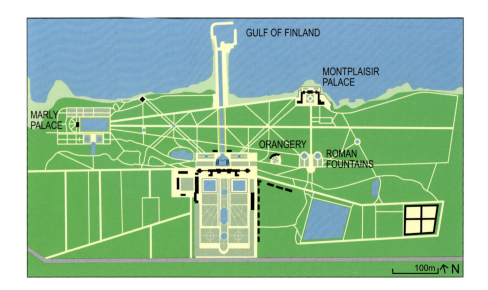

GULF OF FINLAND

MONTPLAISIR PALACE

MARLY PALACE

ORANGERY

ROMAN FOUNTAINS

100m N

7.36 Peterhof, St. Petersburg

diamonds, whilst the flashing lights beneath had an indescribably brilliant effect; the fine bronze figures untarnished glittered like statues of gold in the rays of thousands of beaming stars.[31]

Notes

1   Bazin, G., *Baroque and Rococo*, London: Thames & Hudson, 1964. p. 6.
2   Bazin, G., op. cit., pp. 6–7.
3   Descartes, R., *Discourse on Method, and other writings*, transl. with an introduction by Sutcliffe, F. E., Harmondsworth: Penguin Books, 1968.
4   Fauvel, J., *et al.*, *Let Newton Be!* Oxford: Oxford University Press, 1988, p. 187.
5   Padovan, R., *Proportion: Science, Philosophy, Architecture*, London: Spon, 1999, pp. 137–49.
6   Pope, A., *An Essay on Criticism*, 1711.
7   Bazin, G., op. cit., p. 8.
8   Gothein, M-L., *A History of Garden Art*, London: J. M. Dent, 1928, Vol 1, p. 307.
9   ——, op. cit., Ch. 7, p. 10.
10 *New Advent Catholic Encyclopedia*, http://www.newadvent.org/cathen/14033a.htm.
11 Steenbergen, C. and Reh, W., *Architecture and Landscape: The design experiment of the great European gardens and landscape*, Prestel, 1996.
12 Gothein, M-L., op. cit., p. 345.
13 ——, op. cit., Ch. 12, p. 5.
14 Le Blond, *The Theory and Practice of Gardening (of A. J. Dézallier d'Arganville)*, London: Lintot, 1728.
15 Kip, J. and Knyff, J., *Britannia Illustrata, or Views of several of the Queen's palaces, also of the principal seats of the nobility and gentry of Great Britain*, 1707.
16 Hahr, A., *Architecture in Sweden*, Stockholm: Bonniers Boktryckeri, 1938, p. 37.
17 *Swedenborg Digital Library*, http://www.swedenborgdigitallibrary.org/ES/epic4.htm.
18 John Evelyn, 1645. The text is taken from William Bray's 1818 edition of Evelyn's *Diary*.
19 Wölfflin, H., *Renaissance and Baroque*, London: Collins, 1964, p. 157.
20 Masson, G., *Italian Gardens*, London: Thames & Hudson, 1961, p. 116.
21 Evelyn, J. 1646. The text is taken from William Bray's 1818 edition of Evelyn's *Diary*.
22 Gothein, M-L., op. cit., p. 52.
23 Woodbridge, K., *Princely Gardens. The origins and development of the French formal style*, London: Thames & Hudson, 1986, p. 188.
24 Wharton, E., *Italian Villas and their Gardens*, New York: The Century Co., 1904, p. 94.
25 Quoted in Hobhouse, P. and Taylor, P., *The Gardens of Europe*, London: George Philip Ltd, 1990, p. 89.
26 Woodbridge, K., op. cit., p. 213.
27 Loudon, J. C., *Encyclopaedia of Gardening*, London: Longman, 1822, p. 33.
28 Young, A., *Travels During the Years 1787, 1788, and 1789*, Bury St. Edmunds: Rackham, 1792–4.
29 Gothein, M-L., op. cit., Vol. 2, p. 199.
30 Loudon, J. C., op. cit., p. 50.
31 Anon., *The Englishwoman in Russia: Impressions of the society and manners of the Russians at home*, by a Lady two years resident in that country, London, 1855, p. 21.

Chapter 8

Neoclassical and Romantic gardens 1700–1810

History and philosophy

Even in the Protestant countries, baroque gardens continued to be made during the eighteenth century. But a radical departure also took place, eventually to be described as the landscape garden. Historians enjoy tracing its origins. There are many candidates for the role of prime cause and it is unlikely that agreement will be ever reached. The position taken in my book, *English Garden Design: history and styles since 1650*, was that the departure resulted from a coalition of six key ideas: empiricism, Neoplatonism, constitutional democracy, landscape painting, rural retirement and Chinese gardens.[1] Today, I view empiricism as the king and rationalism as Prime Minister.

The role of political parties in representing coalitions of interest was devised in the eighteenth century and came to be regarded as the most reasonable and natural style of government. Conversely, the divine right of kings to stand above the law, taxing, imprisoning and torturing their subjects, came to be seen as unenlightened, unreasonable and unnatural. Paintings of idealised landscapes incorporating classical subjects were admired as representations of a harmonious calm between mankind, nature and the gods. Roman ruins were venerated. Men dreamed that adherence to natural law would allow god-fearing shepherds, shepherdesses, improvers and rational gentlefolk to enjoy peace on earth. The English Civil War had given the leading political theorist of his day, Thomas Hobbes, personal experience of a 'state of nature' with 'a condition of war of everyone against everyone' and with the life of man 'solitary, poor, nasty, brutish and short'.[2] Advocates of the new style planned for a better world,

8.1 Sanssouci provides the best indication of how gardens might have evolved had there not been a radical departure from the baroque: (clockwise from top left) Chinese tea pavilion, fountain below wine-hill, historic mill and Mount of Ruins

symbolised by ideal landscapes with Roman references. The four phases in the development of this ideal landscape will be categorised as: Augustan, serpentine, Picturesque and landscape, with the fourth of these phases discussed in the next chapter. They were influenced by the Enlightenment response to the baroque, known as neoclassicism, and by the growth of the Romantic movement.

The term 'English landscape garden' does not place the new ideas in an art-historical category. Opinions vary as to which of the categories of eighteenth-century art – neoclassical, rococo and Romantic – provides the most appropriate label for the new movement in garden design. Bazin, whose precise summary of the baroque was quoted at the start of the previous chapter, sees the landscape garden as 'in fact the principal contribution of Great Britain to the Rococo style'.[3] Gombrich associates the new style with the classicism of Claude and Palladio.[4] Pevsner sees it as 'a truly Romantic conception'.[5] Jansen (with whom I agree) identifies the artistic parents of the new approach as classicism and Romanticism:

> Long regarded as opposites, the two seem today so interdependent that one name would serve for both, if we could find it. ('Romantic Classicism,' which has been proposed, has not won wide acceptance.) The two terms are too unevenly matched – like 'quadruped' and 'carnivore.' Neoclassicism means a new revival of classical antiquity, more consistent than earlier classicisms, while Romanticism refers to an attitude of mind that may reveal itself in any number of ways. The word derives from the late-eighteenth-century vogue for medieval tales of adventure (such as the legends of King Arthur or the Holy Grail, called 'romances' because they were written in a Romance language, not in Latin).[6]

The first work discussed in Part 4 of Jansen's *History of Art* is Chiswick House in London, inspired by an Italian architect's vision of the ancient world. Andrea Palladio (1508–1580) was inspired by reading Vitruvius and sketching Roman ruins. He developed a simple classicism which appealed equally to the wealthy farmers who were his clients and, two centuries later, to their English counterparts. Landowning farmers in the Veneto and in England wanted open views of their fields uncluttered by wasteful gardens and Renaissance frippery.[7] Claude Lorraine (1600–1682), who has 'at all times been considered the greatest of landscape painters',[8] drew antique and ideal landscapes. The mythological scenes identified by his titles are 'the primordial element, from which the entire composition is conceived'[9] and, in the greatest of his paintings, the themes were drawn from Greek myths told in the *Metamorphoses* of Ovid or of Apuleius. Claude painted a romantically classical world adorned with temples and populated by gods, heroes, shepherds and shepherdesses.

Claude's world drew from the landscape of Greece and Rome, but not from their gardens. Comparing his paintings with the quotations from Homer in Chapter 3 reveals this: we see no walled cities, palace courtyards or productive gardens with 'beautifully

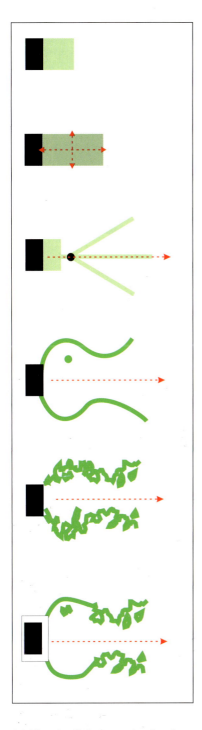

8.2 Thumbnail diagrams showing the geometrical evolution of garden plans after the Renaissance

8.3 Chiswick House and park, designed by Lord Burlington and William Kent, was a statement of their love for classical landscapes

8.4 Claude Lorrain: *Landscape with the Father of Psyche sacrificing at the Temple of Apollo* (1662)

arranged beds of flowers that are in bloom all the year round' (see p. 55). Instead, Claude painted antique landscapes with sacred groves in which mythological and biblical events are depicted. The subject of Claude's *Landscape with the Father of Psyche Sacrificing at the Temple of Apollo* (1662; 8.4) comes from Apuleius. Venus, jealous of Psyche's wonderful beauty, asked Cupid to make her fall in love with a detestable man. Psyche's father learned of his daughter's fate at an altar outside a temple in a grove sacred to Apollo. In Renaissance Italy the story was given a Neoplatonic interpretation, as an 'account of the progress of the soul in its search for, and ultimate union with, divine Beauty'.[10] Such were the scenes Claude painted – and many are their delights.

The respective roles of gardens and groves were as separate in the ancient world as they became in eighteenth-century Europe. Though not without a spiritual dimension, the primary roles of French baroque estates were courtly gatherings and stag hunts. The role of English landscapes, in marked contrast, was to provide a balm for the soul. In his *Essay . . . on the Use of Studying Pictures, for the Purpose of Improving Real Landscape* (1794), Sir Uvedale Price wrote:

> The peculiar beauty of the most beautiful of all landscape painters is characterised by *il riposo di Claudio*, and when the mind of man is in the delightful state of repose, of which Claude's pictures are the image – when he feels that mild and equal sunshine of the soul which warms and cheers, but neither inflames nor irritates – his heart seems to dilate with happiness, he is disposed to every act of kindness and benevolence, to love and cherish all around him.[11]

Kenneth Clark described this as 'the most enchanting dream which has ever consoled mankind'.[12] Imagine stepping from a frenzied baroque ballroom onto a still terrace with the sun setting beyond a dark valley and stars appearing in the night sky: this contrast represents the psychological divide between baroque and landscape gardens. Inside, everything is sprightly. Outside, the soul yearns to fathom the mysterious yet ordered nature of the universe with whatever help can be obtained from reason, imagination, empirical observation or the lips of one's partner. Landscape gardens evolved during the eighteenth century, in step with the progression from neoclassicism to Romanticism. The closest forebear of Chiswick House, artistically, conceptually and chronologically, is the Sacro Bosco which Duke Vincino Orsini made in the valley beneath the walled city of Bomarzo (see p. 152). I would like to know whether the designers of Chiswick House knew this place.

There is a tendency for British garden historians to view the inception of the landscape garden through the distorting lens of patriotism. Plucky British designers, spurning autocracy and motivated by high ideals drawn from poetry, painting, reason, nature and democracy, are said to have originated a glorious new style which conquered first Britain, then Europe. French historians like Bazin, tend to see matters through a different lens, finding *le style Anglo-Chinois* to be an effete scion of the baroque, pushing out baleful tentacles from the long shadow of Chinese art.

The characteristic which landscape gardens unquestionably shared with baroque gardens, and classical art, was dependence on the axiom, derived from Plato's Theory of Forms, that 'art should *imitate* nature'. It is embodied in the following quotations:

- Aristotle: 'Epic poetry, tragedy, comedy, lyric poetry . . . are, in the most general view of them, modes of imitation'[13]
- Cicero: 'I follow Nature, the best of guides, as I would a god'[14]
- Plotinus: 'What is beyond the intellectual principle we affirm to be the nature of Good radiating beauty before it'.[15]

8.5 Bomarzo in Italy and Rousham in Oxfordshire, both have re-created sacred groves

- Du Fresnoy: 'a learned Painter should form to himself an Idea of perfect Nature'[16]
- Dézallier d'Arganville: 'If one wishes to lay out a garden it must be borne in mind that one must stay closer to nature than to art'[17]
- Salmon: 'The work of the painter is to express the exact imitation of natural things; wherein you are to observe the excellencies and beauties of the piece, but to refuse its vices'[18]
- Temple: 'greater sums may be thrown away without effect or honour, if there want sense in proportion to money, or if Nature be not followed; which I take to be the great rule in this, and perhaps in everything else'[19]
- Pope: 'First follow NATURE, and your Judgment frame/By her just Standard, which is still the same'[20]
- Walpole: 'Kent . . . had followed nature, and imitated her so happily, that he began to think all her works were equally proper for imitation'[21]
- Reynolds: 'The great style in art, and the most perfect imitation of nature, consists in avoiding the details and peculiarities of particular objects'[22]
- Dryden: 'those things, which delight all ages, must have been an imitation of Nature'[23]
- Downing: 'By Landscape Gardening, we understand not only an imitation, in the grounds of a country residence, of the agreeable forms of nature, but an expressive, harmonious, and refined imitation'.[24]

What did change in eighteenth-century England was the predominant interpretation of the axiom. 'Nature', in neoclassical art theory, meant the world of the universal forms. In Romantic art theory, 'Nature' meant the world of the particulars. It was a change from the *nature of the world* to the 'world of *nature*'. The period 1780–1830 saw the flood tide of Romanticism, but the movement began softly, grew to a torrent, and subsided gradually, leaving permanent tidemarks on the world's psyche. This chapter deals first with England and then with other parts of Europe.

Pre-1700

According to Pevsner, European Romanticism began with a hint from Sir William Temple:

> What I have said of the best forms of gardens, is meant only of such as are in some sort regular; for there may be other forms wholly irregular, that may, for ought I know, have more beauty than any of the others . . . something of this I have seen in some places, but heard more of it from others, who have lived much among the Chinese; a people, whose way of thinking seems to lie as wide of ours in Europe, as their country does.[25]

This passage is one of the most amazing in the English language. It started a line of thought and visual conceptions which were to dominate first England and then the World for two centuries. It is the first suggestion ever of a possible beauty fundamentally different from the formal, a beauty of irregularity and fancy.[26]

Pevsner specifically identified a twisty stream south–east of Temple's walled garden at Moor Park, outside Farnham in Surrey, as the first hint of Romanticism in the visual arts (Figure 8.6). After being involved as a diplomat in the murky religious wars of the seventeenth century, Temple retired to Moor Park to reflect on life, cultivate his garden, and compose some of the best English essays of the period. He had two classical predecessors: Horace, who withdrew from the civil strife of Rome to savour the pleasures of country life, and Epicurus, the Greek philosopher who withdrew to a 'grove of Academe' (see p. 58) to teach the value of simple pleasures as compared with the deceits of glory and power. Temple's essay *Upon the Gardens of Epicurus* may have been in Voltaire's thoughts when he had Candide conclude, '*il faut cultiver notre jardin*' ('we must cultivate our garden', in the sense of 'mind our own business').

1700–1750

The advance of Romanticism, which saw enclosed gardens evolve into open landscapes, was traced with great skill by Christopher Hussey.[27] An early step was the layout of estates in what Switzer described as a 'forest style'.[28] They used baroque geometry but for a life of rural retreat and practical husbandry. Two of the most celebrated steps were the retention of Wray Wood and the design of Henderskelf Lane,

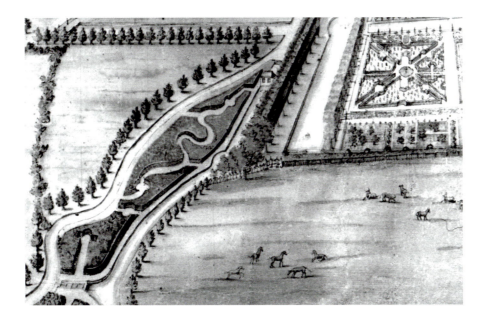

8.6 According to Pevsner, Moor Park in Surrey was the first designed landscape to incorporate a deliberately serpentine line

both at Castle Howard. Hussey commented that the low hill on which they lie is 'historic ground, since it became the turning-point of garden design not only at Castle Howard but in England'.[29]

In 1700 the low hill was occupied by a stand of mature beech trees. George London and Stephen Switzer advised Lord Carlisle on the layout of the grounds: London wished to drive an avenue along the north front of Castle Howard, then up the hill to make Wray Wood a star of baroque avenues. Switzer wrote, in 1718, that George London's proposal 'would have spoil'd the Wood, but that his Lordship's superlative genius prevented it'.[30] Wray Wood was retained and furnished with labyrinthine paths and waterworks to make what Switzer judged an 'incomparable Wood the highest pitch that Natural and Polite Gardening can possibly ever arrive to'. Hussey suggests that since Switzer was an expert in waterworks it may in fact have been he, rather than Lord Carlisle, who had the 'superlative' notion of conserving Wray Wood. If so, it was an elegant way of clothing a boast in flattery of a patron.

8.7 Cirencester Park, Gloucestershire, is the best example of the forest style of estate layout

Henderskelf Lane is the path which skirts the southern flank of Wray Wood and joins Castle Howard to the Temple of the Four Winds. This ancient track, according to the logic of the baroque, should have been straightened or eliminated. Instead, it was made into a serpentine walk commanding a prospect of the neoclassical landscape which Lord Carlisle formed. Henderskelf Lane has a family resemblance with the serpentine grass terrace at nearby Duncombe. Its owner had married a Howard girl and planned to extend the terrace for three miles along the hillside to join a third serpentine walk, made at Rievaulx in the 1740s – a Romantic conception indeed.

Some of the other well-known steps in the evolution of landscape gardens are as follows:

- Vanburgh's proposal for saving £1,000 by keeping Old Woodstock Manor in Blenheim Park, Oxfordshire, as a picturesque feature in the view

8.8 Castle Howard, Yorkshire, represents a classical landscape, with a temple, a mausoleum, statuary, an obelisk, a Roman bridge, 'city' walls, a pyramid and even a long straight Roman road with triumphal arches

8.9 Henderskelf Lane at Castle Howard (above) and the Terrace at Duncombe (both in Yorkshire) are classic examples of the serpentine line

- The acceptance of site irregularities at Bramham Park, Yorkshire, to create a garden axis independent of the house axis
- Formation of the irregular grove at Melbourne, Derbyshire, which Hussey describes as 'the classic example in England of the first movement away from an entirely regular conception of garden-design which eventually led to landscape'[31] (as at Bramham, the axis of the garden was not related to the house axis)
- Use of the accidental diagonal provided by an old lane at Stowe, Buckinghamshire, to form the 'Great Cross Lime Walk' (it crosses at 70° instead of the usual 90°)
- Extensive use of the ha-ha (sunk fence) at Stowe to bring the view of the countryside into the garden
- Charles Bridgeman's design for joining up a series of small ponds in Hyde Park, London to form the large lake which is known, eponymously, as 'The Serpentine'.

Each of these examples is a step from:

- Regularity to irregularity
- Rationalism to empiricism
- Neoclassicism to Romanticism
- Formal (in the Platonic sense) to informal (in the Romantic sense).

A remark by A. O. Lovejoy, read by Frank Clark to his class of 1969, inspired the above analysis and the present book:

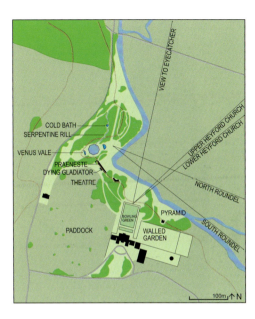

8.10 Rousham, Oxfordshire, has England's most beautiful example of a serpentine line

In one of its aspects that many-sided thing called Romanticism may not inaccurately be described as a conviction that the world is an *englischer Garten* on a grand scale. The God of the seventeenth century, like its gardeners, always geometrized; the God of Romanticism was one in whose universe things grew wild and without trimming and in all the diversity of their natural shapes.[32]

Some of the best eighteenth-century English gardens were made under the auspices of both Gods. Duncombe Park, Yorkshire (1713–1750), Studley Royal, Yorkshire (1715–1730), Rousham, Oxfordshire (1726–1739), Stourhead, Wiltshire (1726–1739), and Middleton Place, South Carolina, USA (1741) are brilliant examples of the way in which a classically-ordered concept, rich in allegory, can develop from an imaginative response to the genius of a place. The Latin phrase *genius loci* meaning 'the guardian spirit of a place' derives from the notion that places are inhabited by gods with the outward appearance of humans. English designers used it to mean 'the essential character of a place', but were pleased to erect statues of Greek and Roman gods in their groves of Romantic classicism.

1750–1783

These dates cover the independent career of Lancelot 'Capability' Brown. His career having reached a peak the 1770s, he died the most celebrated garden designer of the century. Then the criticism began. His reputation was besmirched by 1793 and remained so until reassessed by Marie-Luise Gothein after 1913. Brown was then restored, like a pagan statue, to an honoured place in the sacred grove of garden heroes.

8.11 (top and above) Stourhead in Wiltshire and Studley Royal in Yorkshire have an air of classical perfection

8.12 (right) Middleton Place, South Carolina, belongs to the same group as Rousham and Studley Royal

In 1751 Brown had been head gardener at Stowe for ten years and had seen great works under the overall direction of William Kent. It is thought that Brown and Kent were jointly responsible for the Grecian Vale, one of the last projects at Stowe. It had classical overtones but was executed with more feeling for the composition of land-form and woods than is shown in Kent's drawings for other projects. Serpentine lines became Brown's trademark after he left Stowe. He was not averse to the occasional temple when it improved the composition, but there is no reason to think he had any taste for allegory, symbolism or the landscapes of antiquity. One could describe his style as nature-like, or nature-esque.

During the 32 years of his career as an independent designer Brown's style hardly changed. The characteristic features of his work are circular clumps of trees, a grassy meadow in front of the house, a serpentine lake, an enclosing belt of trees and an encircling carriage drive. Hussey remarks that Brown was 'a practical man in the grip of a theory'.[33] The diagram (8.42) shows the theory. Brown's interest in serpentine shapes was quickly recognised, and comparisons were drawn between Hogarth's line of beauty, the outline of a woman's body and a Brownian park. *The World* recorded in 1753 that 'a young lady of the most graceful figure I ever beheld' came to London:

'To have her shape altered to the modern fashion'. That is to say, to have her breasts compressed by a flat straight line. I protest, when I saw the beautiful figure that was to be so deformed by the stay maker, I was as much shocked, as if I had been told that she was come to deliver up those animated knowls

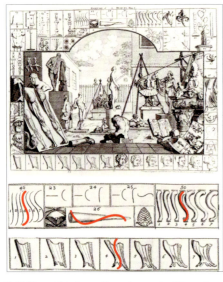

8.14 Hogarth's line of beauty, marked by red lines (from Analysis of beauty, 1753)

8.15 The Leasowes, near Halesowen, West Midlands: Shenstone's ornamental farm, now a golf course, had fields, ponds, a grotto and seats with poetic inscriptions. The seat was part of a restoration scheme and the poem incorporated by the photographer

of beauty to the surgeon – I borrow my terms from gardening, which now indeed furnishes the most pregnant and exalted expressions of any science in being. And this brings to mind the only instance that can give an adequate idea of my concern. Let us suppose that Mr Brown should, in any one of the many Elysiums he has made, see the old terraces rise again and mask his undulating knowls, or straight rows of trees obscure his noblest configurations of scenery.[34]

The comparison between serpentine lines and women's stays comes from Hogarth's *Analysis of beauty*, first published in 1753. Hogarth observed 'an elegant degree of plumpness to the skin of the softer sex', and drew diagrams to show how closely an ideal stay resembles the line of beauty. The beautiful Lady Luxborough, banished by her boorish husband to his Warwickshire estate near the celebrated *ferme ornée*, The Leasowes, borrowed a copy of the book. In her correspondence with the owner of The Leasowes, the poet and gardener William Shenstone, she envied the shape of the letter with which Shenstone's name began, regretting that 'I have not now an S in my name to claim any share in it'.

Dorothy Stroud attributes 211 designs for English parks to Brown. A surprisingly large number of his landscapes remain in good condition, often because they have been adapted to modern use as public parks, farms, golf courses and schools. The best of them are magnificent, probably more so today than when they were seen by Brown's critics in the 1790s. My favourites are the Arcadian glade at Prior Park, Somerset, the Grecian Vale at Stowe, the lakes at Luton Hoo and Blenheim Park, the embankment outside Alnwick Castle, Northumberland, the riverside scenery at Chatsworth, Derbyshire, and the grand views at Petworth, Sussex and Harewood, Yorkshire, which J. M. W. Turner loved to paint.

Some of Brown's other designs are so 'natural' and so 'English' that it is difficult to appreciate them without a survey of the pre-existing site and a plan of the executed works. His lakes sit in comfortable depressions, his woods clothe hills which would resist the plough and his green pastures roll to the rhythm of the English countryside. A large collection of Brown's professional papers, which might have provided more information on what he actually did, was given to Repton by Brown's son and subsequently disappeared.

A variant of the serpentine style, known as the *ferme ornée*, is of particular interest to historians of rural retirement. Maren-Sofie Røstvig comments that 'Instead of penning yet another version of Horace's second epode, Southcote translated the literary ideal into a living reality'[35] at Woburn Farm (*c.* 1735). It was a working farm ornamented with trees, shrubs and temples. 'Ideal farm' would be a good description. In 1746 Shenstone called The Leasowes a *ferme ornée*, but he did not include the term in his 1764 classification of garden types. This may be because he had read Burke's argument that beauty does not arise from utility. Burke observed that the wedge-like snout of a pig and the bared teeth of a wolf are useful but not beautiful.

Horace Walpole's essay *On Modern Gardening* (1780) was short, witty, brilliant – and relentlessly partisan. Hunt writes that: 'Walpole's achievement has to be saluted all the more when it is realized that single-handedly he determined (or distorted) the writing of landscape architecture history to this day'.[36] The distortion of most concern is revealed by this famous passage:

But the capital stroke, the leading step to all that has followed, was (I believe the first thought was Bridgeman's) the destruction of walls for boundaries, and the invention of fosses – an attempt then deemed so astonishing, that the common people called them Ha! Ha's! to express their surprise at finding a sudden and unperceived check to their walk . . . At that moment appeared Kent, painter enough to taste the charms of landscape, bold and opinionative enough to dare and to dictate, and born with a genius to strike out a great system from the twilight of imperfect essays. He leaped the fence, and saw that all nature was a garden . . . Kent, like other reformers, knew not how to

8.16 Brown's serpentine mounding made the old fortress at Alnwick, Northumberland, an ornament in the landscape

8.17 Petworth, Sussex, has a beautiful serpentine hill with a feminine curve

8.18 William Hearne's engravings, from Payne Knight's *The Landscape*, contrast the smoothness of the serpentine style with the irregularity of the Picturesque style

stop at the just limits. He had followed nature, and imitated her so happily, that he began to think all her works were equally proper for imitation.[37]

In this paragraph, Walpole distorts historical fact for the convenience of his argument, as follows:

- Baroque gardens were not contained within boundaries. They used the surrounding landscape
- The English did not invent 'Ha! Ha's!' Sunk retaining walls were used to allow outward views from baroque gardens
- Kent did not originate the 'system' of imitating nature.

Walpole commented on Kent's successor: 'It was fortunate for the country and Mr Kent, that he was succeeded by a very able master; and did living artists come within my plan, I should be glad to do justice to Mr Brown; but he may be a gainer, by being reserved for some abler pen.' The touch of sarcasm in that 'may' is telling: always attuned to the tides of taste, Walpole probably realised that Brown's work was not 'natural' in what was becoming the 'modern' sense.

1783–1813

It should be no surprise that the next step on the road to Romanticism was taken by a vicar. Theologians, also influenced by empiricism, increasingly saw 'the wonder of creation' as being the visible world, rather than the abstract realm of the Platonic Forms. William Gilpin (1724–1804) was described as 'Master of the Picturesque and Vicar of Boldre'.[38] His essay *On Prints* (1768) and his great series of Picturesque *Tours*, published between 1782 and 1809, awakened British tourists to the natural delights of the River Wye, North Wales and 'the Mountains and Lakes of Cumberland and Westmoreland'. He then wrote three *Essays* on the heartland of eighteenth-century garden theory: landscape painting and the appreciation of nature.[39] Gilpin reveals a passion for rough, shaggy scenery, commenting that although 'the picturesque traveller is seldom disappointed with pure nature, however rude' he is 'often offended with the productions of art' and 'frequently disgusted' by the timidity of modern gardens: 'How flat, and insipid is often the garden scene, how puerile, and absurd! The banks of the river how smooth, and parallel! The lawn, and its boundaries, how unlike nature!' For Brown's style, this was a death sentence.

Gilpin said that if a modern landscape painter were to attempt a garden scene he would need to consult Claude on how to:

Turn the lawn into a piece of broken ground: plant rugged oaks instead of flowering shrubs: break the edges of the walk: give it the rudeness of a road: mark it with wheel-tracks; and scatter around a few stones, and brushwood; in a word, instead of making the whole smooth, make it rough; and you make it also picturesque.[40]

Sir Uvedale Price applied Gilpin's idea to landscape design in *An essay on the Picturesque, as compared with the Sublime and the Beautiful; and, on the use of studying pictures, for the purpose of improving real landscape*. Price echoed Gilpin's opinion that 'whoever views objects with a painter's eye, looks with indifference, if not disgust, at the clumps, the belts, the made water, and the eternal smoothness and sameness of a finished place'. Price jested that Brown would consider the 'finest composition of Claude' to be 'rude and imperfect', with some 'capability' for improvement[41] – which, I suggest, was like saying he would remove the blood and nails to 'improve' a *Crucifixion*. Though Price did not argue for gardens to be wholly sublime, in Burke's sense of 'fitted . . . to excite the ideas of pain and danger',[42] his *Essay on the Picturesque* incited readers to make gardens picturesque in the sense of rough, varied, and intricate.

Price's friend and neighbour, Richard Payne Knight, possessed the incautious hauteur of an immensely wealthy man. Downton Castle, five miles west of Ludlow in Herefordshire, was designed with a classical interior and gothic exterior. Then: 'large fragments of stone were irregularly thrown amongst briers and weeds, to imitate the foreground of a picture'.[43] Repton believed this to be a temporary 'experiment' but John Claudius Loudon observed their presence a decade later, adding that the rocks were 'quite unconnected with each other'.[44] Downton Vale was rich in Gilpinesque, Christian, thorns. The young Loudon was an ardent admirer of Price, Knight and romantic irregularity. His first book told the world that:

> I believe that I am the first who has set out as a landscape gardener, professing to follow Mr Price's principles. How far I shall succeed in executing my plans, and introducing more of the picturesque into improved places, time alone must determine.[45]

Loudon arrived in England at the age of 20 and within a decade gave up the attempt to establish himself as a landscape gardener. From the surroundings of Edinburgh he remembered the naturally picturesque valley of the Water of Leith and an unnaturally hideous park designed by a pupil of Brown's. The brook running through the park had, Walter Scott later observed, been 'twisted into the links of a string of pork-sausages' (Scott was also a disciple of the Herefordshire squires).

Loudon's early work shows the influence of Price and Knight's plea for the Picturesque. The sketches and plans published in *Country Residences* (1806) contrast 'Mr Brown's style' with 'the modern style' as practiced by Mr Loudon (Figure 8.19). It is plain that 'the modern style' is more deserving of the description 'irregular' than any other style in garden history. Little survives of Loudon's built work from this period but in the grounds of Barnbarrow (now Barnbarroch) in Wigtownshire, Scotland, natural regeneration has created some of the effects which Loudon sought to attain by art.

The year 1813, chosen to end this period, is marked by two events discussed in the next chapter – Repton's conversion to the Mixed style, and Loudon's European tour, after which he followed Mr Price no further.

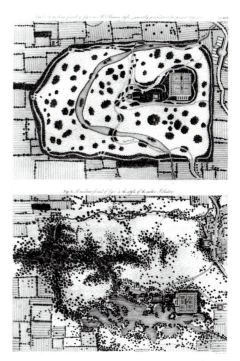

8.19 J. C. Loudon's diagrams of the serpentine and Picturesque styles, which he described as 'Mr Brown's style' and 'the style of the author, J. Loudon' respectively

8.20 Plan of Petworth

8.21 Classical landscape gardens: (from top) Castle Howard, Claremont and Studley Royal

England

It is as well to begin with a comment on the use of the word 'landscape' joined to 'gardens'. Timothy Nourse associated the two words in 1699. Addison was the first, in 1712, to speak of 'making' a landscape. Shenstone was the first, in 1754, to speak of a 'landscape gardener'. Lancelot Brown, now the most famous 'landscape gardener', in fact called himself a 'place-maker' (c. 1760); Humphry Repton was the first professional designer to call himself a 'landscape gardener' (c. 1794) but often used 'improver' as an alternative. The nineteenth century was the heyday of landscape gardening as a professional activity. In 1986, these considerations persuaded me to avoid the word 'landscape' in connection with styles of garden design.[46] 'Landscape garden' is used in this chapter as a general term for the set of styles which originated in the eighteenth century and 'landscape style' is used, in the next chapter, for a specific style which integrated the Augustan, serpentine and Picturesque phases of the landscape garden.

The first generation of English landscape gardens was inspired by a vision of the landscape of antiquity, shaped by landscape paintings and Grand Tours. Italian scenery dominated the vision because Greece, then part of the Ottoman Empire, was much less easy to visit. Naming the style 'Augustan' follows the use of this term for the Augustan Poets who, like Pope, wished to recreate the glory of Rome in the age of its first emperor, Augustus (27 BC–14 AD). Chiswick, Claremont, Rousham, Stowe, Castle Howard, Painshill and Stourhead are the most important Augustan landscapes. The leading designers were the garden owners themselves, with professional assistance from William Kent, Stephen Switzer and Charles Bridgeman. They are classical landscapes with statues, grottoes, temples and roofed bridges. The latter were often inspired by the work of Andrea Palladio (see Chapter 6).

The second generation of English landscape gardens, described as 'serpentine', showed less concern for the romance of antiquity and more for the naturally flowing geometry of landform, woods and lakes. It was as well suited to England's geography as Renaissance gardens had been to Tuscany and the High Baroque to Northern France. All the important examples – Blenheim, Petworth, Prior Park, the changes at Stowe and some 40 other estates – were designed by Lancelot 'Capability' Brown. Many of his lesser projects have become golf courses, which tells us something about their mock-Arcadian character. The principal features were a serpentine tree belt, circular clumps, a naturalised body of water and curvaceous lawns sweeping up to the windows of Palladian mansions.

The third generation of English landscape gardens is described as 'Picturesque' (with a capital 'P' to mark its use as a specialised aesthetic term for a type of scene midway between Burke's concepts of the Sublime and the Beautiful). In England, Picturesque gardens involved worship of Mother Nature, who was displayed in all her natural glory, unadorned by temples or other follies. It was a type of 'natural' scenery well suited to city-centre parks. In continental Europe the making of natural landscapes with romantically pagan temples became a badge of support for Enlightenment values.

8.22 The wavy lines of the lake at Stowe, Buckinghamshire, (above) and the woods at Prior Park, Somerset, (left) form a pleasing contrast with their Palladian bridges

8.23 The amphitheatre at Claremont, Surrey, was intentionally classical

8.24 Brown's lake, at Blenheim, Oxfordshire, has a flowing geometry

8.25 St James's Park, London, provides a romantic setting for the Horse Guards building

France

Louis XVI loved country pursuits and was sympathetic to the calls for reform from the *philosophes*. His journey to the scaffold in 1793 was a consequence of his failure to persuade the nobility and clergy to pay taxes or accept change. Louis' gloomy awkwardness affected his marriage to Marie Antoinette, fourteenth child of the Empress of Austria. 'Her tragedy was that she had to be a queen. Nature had made her a brave, charming, warm-hearted, and indiscreet girl, who only wanted to be happy and to make others happy'. But in France 'Her slightest indiscretion was magnified into a scandal, her mildest witticism into an insult.'[47] Between 1774 and 1784 Louis allowed her to create an expensive but delightful retreat: the landscape garden and *Hameau de Trianon* at Versailles. To the king, it was a fashionable gift, perhaps symbolic of the more natural approach to life, society and government he favoured. To the queen, it was a place to escape from the intrigues and formalities of palace life. To Parisian journalists, it was wanton royal profligacy, a place for the Queen to enjoy the pornographic adventures of which she was so often accused. To some historians, it was 'the first distinctly English landscape garden on the Continent'.[48]

8.26 A romantic area beside the Petit Trianon

The new garden at Versailles was made beside an older garden and building, the *Petit Trianon*. Marie Antoinette chose the English fashion for her garden, which was made in two stages. First, Madame de Pompadour's baroque garden was complemented with an informal layout of walks, streams and woods, embellished with a circular Temple of Love. Second, the informal layout was extended, between 1778 and 1782, and provided with a fashionable accessory: an ornamental hamlet (*hameau*). Antoine Richard, its designer, had travelled in England and visited both Stowe and Kew. The hamlet has a bucolic group of thatched buildings beside a small lake. There is a dairy, a fisherman's house, a mill and a house for the Queen.

> Here Marie Antoinette trifled away the last years of her glory with her ladies
> and cavaliers. No threatening voice of the coming revolution penetrated to
> that rippling lake, where they played blind-man's-buff on the banks; or to the
> beautiful round temple, whence the little god of love looked down on their
> happy games. The noble groups of trees that were set round the lake were
> calmly growing higher and higher; men who were used to this pretty little
> place shuddered to think of the long broad avenues at Versailles, where one
> was lost and felt so small. Versailles slept the sleep of the giant, slept through
> every danger that threatened, until the day of its awakening came.[49]

Marie Antoinette's garden is a convenient symbol of the days before 14 July 1789 but the French royal family, like Britain's, had lost its leading role in the art of garden design. The author of a careful study, *The Picturesque Garden in France* wrote that: 'The first irregular French garden has yet to be identified. One of the earliest, however, is Ermenonville',[50] not the *Hameau* at Versailles. Ermenonville's owner and designer was the Marquis de Girardin, who had been a French officer during the Seven Years

8.27 Romantic additions were made to Versailles, for Marie Antoinette and others

War. Like many French intellectuals, he hastened to visit England after the Treaty of Paris ended hostilities in 1763. Girardin found much to admire, and was particularly struck by William Shenstone's *ferme ornée* at The Leasowes. Girardin's writings on garden design were published in English in 1777 as the *Essay on Landscape or, on the means of improving and embellishing the country round our habitations*. He wrote:

> This change of things then, from a forced arrangement to one that is easy and natural will bring us back to a true taste for beautiful nature, tend to the increase of agriculture, the propagation of cattle, and, above all, to more humane and salutary regulations of the country, by providing for the subsistence of those, whose labour supports the men of more thinking employments who are to instruct, or defend society.[51]

A distinctive feature of Ermenonville was the owner's determination to combine 'use with beauty': Girardin was both a scenic and an agricultural improver. His *hameau* was a working model farm, not a model of a working farm. Another much-admired *hameau*, preceding Marie Antoinette's, was made at nearby Chantilly.

Ermenonville drew upon ideas propagated by the Enlightenment philosophers who paved the road to the French Revolution: Montesquieu (1689–1755), Voltaire (1694–1778) and Rousseau (1712–1778). Montesquieu and Voltaire favoured constitutional monarchy on the English model. They saw, admired and praised English gardens. Rousseau believed all men should be free, equal and virtuous. His famous words, in *Du contrat social*, proclaim: 'Man was born free, and everywhere he is in chains'. In *Emile*, a man explained that he had to write because he had to live; the aristocrat replied, 'I fail to see why'. In Rousseau's *Nouvelle Héloïse* (1761) Julie took her lover into a wilderness with no trace of artificiality. Unlike Marie Antoinette, Rousseau married for love, choosing an illiterate chambermaid. His call for natural rights was heard throughout Europe: men, children and gardens should be allowed to express their inner natures – with the 'nature' in question being discovered through empirical observation. In 1778, Rousseau was buried on an island at Ermenonville which became a place of pilgrimage to be copied elsewhere.

Though influenced by the same coalition of ideas as Britain, the weighting of its constituents and the resultant design style differed in France and in those parts of Europe which saw England through a French glass. The Augustan phase of the landscape garden and its supposed Chinese origin were the dominant influences, William Kent and William Chambers the leading innovators. Stowe and Kew were the most admired gardens. The serpentine phase of the landscape garden, as pursued by Brown, received little attention in France. French landscape gardens were characterised by a profusion of small buildings and the avoidance of straight lines. But 1763–1789 was too short a period for the style to reach maturity. The Parc Monceau in Paris, a prime example, is rich in small buildings but weakly composed; buildings, landform, woods, water and paths are spotted about. French gardens decayed during

8.28 An imitation of Rousseau's burial island, at Wörlitz, near Dessau

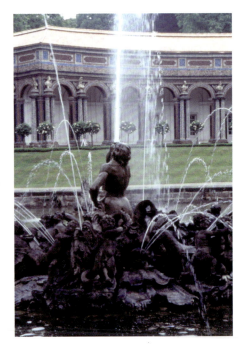

8.29 The rococo fountain at the Ermitage, which belonged to Frederick the Great's sister, Louisa Ulrika

8.30 Ilm Park, Weimar, designed by Johann W. Goethe, influenced German romanticism

the revolutionary period (1789–1815). When the old families recovered their property, they had neither the wealth nor the inclination to repair the ancestral symbols of aristocratic privilege. Instead, they turned to a Mixed style of informal plantings and buildings (see Chapter 9).

Germany

A love of forests and nature had run deep in German culture since pre-Christian times. Under the influence of the Romantic Movement, it burgeoned. Poets wrote of it, philosophers theorised about it, and princes used landscape gardens to demonstrate the enlightened nature of their despotism. In the eighteenth century, Germany came under the domination of Prussia's Hohenzollern kings: Frederick-William I (1688–1740) and his son, Frederick II (1712–1786), called Frederick The Great. Frederick-William I, an impressively efficient ruler, left Prussia with a brimming treasury, a highly trained army and a son reared in a blisteringly un-Enlightened manner. In 1730, aged only 18, the boy was accused of 'deserting' his militaristic home, court-martialled, imprisoned in a dank cell and made to watch his best friend being executed as a 'co-conspirator'. The experience contributed to Frederick II becoming the first of Europe's enlightened despots. Unfortunately, he also wished to shine in battle. To learn about war, Frederick read history. To learn about the Enlightenment, he turned to Voltaire. To learn about culture and the arts, he turned to the *ancien régime* that Voltaire despised. Frederick spoke French better than German and loved the literature, painting, music, architecture and gardens of France.

Frederick-William I, also a Francophile, had employed a pupil of Le Nôtre to design the first baroque palace garden in Prussia, the Charlottenburg. Frederick II associated the site with brutality, and decided to make a new house and garden in the relaxed lakeside suburb of Potsdam. His project was influenced by French rococo ideas and its name, Sanssouci ('without care'), reveals both the design aim and its inspiration. As a poet, a philosopher and a gardener, Frederick wanted his home to evoke that of a Roman poet, not a Caesar. He told Ligne that 'I used Vergil's *Georgics* as a gardener's Guide'.[52] Sanssouci, planned as a rural retreat, was never the hub of a groaningly sybaritic court.

There were other departures from baroque practice: first, the house was set to one side of the prime axis, instead of being a focus for radial avenues. Second, Frederick placed a wine-hill-terrace in front of the palace windows, instead of an embroidered parterre. It was a most unusual feature, functional, curved and glazed with French windows. Third, the Tea Pavilion was rococo. Fourth, the owner's enlightened submission to the rule of law was demonstrated by allowing a miller to bring a suit against him to prevent the removal of his mill. It survives (Figure 8.1). Frederick's garden is unique but something can be done to set its design in a context.

Frederick did not see the famous gardens of Italy or France, because his foreign 'travels' were always at the head of an army. The gardens he knew belonged to German courts. Of these, the Ermitage, made by his favourite sister, is likely to have been the most influential. As its name suggests, it was a retreat, and it had features in common with Sanssouci: it is rococo; it is on a hilltop; it has axes at right-angles to one another; it has a gay spirit; it contains a collection of classical structures. Another sister added Chinese buildings to Drottningholm (see p. 213). For Sanssouci, Frederick commissioned features in classical and romantic styles: busts of Roman Emperors (1744), an Egyptian obelisk (1747), a Neptune Grotto (1751), a Chinese Tea Pavilion (1754), and, most appropriately, a Mount of Ruins. During the Seven Years War (1756–1763), Prussian estate owners became as interested in English gardens, as they were in the English gold that supplied Prussia's war chest. *La Nouvelle Héloïse* fanned the flames of enthusiasm for Dame Nature.

Sanssouci and Stourhead were both made between 1745 and 1785, and the ideas that led to their creation are not so far apart as one might suppose. The owners of both were attracted by landscape painting, rural retirement, chinoiserie, classicism, rationalism and empiricism. Bankers like Hoare, the creator of Stourhead, favoured constitutional democracy. Enlightened despots like Frederick, considered democracy unworkable. Both agreed that 'art should imitate nature'. We thus have a list of similarities. The differences were that Frederick looked to modern France rather than Ancient Rome to learn about 'nature', and that he preferred the landscape paintings of Watteau to those of Claude or Poussin. In art-historical terms, the rococo garden at Sanssouci and the landscape garden at Stourhead are both departures from the baroque style which, in the 1770s, was 'dying in the climate of rationalism'.[53] Had the landscape garden not been devised, Sanssouci might have been the seminal garden design of the period.

The first Romantic landscape garden in Germany was made at Wörlitz by Prince Franz von Anhalt-Dessau, between 1765 and 1817. Though surrounded by Prussia, the Prince retained his independence. He liked the English gardens which were admired in France, belonging to the Augustan phase of the landscape garden: Claremont, Stourhead and Stowe. But Wörlitz was low-lying and flood-prone, unlike the English sites. This was turned to great advantage: nature's flood was allowed to enter the garden. Water dominates the design and visitors have to choose between a long walk and a series of short boat trips. The buildings that punctuate the garden are in classical and Romantic styles, with the choice of classical structures influenced by Winckelmann. Taking a Platonic view, Winckelmann found in Greek art a 'noble simplicity and supreme calm'.[54] Wörlitz has a Palladian villa, an Elysium and a Temple of Venus. The romantic features include a Gothic House, a Swiss Bridge and a symbolic Isle of Poplars to commemorate Rousseau's tomb at Ermenonville. The Georgium, with Wörlitz part of Prince Franz's 'garden kingdom', is a landscape park with artificial ruins and a classical temple.

Use of classical and romantic elements became characteristic of German gardens. A Danish Professor of Philosophy and Aesthetics at Kiel University, Christian Hirschfeld, published a *Theory of Garden Design* in 1779, recommending 'both the English landscape garden that was popular at the time and the French baroque garden,

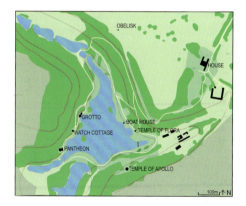

8.31 Plan of Stourhead

8.32 A Roman ruin made at the Georgium

8.33 The landscape park at Wörlitz, near Dessau, is dominated by water

8.34 Goethe's work at the Ilm Park, Weimar, did much to popularise romantic gardens in Germany

in order to create a specifically German garden'.[55] In England, baroque gardens were destroyed. In Germany, baroque gardens were modernised by ringing them with landscape parks. There were many happy marriages, with good examples at Schwetzingen, Nymphenburg and Herrenhausen. The designers of completely new gardens turned to Hirschfeld for advice on landscape gardens. He recommended use of the 'strict English line' of Capability Brown, meaning the serpentine line, hitherto unused in Germany. Though Hirschfeld advised self-restraint with regard to the use of small buildings, they were prominent in his illustrations.

Hirschfeld's *Theory of Garden Design* and the Wörlitz landscape garden attracted the attention of Germany's leading poet and writer. Johann Wolfgang von Goethe (1749–1832) balanced the romantic and classical in his thoughts, always seeking both the unity and the individuality of nature. In 1777, the Duke of Saxe-Weimar asked for help with the layout of the Ilm Park in Weimar, beside which Goethe lived. In the spirit of Hirschfeld, it is a Brownian composition of woodland and grassland with a minimum of classical allusion. Order restrains chaos. The River Ilm provides a serpentine water feature and there is no trace of the rococo. Goethe's endorsement of the new approach was highly influential.

Prince Pückler-Muskau (1785–1871) inherited a large estate at Muskau and purchased additional land, in what is now Poland, to create a vast landscape garden (6sq km, containing 27 km of paths). The topography has a rolling character and the style is serpentine. The design was highly regarded by the American historian, Norman T. Newton:

8.35 Muskau had one of Europe's largest landscape parks

The whole scheme was tied together with a flowing system of roads, paths, and bridges that provided routes of great variety and ingenuity as described by Pückler in 'the three carriage drives' on which he conducts the reader in his book. The crowning glory of the park, however, is the firm integrity of its magnificent pastoral spaces. Here Pückler seems to have revealed most clearly the innate understanding of spatial structure – the awareness of spaces as components of design – sought in vain among the usual English landscape gardening works.[56]

Pückler-Muskau had toured English gardens and regarded himself as more a follower of Repton than Brown. In my view, Pückler-Muskau's first project, Muskau, was more Brownian and his second, Branitz, more Reptonian. Neither project belongs to the Picturesque phase of the landscape garden. The natural landscape at Muskau was well suited to the creation of 'magnificent pastoral spaces'. At Branitz, because of the smaller and flatter site, it was easier for Pückler to create the Mixed style effects associated with Repton's later writings and nineteenth century projects (see Chapter 9). Branitz has a Pyramid Lake, a Serpentine Lake, a Blue Garden, a Smithy Garden, a Rose Mount, a Moon Mount and Island of Venus, an iron Kiosk and a series of waterways.

Pückler-Muskau was an owner-designer and author. The leading professional designers of German landscape gardens were Peter Josef Lenné (1789–1866), who designed the Potsdam landscape, and Friedrich Ludwig von Sckell (1768–1834), who surrounded Schwetzingen with a landscape garden and made the famous Englischer Garten in Munich.

8.36 The German section of the Muskau estate

8.37 (left) The baroque garden at Nymphenburg was ringed with a romantic park

8.38 (right) The Englischer Garten in Munich was designed by von Sckell

Russia

Catherine the Great (1729–1796) introduced the landscape garden to Russia. She was Prussian by birth and had attracted the admiration of Frederick the Great, who, when Catherine was only 14, insisted on her attendance at a court dinner. Frederick supported her marriage to Peter III and concluded a vital alliance with her after the Seven Years War. Like him, she preferred to speak French and, for artistic and intellectual guidance, always looked abroad. To Diderot, she sighed: 'All your work is done upon paper, which does not mind what you do to it: it is all of a piece, pliable, and presenting no obstacles either to your pen or to your imagination. But I, poor Empress, must work upon the human skin, which is terribly ticklish and irritable'.[57] Landscape design, which compares with drawing on 'the bark of a tree',[58] appealed to Catherine as a symbol of how an Enlightened Empress should conduct her affairs. Politically, she was an enlightened autocrat who questioned and then extended the practice of serfdom. Culturally, she had a liberal enthusiasm for the Enlightenment. Sexually, she favoured young men. Catherine commissioned landscape parks for herself, at Tsarskoe Seloe, and her son, at Pavlosk.

The landscape garden at Tsarskoe Seloe (*c*. 1770) is separated from an older, baroque garden (*c*. 1750) by a covered walk, known as the Cameron Gallery. From it, Catherine could view both gardens, symbols of old and new Russia. She employed a German-born, English-trained landscape designer (John Busch) for the new park. For the buildings she employed a Russian, Vasily Neyelov, whom she sent to visit England, and a Scotsman, Charles Cameron, who married Busch's daughter.

The setting of the Palladian Bridge was inspired by Stowe. There are excellent Chinese pavilions and a Chinese Village. Since it was made for an Empress, Tsarskoe Selo has an opulent grandeur uncommon in landscape parks. The Orlov Column in the lake commemorates Catherine's most dashing lover. The park was given the name Pushkin by the Soviets, in 1937, to mark the 100th anniversary of the death of

Russia's great Romantic poet, who also loved the park. The family of Russia's last Tsar, Nicholas II, lived in the Alexander Palace before being exiled and shot in 1917. Despite Catherine's modernising liberalism, Tsarskoe Selo eventually played the role of Russia's Versailles.

Pavlosk was designed by Charles Cameron for Grand Duke Pavel, whose German wife was the chief influence on the design. The Duke resented his mother's involvement but the Duchess adored the landscape garden. The Temple of Friendship, built to please her mother-in-law, was the first of some 60 garden buildings in an immense park (10 sq km). The River Slavyanka was dammed and bridged. Lakes were dug. The Apollo Colonnade was made into a real ruin by a great storm in 1817. There is a Temple of the Three Graces, a thatched dairy, a hermit's cell and a Mausoleum for the Emperor Pavel. Loudon visited Pavlosk in 1812 and judged it the best design of its type in Russia. He believed 'Brown furnished a design', which is unlikely. The profusion of small buildings in diverse styles suggests Cameron was most interested in the Augustan phase of the landscape garden.

Scandinavia

In Denmark, some baroque gardens, including Fredensborg and Glorup, were remodelled in the landscape style. In Norway, a landscape garden was made at Bogstad Manor outside Oslo *c.* 1780. In Sweden, a landscape garden was added to the royal estate at Drottningholm, where Frederick the Great's sister had built a Chinese pavilion after her country made peace with Prussia in 1763. Both siblings were energetic and ambitious. Louisa Ulrika was queen during the Period of Liberty (1718–1772). Her son, Gustavus III, reverted to despotism but, wanting to represent himself as enlightened, employed F. M. Piper to design landscape parks at Drottningholm and Haga. Gustavus was a theatre-loving aesthete. Haga was planned on a dramatic scale in dramatic scenery, drawing upon both the Augustan and serpentine phases of the landscape garden. It has a neoclassical Royal Pavilion, built after an Italian tour undertaken by Gustavus in 1782, a 'Roman battle tent', designed in 1790 by Jean-Louis Desprez, (1737–1804), a Chinese Pagoda, a Turkish Pavilion and a brightly coloured Ekotemplet used as a summer dining room. Gustavus III was assassinated by a nobleman who thought him too despotic. His son, who built Haga Slott in 1802, was deposed for the same fault. Mere symbols of enlightenment were no longer sufficient.

Southern Europe

The landscape style had some influence on Southern Europe. Irrigation and intensive care allowed the creation of gardens with a serpentine form but dry rocky hills were unsuited to the formation of vast serpentine parks. Usually, an English garden was an addition to a baroque park, as at Caserta in Italy and Aranjuez in Spain. Where larger projects were instigated, as at the Palácio da Pena in Portugal, they drew upon the Augustan and Picturesque phases of the landscape garden.

8.39 Haga Royal Park, Stockholm, is on an enormous scale

8.40 The Palácio da Pena in Portugal is surrounded by a Picturesque park

8.41 A romantic scene in the English Garden at Caserta, Naples

Styles and examples

Forest style

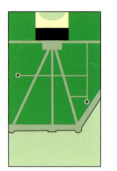

8.42
Forest
style

Use: The view of gardens as rural retreats grew in deliberate contrast to their High Baroque role. Owners shunned courtly life, with the proud aim of imitating Virgil's example by making places which are simultaneously useful and beautiful. Agriculture and forestry became important land uses. Avenues were made by planting new forests, not by cutting rides through existing forests. The name 'forest style' comes from Stephen Switzer. He also called it 'rural' and 'extensive' gardening.

Form: The radial geometry was carried over from the High Baroque. Boundaries were often low retaining walls with bastions at turning points giving views over the surrounding countryside. There was an interest in lines of view, sometimes emphasised by low hedges on the inside margins of avenues, meeting the estate boundary at bastion points.

Cirencester Park 1715

As it is 8 km long and 4.8 km wide, the leading example of the English forest style requires an informed eye and an enthusiasm for walking. Stephen Switzer may have advised on the design. Pope came here over a 30-year period and invested money in Lord Bathurst's forest enterprise. It has a baroque goosefoot of avenues, but the intention was to make a Sabine farm, not to impress visitors with the owner's wealth, power or fashionable taste. The best view of the park is from the top of Cirencester's church steeple, not from the great man's house.

8.43 Cirencester Park, Gloucestershire

Alexander Pope was closely connected for thirty years with Lord Bathurst's creation of Cirencester Park, or rather the series of conjoined parks that stretches from the town of Sapperton, five miles to the west. The outcome is the largest and most impressive example surviving of 'extensive or forest gardening' – as Stephen Switzer in 1714 termed the earliest kind of landscape gardening . . . The creation of the great park at the geographical and historical focus of the Cotswold uplands, on what had previously been predominantly open sheepwalks, was an undertaking as visionary as sustained.[59]

Augustan style

Use: Owners looked back, before the baroque, before the Renaissance, before the Middle Ages, to the Roman roots of western culture. They wanted gardens which recalled the classical landscape of antiquity, suitable for use as places to reflect on literature, history, natural science and the affairs of the day. Discussions with friends might take place while strolling through the grounds or taking tea on a well-placed garden seat. Classical ornament and allusion contributed to the theme. For landowners who had been on a Grand Tour, an Augustan garden became a symbol of their travels and a place to display souveniers, including urns, statues and quotations from Roman poets.

Form: The first 'landscape gardens' in England drew upon visions of Rome's landscape in the time of the Emperor Augustus. There were classical groves with woods, water, grass and small temples as in Graeco-Roman groves (sanctuaries). William Kent was the first professional designer to give physical form to this vision. The diagram shows part of the garden as a carry-over from the baroque and part as an early exercise in the re-creation of a classical Italian landscape. Between 1720 and 1745 the placing of temples and statues was more important than the plan geometry.

8.44
Augustan
style

Chiswick 1725

'Chiswick is a prime example of Palladio made to speak good English – the architectural equivalent to what Pope was doing for Homer in the 1720s.'[60] Indeed, the garden at Chiswick was sufficiently changed by 'landscape' ideas for Pope to see it as the first garden in which 'the genius of the place' had been duly consulted. Lord Burlington, the owner and chief designer, was assisted by Charles Bridgeman and William Kent. They aimed to make an Augustan villa, but with the architecture modelled on Palladio's Villa Rotunda of 1550. Buildings and obelisks were placed at the termination of avenues, in the baroque manner. Classical busts, sphinxes, columns and an exedra

8.45 Lord Burlington's villa at Chiswick, West London, in 1736 and in 2003

evoked the landscape of antiquity. William Kent helped with the classical allusions, designed a rustic cascade and gave the canal a mildly serpentine shape. The area between the canal and the house, occupied by a maze in 1730, was the first to be treated as a classical landscape. Since Kent's style became influential, we are fortunate that it survives.

The garden was in a poor state when Frank Clark (quoted below) wrote about its condition. It is being restored, but this is a difficult task because there were five important stages in the garden's evolution:

- A 1707 drawing by Knyff showed a simple Renaissance garden with grass plats and knots. This has gone, except for the path on the north front of the house
- By 1730 Lord Burlington had made a 'Roman' garden, which drew something from the baroque and something from Robert Castell's *Villas of the Ancients*.[61] It had avenues, geometrical pools, an amphitheatre, a maze and several small pavilions
- By 1733 William Kent was recognised as having introduced a 'natural taste in gardening', probably in the area between the house and the canal. A maze was removed and the area treated in a manner which became famous as 'the English style'
- By 1753, the year of Lord Burlington's death, the exedra was planted, an orangery built and more of the land fronting the canal 'naturalised' by removing the basins of water
- By 1858 several Dukes of Devonshire had made further changes to the estate. These included demolition of the old house and some of Burlington's temples. A conservatory and an 'Italian' garden were added.

The gardens of Chiswick Park are now a public park. They are, or they should be, a public monument. Here lies buried under bamboo, rhododendron and worn turf, the first of the experimental irregular gardens. The grounds are rich in association and historical memories.[62]

Stowe 1730

Stowe has many beautifully composed classical scenes. It lacks cohesion but the design history is fascinating:

- In the 1690s Stowe had a modest, Early Baroque parterre garden, owing more to Italy than France
- After 1710 Charles Bridgeman, as garden designer, and John Vanburgh, as architect, designed a baroque park, inspired by the work of inspired by the famous garden designers, London and Wise

- In the 1730s William Kent and James Gibbs were appointed to work with Bridgeman. Stowe began to evolve into a series of classical scenes to be appreciated from a perambulation rather than from a central point
- Brown made a Grecian Vale.

Kent's Temple of Ancient Virtue (1734) looks across the Elysian Fields to a Shrine of British Worthies. A Palladian Bridge was made in 1744. Lancelot 'Capability' Brown was appointed head gardener in 1741. He worked with Kent until the latter's death in 1748 and his own departure in 1751. Bridgeman's Octagonal Pond and 11-acre Lake were given a 'natural' shape and Brown contributed the Grecian Vale.

> Stowe appears to have been the first extensive residence in which the modern style was adopted . . . Kent was employed . . . in the double capacity of architect and landscape-gardener; and the finest buildings and scenes there are his creation. The character of Stowe is well known: nature has done little; but art has created a number of magnificent buildings by which it has been attempted to give a sort of emblematic character to scenes of little or no natural expression. The result is unique; but more, as expressed by Pope, 'a work to wonder at', than one to charm the imagination.[63]

> Landscape design can be said to have originated at Stowe and Castle Howard . . . The outstanding monument of English landscape gardening is also its most complete 'living document': a visual epic of social and political as well as of aesthetic history. Soon after its inception Pope considered the new garden 'a place to wonder at' and by the mid-century its scenery was generally accepted as the finest physical expression of the age's aesthetic concept of Ideal Nature, This was the more influential owing to Stowe's being the chief seat of the Whig political establishment . . . Stowe's scenery remained almost as influential in shaping the continental conception of *le jardin anglais* as had been Versailles for that of the Grand Manner.[64]

Wörlitz Germany 1765

The first landscape park in Germany was inspired by Prince Franz Anhalt-Dessau's visits to Claremont, Stourhead and Stowe. It forms part of a collective project covering a 25 sq km area. There is a Temple of Flora, a Temple of Venus, A Gothic House, a Nymphaeum, a classical bridge and a Rousseau island. The estate can be divided into five sections:

- The Schloss Garten, modelled on Stourhead but intended as a private garden
- The Neumark Garten, with a canal, islands and a circular building modelled on a temple at Stowe

8.46 The landscape garden at Stowe, Buckinghamshire, in 1739 and 1980

8.47 Wörlitz, near Dessau

- The Gothic House, Temple of Venus and Temple of Flora
- The garden on the north–east shore of the lake
- The New Gardens, with mementoes of Italy.

Wörlitz has many interesting scenes, which can be enjoyed like a postcard collection.

It is beautiful without end here. Yesterday, as we walked by canals and groves it touched men how the Gods could allow the Prince to create such a dream around himself. Travelling through, it seems like a fairy-tale and has the character of Paradise.[65]

Serpentine style

8.48 Serpentine style

Use: A circumferential track allowed owners to enjoy what Hussey, quoting Burke, described as the 'sense of being swiftly drawn in an easy coach on a smooth turf, with gradual ascents and declivities'.[66] Parkland was used for grazing, allowing visitors to note that, although the owner was extremely rich, resources were used productively instead of being wasted on boastful display. In Continental Europe writers, including Goethe and Rousseau, admired the naturalness of the style. Its adoption became a badge of an estate-owner's adherence to Enlightenment values.

Form: The hallmarks of this style were a lawn sweeping to the house front, circular clumps, a serpentine lake, an encircling tree belt and a perimeter carriage drive. This combination is sometimes known as the 'English landscape garden' or 'Brownian' style. The adjective 'serpentine' draws attention to use of a free-flowing 'line of beauty'. Lancelot Brown's approach was significantly more abstract than the Augustan style, making less use of garden buildings and more use of serpentine lines in the design of lakes and woodlands.

Blenheim 1760

The palace, designed by Vanbrugh *c.* 1705, was the nation's reward to the first Duke of Marlborough for his victories against Louis XIV. Henry Wise, working with Vanbrugh, designed the garden in an Anglo-Dutch style with military overtones – mock fortifications and regimented parterres. The first Duke died in 1722. During the 1720s his wife, Sarah, canalised the River Glyme and spanned it with a triumphal bridge. In 1764, the 4th Duke commissioned Lancelot Brown, then at the apogee of his fame. Brown transformed the canal into a serpentine lake. He also naturalised the woods, designed a cascade and placed clumps of trees in strategic positions.

The ninth Duke commissioned Achille Duchêne in the 1930s to design a terrace and water parterre as transitional features between the palace and its landscape setting.

Blenheim, leaving its size and classic garb out of the question, is moulded to produce a varied and intricate impression on the eye, by masses of light and

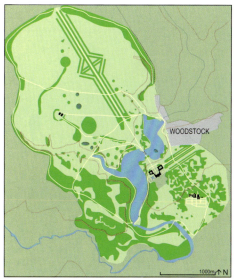

8.49 Blenheim, Oxfordshire

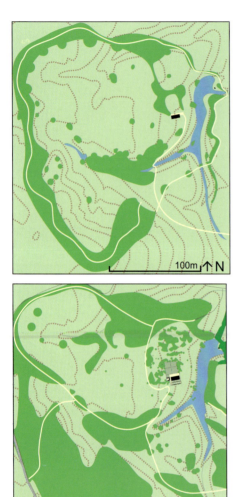

shade, and a dramatic outline built up like an apotheosis of Rubens, the modern 'dwelling' is given features that appeal to the common mind as being in themselves picturesque.[67]

Bowood 1761

Lancelot Brown's design for the park at Bowood, Wiltshire, was a clear example of his style, with circular clumps, an encircling tree belt and a serpentine lake. The plan of the park today shows that the principle of his design has survived. The lake discharges via a cascade designed by Charles Hamilton of Painshill and there is a small Doric temple beside the lake. In order to create a landscape transition, George Kennedy was asked to design an 'Italian garden' in 1851. It has terraces, balustrades, urns and steps. The north section of the park is now a golf course, which retains its structure but mars its texture.

[Brown's] bill for this work, £4,300, included such common trees and shrubs as ash and hawthorn – twelve thousand hawthorns cost him £50 – but his client had to pay extra for some exotic trees. Bowood Park has not been much altered since Brown worked on it, and is one of the best places now left to us where his style can be studied.[68]

Englischer Garten, Munich 1789

The oldest public park in Germany was promoted by Count Rumford, an American, and designed by Friedrich von Sckell. The central feature is the circular Monopteros Temple. It stands on a mound and overlooks a grass meadow with a lake. Von Sckell was the court gardener to Elector Carl Theodor. He designed a people's park for the

8.50 Bowood, Wiltshire, as designed by Brown (above) and in 2000 (below)

8.51 The Englischer Garten, Munich

purpose of exercise and recreation. It is one of Europe's largest city parks (5 km by 1.5 km) and a popular area for nude sunbathing, contributing to its Arcadian ambience in summer.

> [Von Sckell] walked through the terrain in person indicating where the pathway should go, in order to be sure that walkers would be able to see ... 'the city of Munich in the foreground and the age-old Hirschanger wood in the background along with the other beauties of nature'. Crown and countryside, the spheres of courtly and rural society, were to be linked by means of curving paths of this kind.[69]

Picturesque style

Use: Picturesque estates were designed to stimulate the mind with scenery composed according to the principles of landscape painting. They were not intended for domestic pleasure, social gatherings or hunting. The Picturesque was primarily an aesthetic conception. Clients, one must suppose, can have found few other uses for parks and gardens designed in this manner, but their maintenance budgets would have been gratifyingly low.

Form: Enthusiasm for the Picturesque resulted in the most irregular plans in garden history. As advocated by Gilpin, Price and Knight, and as illustrated by the drawings in Loudon's *Country Residences*, they were jagged in every detail, except for the kitchen ground. The style is best viewed in elevation.

8.52
Picturesque style

Hawkstone 1790

The design history of Hawkstone awaits further investigation but it appears to have been conceived under the torrent of Picturesque enthusiasm unleashed by Gilpin in the late eighteenth century. The park was made by Sir Roland Hill and his son in dramatic countryside with hills, woods and rocks. *Rhododendron ponticum*, introduced to Britain *c.* 1770, has overrun the site.

> In the eighteenth and nineteenth centuries it was ranked as one of the principal attractions of England ... When Dr Samuel Johnson visited Hawkstone in 1774 he wrote 'By the extent of its prospects, the awfulness of its shades, the horrors of its precipices, the verdure of its hollows, and the loftiness of its rocks, the ideas which it forces upon the mind are the sublime, the dreadful and the vast'[70]

View of Barnbarrow from the East, as it appeared in 1805.

View of Barnbarrow from the East, as it will appear when the alterations at present executing have been three years completed.

8.53 Barnbarrow, Wigtownshire

8.54 (right) Hawkstone, Shropshire

Barnbarrow 1806

Loudon published designs for converting the house and estate to the Picturesque style. They were not fully implemented but the house and garden have fallen into a ruinous condition and one could scarcely hope to find a better example of the character which Loudon intended. The estate is not open to the public.

Rocks may be shewn by removing earth, and forming breaks and abruptnesses in the surface. This may be done in several ways; but those are to be preferred which shew a perpendicular surface, or upright front of rock . . . Many examples of this kind occur in the different parts of Barnbarrow.[71]

Notes

1 Turner, T., *English Garden Design: History and styles since 1650*, Woodbridge: Antique Collectors Club, 1986.

2 Hobbes, T., *Leviathan, or the Matter, Forme, & Power of a Common-wealth, ecclesiasticall and civill*, London: Andrew Crooke, 1651, Part I, Ch. 13.

3 Bazin, G., *Baroque and Rococo*, London: Thames & Hudson, 1964, p. 262

4 Gombrich, E. H., *The Story of Art*, London: Phaidon, 1995, p. 460.

5 Pevsner, N., *An Outline of European Architecture*, London: Pelican, 1963, p. 350.

6 Jansen, H. W., *A History of Art*, London: Thames & Hudson, 1962, p. 453.

7 Ackerman, J. S., *Palladio*, London: Penguin, 1966, p. 78.

8 Röthlisberger, M., *Claude Lorrain*, New York: Hacker Art Books, 1979, p. 3,

9 ——, op. cit., 1979, p. 23.

10 Hall, J., *A History of Ideas and Images in Italian Art*, London: John Murray, 1983, p. 265.

11 Price, Sir U., *An Essay on the Picturesque, as compared with the Sublime and the Beautiful; and on the use of studying pictures, for the purpose of improving real landscape*, London, 1794, p. 109.

12 Clark, K., *Landscape into Art*, London: Penguin, 1956, p. 67.

13 Aristotle, *Poetics*, transl. Twining, T., 1789.

14 Cicero, *On Old Age*, trans. E. S. Shuckburgh, New York: Collier & Son, 1909, Para 2.

15 Plotinus, *The Enneads*, transl, MacKenna, S. and Page, B. S., Sixth Tractate, 'On Beauty'.

16 Du Fresnoy, C. A., *The Art of Painting, translated by Mr Dryden*, p. XVI, 1695.

17 d'Arganville, D., *La Théorie et la Practique du Jardinage*, 1713. Quoted in Toman, R., *European Garden Design*, Kömann, 2000, p. 228.

18 Salmon, W., *Polygraphice*, London, 1672.

19 Temple, W., 'Upon the gardens of Epicurus', in *Works*, London, 1814, Vol. III.

20 Pope, A., *An Essay on Criticism*, 1711.

21 Walpole, H., 'On Modern Gardening', in *Anecdotes of Painting in England*, 1780, Vol. 4.

22 Barrell, J., *The Political Theory of Painting from Reynolds to Hazlitt*, New Haven and London: Yale University Press, 1986.

23 Quoted in Willey, B., *The Eighteenth-century Background: Studies on the Idea of Nature in the thought of the period*, Penguin, 1962, p. 26.

24 Downing, A. J., *Treatise on the Theory and Practice of Landscape Gardening adapted to North America with a View to the Improvement of Country Residences*, New York: Moore & Co., 1859, Section II, p. 51.

25 Temple, W., op. cit., Vol. III.

26 Pevsner, N., *Studies in Art, Architecture and Design*, London: Thames & Hudson, 1969, Vol. 1, p. 82.

27 Hussey, C., *English Gardens and Landscapes 1700–1750*, London: Country Life, 1967, p. 123.

28 Switzer, S., *Iconographic Rustica*, London, 1718, Vol 1, p. xv.

29 Hussey, C., op. cit., p. 123.

30 Switzer, S., *Iconographia Rustica*, London, 1718, Vol. 1, p. 124.

31 Hussey, C., op. cit., p. 61.

32 Lovejoy, A. O., *The Great Chain of Being*, Harper Torchbook, 1960, p. 16.

33 Hussey, C., *The Picturesque*, London: Frank Cass, 1927, p. 137.

34 *The World* 13 December 1753, no. 50.

35 Røstvig, S. M., *The Happy Man. Studies in the metamorphoses of a classical ideal*, Oslo: Norwegian Universities Press, 1962, Vol. 2., p. 42.

36 Hunt, J. D., *Greater Perfection: The practice of garden theory*, London: Thames & Hudson, 2000, p. 208.

37 Walpole, H., op. cit.

38 Templeman, W. D., *The Life and Work of William Gilpin (1724–1804), Master of the Picturesque and Vicar of Boldre*, Urbana: The University of Illinois Press, 1939.

39 They were entitled *Three Essays on Picturesque Beauty, on Picturesque Travel and on Sketching Landscape*, London, 1972.

40 Price, Sir U., op. cit., p. 9.

41 Ibid.

42 Burke, E., *An Essay on the Sublime and Beautiful*, 1898 edn, London, p. 44.

43 Loudon, J. C. (ed.), *The Landscape Gardening and Landscape Architecture of the Late H. Repton Esq*, London, 1840, p. 354.

44 Loudon, J. C. , *Country Residences*, London, 1806, p. 371.

45 ——, *Observations . . . on the Theory and Practice of Landscape Gardening*, Edinburgh, 1804, p. 241.

46 Turner, T., op. cit., p. 43.

47 Gotheim, M. L., *A history of garden art*, London, J. M. Dent, 1928, Vol 2, p. 255.

48 Kluckert, E., *European Garden Design*, Cologne: Könemann, 2000, p. 208.

49 Ericson, C., *To the Scaffold – The life of Marie Antoinette*, Robson Books, 2000.

50 Wiebenson, D., *The Picturesque Garden in France*, Princeton University Press, 1978, p. 81.

51 Girardin, R.-L., *An Essay on Landscape, or on the means of improving and embellishing the country round our habitations*, London, 1783, p. 149.

52 Fraser, D., *Frederick the Great*, London: Allen Lane, 2000, p. 531.

53 Holborn, H., *A History of Modern Germany, 1648–1840*, London: Eyre & Spottiswoode, 1965, p. 322.

54 ——, op. cit., p. 323.

55 Kluckert, E., op. cit., 2000, p. 406.

56 Newton, N. T., *Design on the Land: The development of landscape architecture*, Harvard: Belknap Press, 1971, p. 237.

57 Thompson, J. M., *Lectures on Foreign History*, 1494–1789, Oxford: Basil Blackwell, 1925, p. 375.

58 Turner, T. *City as Landscape*, London: Spon, 1998, p. 38.

59 Hussey, C., op. cit., p. 78.

60 Hunt, J. D., *William Kent, Landscape Garden Designer. An assessment and catalogue of his designs*, London: Zwemmer, 1987, p. 67.

61 Castell, R., *The Villas of the Ancients illustrated by The Author*, London, 1728.

62 Clark, H. F., *The English Landscape Garden*, 1948, p. 37.

63 Loudon, J. C., *Encyclopaedia of Gardening*, 5th edn., 1835, p. 320.

64 Hussey, C., op. cit., p. 89

65 Von Goethe, J. W. *Italian Journey*, 1778.

66 Hussey, C., introduction to Stroud, D., *Capability Brown*, London: Faber & Faber, 1975, p. 31; Burke, E., op. cit., p. 170.

67 Hussey, C., op cit., 1927, p. 186.

68 Hyams, E., *Capability Brown and Humphry Repton*, London: J. M. Dent, 1971, p. 42.

69 Kluckert, E., op. cit., p. 415.

70 McBride, D., *A History of Hawkstone*, Shrewsbury: MPS, 1987.

71 Loudon, J. C., op. cit., 1806, Vol. II, p. 369.

Chapter 9

Eclectic gardens
1800–1900

History and philosophy

Around 1800, garden design theory struck a problem that, even today, is scarcely resolved. Gothein's analysis was that practitioners had ceased to 'look for art at all',[1] so that, 'the whole of the nineteenth century must complete its tale of sins before the foundations are shattered'.[2] Nineteenth-century architecture suffered a comparable fate. It was seen, with less clarity, as the dilemma of which historic style to apply in which circumstances. Artists also turned to historic themes but some individuals, less dependent on patronage than designers, were able to chart their own futures – a freedom that permitted the realisation of a personal vision. Gombrich commented that

9.1 Art or nature? As part of Blenheim Park in Oxfordshire, this must be classified as a work of art

'it was only in the nineteenth century that the real gulf opened between the successful artists – who contributed to "official art" – and the nonconformists, who were mainly appreciated after their death'.[3] Garden designers, like architects, and 'successful' artists, neglected the quest for art to imitate 'the nature of the world'. They saw only the superficial 'world of nature', soon to be captured by photography.

Quatremère de Quincy, an astute French critic, was one of the first to appreciate the garden designer's problem. In 1823 he explained the dilemma facing the 'irregular system of landscape gardening' as follows:

> What pretends to be an image of nature is nothing more or less than nature herself. The means of the art are reality. Everyone knows that the merit of its works consists in obviating any suspicion of art. To constitute a perfect garden, according to the irregular system of landscape gardening, we must not have the least suspicion that the grounds have been laid out by art.[4]

What could the designer do? It appeared that:

- To be works of art, gardens must imitate nature
- If they imitate nature, gardens cannot be works of art.

The first proposition had been agreed by all since ancient times. It is the foundation of Neoplatonic aesthetics. The second proposition arose from the empiricist aim, explained in the previous chapter, of creating 'natural' gardens using native plants, rocks, water and jagged lines. Picturesque gardens became indistinguishable from Mother Nature herself: romantic, wild, unadorned, intensely desirable – but impossible to live with. In Britain, and elsewhere, garden design reached an impasse which cannot be explained using the usual British design-historical categories of 'Stuart' 'Georgian' and 'Victorian' Gardens. These labels do not illuminate the why or wherefore of garden design.

When there was no obvious way forward, most designers turned backward: they reproduced ancient styles and combined them in new ways. This opened a debate that led to a Great Turning Point, and four design approaches:

- The landscape style: using ideas selected from the past in a structured sequence
- The Mixed style: using design styles selected from other countries and displayed as if in a museum
- The gardenesque style: using plants selected from favourite regions of the world and arranged to display their individuality
- Nationalistic styles: using design ideas selected from glorious eras in the histories of the nations in which the gardens were made.

The word 'selected' is used in each of the above accounts to underline their common aspect. 'Eclectic' derives from the Greek *eklektikos*, meaning 'to select or pick out'. In

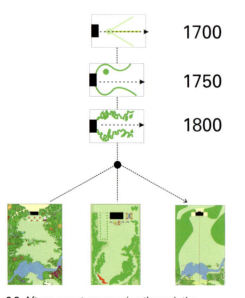

1700

1750

1800

9.2 After a sweet progression through the eighteenth century, garden design theory branched confusingly, as did design styles

Ancient Greece, the Eclectics were philosophers who, on principle, selected and combined the best ideas from every source. Systematic philosophers disdain the practice but most of us do it to a greater or lesser extent.

In the absence of a workable design theory, eclecticism ran amok in the gardens of the nineteenth century. The landscape style was most popular in Britain and Germany. In Britain it led to the addition of terraces and woodland gardens to Brownian parks; in Germany, Picturesque parks were wrapped round baroque gardens. The Mixed style was popular in most parts of Europe and also in North America. The gardenesque style affected botanical gardens everywhere and private woodland gardens in Britain. Nationalism affected most countries. Before examining these approaches in detail, one point should be emphasised: some of the resulting gardens were of high quality. One may find them lacking in a spiritual or artistic dimension but this is akin to criticising Berlioz for not being Bach, or a house for not being a church. The four approaches rested on a sophisticated theoretical debate, which also created the modern profession of landscape architecture. In the longer term, the ideas were of more importance than their design consequences.

The Great Debate

Between 1793 and 1815, while continental Europe was in thrall to Napoleon, three English squires – Sir Uvedale Price, Richard Payne Knight, and Humphry Repton – conducted a discussion of garden theory. Most nineteenth century garden theorists, including J. C. Loudon, Prince Pückler-Muskau, Frederick Law Olmsted and Gertrude Jekyll, took this debate as the starting point for their own deliberations. It also had a deep influence on twentieth-century town and country planning. The principles of Mr Price, the theories of Mr Knight, the works of Mr Repton and the phenomenal literary output of Mr Loudon spread round the world, aided by the improvement in transport and the industrialisation of book production. The debate itself centred on the classic themes of utility, firmness and beauty (see Chapter 1).

Knight was a wealthy dilettante, the grandson of an ironmaster and the brother of a famous horticulturalist. He opened the debate with a Gilpinesque attack on Brown's style of landscape gardening.[5] The illustrations supporting his argument showed Brown's work as 'bald and shaven' in contrast with the romantic charm of Dame Nature. A jibe against Repton was included, because he had proclaimed himself Brown's successor. Repton was hurt, and worried that his business might suffer. He entered the debate, emphasising utility, and poked fun at Knight for placing picturesque rocks on his front lawn (see p. 201). Price agreed this was impractical but joined Knight in writing lyrically about Dame Nature's seductive beauty and harmony with the 'masculinity' of classical architecture. A compromise was reached, in the best tradition of English diplomacy.

In 1986, albeit unrequested, I put my services as a technical editor at the disposal of the departed squires by writing a collective opinion for them to give a client who wished to 'improve his estate'.[6] An edited version of this opinion follows.

9.3 Linderhof, Bavaria: it is not known if Ludwig II was influenced by the three English squires but he developed a similarly eclectic enthusiasm. Linderhof has a transition from art to nature, a terrace for social events, a serpentine park, a sublime background and exotic buildings in various styles

Good morning. We have completed a study of your estate and Mr Repton has made sketches from several viewpoints. The changes we propose are designed to fit the existing site and create improvements. The new landscape should be useful and beautiful, with a smooth transition from your house to Nature.

We can best explain this idea by referring to the work of the great landscape painters of Italy. The *foreground* of your view should be a terrace with a profusion of flowers. It should be Beautiful and well-kept for family use, with something of the character of a garden scene by Watteau. The *middle ground* should be a noble park, laid out with a view to Picturesque effect but available for agriculture. Claude and Poussin show how sheep and herdsmen can make scenery Picturesque. The *background* should be Sublime. We recommend opening views to the wild scenery beyond. Each of the three grounds can contain more than one type of character but the Beautiful should predominate in the foreground, the Picturesque in the middle ground and the Sublime in the background.

Your new mansion should be carefully placed: to have a good microclimate and to command fine views. It should dominate the foreground but should only be an incident in the landscape when seen from afar. Lancelot Brown, though he did not appreciate wild nature, had good taste in the selection of sites and in the composition of parkland with woods and water. As to the choice of an architectural style, we recommend an Italian style for Claudian sites and a Grecian style for Poussinesque sites. But for English parkland, like yours, we advise the old castle style.

Finally, we propose a small Palladian temple overlooking the lake so that we can join you for an outdoor repast in summer. It should rest on the brow of the hill, to be seen from your drawing room, and we suggest that you inscribe it with the famous lines by Alexander Pope which have guided our composition:

> To build, to plant, whatever you intend,
> To rear the Column, or the Arch to bend,
> To swell the Terras, or to sink the Grot;
> In all, let Nature never be forgot.
> Consult the Genius of the Place in all
> That tells the waters or to rise, or fall . . . .
> Joins willing woods, and varies shades from shades
> Now Breaks, or now directs, th'intending
> Lines; Paints as you plant, and as you work, Designs[7]

This collective opinion is based on the following principles:

- There should be a grand transition from the realm of art to the realm of nature
- The foreground, near the dwelling house, should be the realm of art
- Exotic plants should be used near the dwelling but not elsewhere in the estate
- The layout should be based on natural composition, as illustrated in the work of the great landscape paintings of Italy
- The design should respond to the character of the locality in terms of climate, materials and design traditions.

In time, the first of these principles led to the landscape style, the second to the Mixed style and the third to the gardenesque style. The fourth principle led to the term 'landscape architecture'. The fifth principle influenced nationalistic approaches to design and the Arts and Crafts movement. Had the principles been better understood by their protagonists and the public, they might have resulted in even better gardens. But scale was a problem. The five ideas worked well on the 300-hectare estates typical of royal and aristocratic gardens. They were less companionable in the small suburban estates of the rising middle class.

The debate is often described as the 'picturesque controversy', because it centred on the relevance of landscape paintings to landscape design, but this label does little justice to the participants. Knight and Price had a keen interest in aesthetic theory. Repton cared about every aspect of the relationship between landform, water, planting, buildings and gardens. All three wished to see a just balance between the Vitruvian values.[8]

The landscape style

Initial capitals have been used in the account of Knight, Price and Repton for the words Beautiful, Sublime and Picturesque, to mark their use as part of a specialised aesthetic vocabulary. As explained by Edmund Burke, 'Beautiful' meant smooth, flowing, like the body of a beautiful woman. 'Sublime' meant wild and frightening, like a rough sea or the views that might be obtained while crossing the Alps on a rocky track in a horse-drawn coach. 'Picturesque' was an intermediate term, introduced after Burke, to describe a scene with elements of the Beautiful and the Sublime. Without its initial capital, 'Picturesque' means 'like a picture'. In what is called the landscape style in this book, Picturesque gardens have a sequential transition from a Beautiful foreground, through a Picturesque middle ground to a Sublime background. Composing gardens like paintings integrated the design ideas of the eighteenth century to create a landscape design concept of significant grandeur and exceptionally wide application.

The landscape style is the chief support for the claim that British designers made a unique contribution to western culture during the eighteenth century. In his 1955 Reith Lectures Nikolaus Pevsner used the term 'English picturesque theory' for what he described as an 'English national planning theory'.[9] Pevsner stated that it 'lies hidden in the writings of the improvers from Pope to Uvedale Price, and Payne Knight' and that it gave English town planners 'something of great value to offer to other nations'. He then asked whether the same can be said 'of painting, of sculpture, and of architecture proper'. His answer was that Henry Moore and other sculptors had 'given England a position in European sculpture such as she has never before held', but that English painting and architecture of the period were of markedly lower quality.

9.4 Beautiful and Sublime: girls in a rough sea and in the garden of York House in London

At the end of the twentieth century, Moore was still regarded as a great artist and the importance of the landscape planning theory identified by Pevsner took on a global relevance.

Partly inspired by Pevsner, I wrote, in *Landscape Planning and Environmental Impact Design*, that 'The idea of forming a graded transition from art to nature remained at the heart of English garden design from 1793 until 1947. When the 1947 Town and Country Planning Act imposed a squeeze on garden size, the transition idea leapt the garden wall and occupied the country. Planners became enthused with the notion that towns should be tightly urban in character and surrounded by a Brownian agricultural hinterland, itself giving way to wildly irregular national parks and areas of outstanding natural beauty. Strict planning controls were imposed on developments in the green belt, so that towns would become denser and the spaces between buildings could develop a townscape character, with urban squares and circuses like those of Renaissance towns'.[10] It provides a good theoretical base for the landscape architecture profession (see p. 243).

9.5 (top left) Sheringham exemplifies Repton's use of terraces to create garden-to-park transitions

9.6 Brown's serpentine park at Harewood House, Yorkshire, was adapted to the landscape style by the addition of a terrace, designed by Charles Barry, in the nineteenth century.

9.7 Blenheim, Oxfordshire (top left), and Howick Hall, Northumberland (top right), have terraces added in the nineteenth century

9.8 Charlottenburg, Berlin (above), has a full transition from 'formal' to 'informal'

The Mixed style

The nineteenth century was more a time of industrial than agricultural revolution. Fortunes were made and eighteenth-century parks were adorned with costly gardens around their mansions. The three squires' original idea had been to make a realm of art (e.g. a terrace) near the house, presumably so that families could enjoy the utilitarian pleasure of afternoon tea while watching children in sailor suits gambol on the lawn. Repton's imagination leapt the terrace. He began recommending a rich mixture of different types of garden:

> There is no more absurdity in collecting gardens of different styles, dates, characters, and dimensions, in the same enclosure, than in placing the works of a Raphael and a Teniers in the same cabinet, or books sacred and profane in the same library.[11]

9.9 The Chinese Dairy at Woburn Abbey, Bedfordshire, an estate for which Repton produced a 'Red Book' of 'before' and 'after' views

9.10 Alton Towers, Staffordshire, was sharply criticised by J. C. Loudon for its eclecticism, though it is often associated with his name

9.11 The twentieth century Theme Park (above) has added to the mixture of features at Alton Towers

This became the eclectics' charter, providing a logical foundation for what Edward Kemp was later to call the Mixed style. Repton was the first theorist to advocate collections of gardens in diverse styles. He saw himself as a successor to Brown, which, in terms of professional status, he was. Later commentators saw Repton as a stylist in the manner of Brown, which he was not. They also saw Loudon as an advocate of the Mixed style, which he never was.[12]

The eclectic trend which Repton began soon led to whole gardens being laid out in styles associated with particular countries: Chinese Gardens, Japanese Gardens, Swiss Gardens, Indian Gardens, American Gardens, Italian Gardens. Sometimes the styles were used in compartments, sometimes they were very mixed. Italian Gardens

9.12 Biddulph Grange, Staffordshire, has an Italian Garden (top right), an Egyptian Garden (lower right) and a garden based on the Great Wall of China (above)

were the most popular. The introduction of exotic plant species from all over the world assisted the mixture of styles. Two of the best eclectic gardens in England – Biddulph Grange and Alton Towers – were in the English Midlands, an important manufacturing region. It may be that manufacturers had the most money or it may be that they had the most interest in foreign parts. At Biddulph Grange, brilliant use is made of tunnels to keep the stylistic zones apart. In other gardens the search for variety and contrast was assisted by elaborate bedding arrangements. Kemp's account of the Mixed style, supports Gothein's opinion that designers forgot to 'look for art at all':

> Serpentine or wavy lines may be regarded as the characteristic features of the mixed style. Its object is beauty of lines, and general variety. Roundness, smoothness, freedom from angularity, and grace rather than dignity or

grandeur, are among its numerous indications. It does not reject straight lines entirely near the house, or in connexion with a flower-garden, or a rosary, or a subordinate building (as a greenhouse) that has a separate piece of garden to it. Nor does it refuse to borrow from the picturesque in regard to the arrangement and grouping of plants . . . It has all the grace of nature without its ruggedness, and the refinement of art apart from its stiffness and severity.[13]

In considering how the chaste manners of the eighteenth century evolved into the nineteenth century's promiscuous eclecticism, one should remember both Repton's theoretical position and the different circumstances of our predecessors. Should you or I wish to see foreign gardens or plants, we can use the internet to view images or

9.13 Branitz in Cottbus, Germany, was designed by an admirer of Repton. The area near the house was considered best suited to the use of exotic bedding plants, painted statues and cast iron

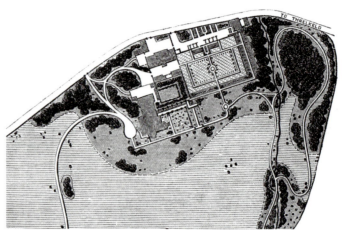

9.14 (above) Brighton, Sussex: the Victorian fashion for carpet bedding endures in public parks

9.15 (right) The Mixed style applied to the area near the house – a design by Edward Kemp

book a flight. Our predecessors heard travellers' tales of amazing places but had to rely on engravings and souvenirs to learn more. Bombay could not be a holiday destination when the ship went via Cape Town, took three months and exposed travellers to incurable diseases. To modern eyes the eclecticism of Victorian gardens may be excessive.[14] To Victorian eyes, it expressed a multicultural enthusiasm and was a means of transporting the imagination to far-away places and far-off times. It should also be remembered that the Augustan style had itself used an eclectic range of garden 'follies'. They, and the Mixed style, were products of Romanticism.

When Ancient Egypt was uncovered by Napoleon, there was a craze for Egyptology: Biddulph has an Egyptian Garden. When serious excavations began at Pompeii, there was craze for Roman Gardens: Schinkel added a Roman Garden to the Potsdam landscape. When plant collectors returned from the mountains, everyone wanted an 'Alpine' garden. Many of the best and worst nineteenth-century gardens were in England, because of her sea-power and wealth. Others were in America, like the Du Pont family's Longwood Gardens in Pennsylvania (1907). Nor did the Mixed style die with the nineteenth century. In the twentieth century it was widely used for theme parks. The original Disneyland, in California, let visitors taste the romance of the Old World and the Wild West without a passport. Disneyland Paris was located outside an Old World capital but its Magic Kingdom was inspired by nineteenth-century romanticism: the Neuswanstein of 'mad' King Ludwig II of Bavaria, or the rebuilt castle of Segovia in Spain. Alton Towers was a fine example of the Mixed style before it became, very appropriately, the location of Britain's largest theme park.

Postmodernist theory did much to legitimate the theoretical basis of eclecticism. The argument, in short, was that modernism was elitist and autocratic; it prescribed a single approach, the International style, as morally and aesthetically acceptable. Postmodernism boasts of being multicultural and multi-ethnic, arguing that east is as good as west, women as good as men, black as good as white, Hindu as good as

Christian and eclecticism as good as rationalism. Repton might well have agreed, and it is a pity that this aspect of his legacy is not better remembered. He was, for example, responsible for persuading the Prince of Wales to build an Indian Pavilion in the heart of Brighton, on the Sussex coast.[15]

The gardenesque style

Loudon began his career with a gutter-low opinion of Repton and no appreciation of the landscape style. He was determined to follow 'the principles of Mr Price' (see Chapter 8), and his lavish two-volume work, *Country Residences*, of 1806, was full of proposals for converting estates laid out in the manner of 'Capability' Brown to 'Mr Price's principles', meaning Picturesque irregularity.[16] One has to doubt the popularity of this style with clients: from the illustrations, it looks, as though Loudon specialised in converting neat parks to tracts of weeds.

9.16 (top left) Repton conceived the Royal Pavilion in Brighton, Sussex, and Nash executed the design

9.17 (top right) The Roman Baths at Potsdam, designed by Karl Friedrich von Schinkel

9.18 (lower left) Longwood Gardens, Pennsylvania: designed by the co-owner of a chemical company. Pierre S. Du Pont was a meticulous engineer with a special interest in fountains. He drew inspiration from books and visits to French gardens

9.19 (lower right) Crystal palaces were built to house exotic plants from distant lands: Buen Retiro, Madrid

Ill-health terminated Loudon's Picturesque quest in the 1810s. But in the 1820s Loudon returned to landscape gardening, this time as an author with a full appreciation of the logical impasse. Drawing intellectual support from Quatremère de Quincy, Loudon proposed that gardens in the irregular, or Picturesque, style should be planted with exotic species, to make them 'recognizable' as works of art entirely distinct from unadorned nature.[17] This aspect of the gardenesque, which Loudon named the Principle of Recognition, was constant. But Loudon spread confusion by using the term in different ways on different occasions. Circular beds could be gardenesque, if they displayed a gardener's skill.[18] An arboretum could be gardenesque, if it showed the individual character of each specimen to best effect. In my view, the best application of the idea was in composing exotic plants in the 'natural' arrangements characteristic of landscape paintings. This led to a genuinely original, and still popular, nineteenth-century idea, one that remains popular today: the woodland garden. It works particularly well in the warm, wet conditions that favour the naturalisation of rhododendron species, including the cypress swamps of the southern United States and the woodland valleys of south–west England.

9.20 (top left) Trebah, Cornwall, has an exotic woodland garden

9.21 (top right) Jardin des Plantes, Angers, designed by Edouard André, has exotic plants in a naturalistic composition

9.22 (below left and right) Kew, Surrey, is a botanic garden with an essentially Gardenesque layout

9.23 Cragside, Northumberland, is immediately recognisable as a work of man, rather than 'wild nature', because of its straight lines (top left) and exotic plants (above)

9.24 Circular beds in Greenwich Park, London

Nationalistic styles

The nationalism that blew through nineteenth-century Europe had its effect on gardens. Despite the fact that Romantic garden theorists, like Christian Hirschfeld[19] in Germany and J. C. Loudon in Britain, had cautioned against mixing styles, their writings fuelled eclecticism. As the nineteenth century drew to its close, writers and designers saw nationalism as a potentially purifying force. Garden historians tend to welcome the influence of nationalistic movements on the appreciation of old gardens,

9.25 Duchêne's recreation of the style of Le Nôtre, at Courances, has an elegant charm scarcely found in the master's own work

but lament some of the speculative (and therefore potentially inaccurate) 'restorations' of gardens carried out in the nineteenth century – rather as Victorian architects have been castigated for their 'restorations' of medieval churches. (A different complaint is made about present-day reconstructions: with their emphasis on archaeological and documentary evidence, they can be so accurate that they are boring.)

France, after the 1870 war with Prussia, was one of the first countries to be touched by artistic nationalism. French critics found fault with German music for aesthetic and nationalistic reasons. The 'Anglo-Chinese' style of garden design was seen as a foreign invader which could be expelled rather more easily than the German army. The France of Louis XIV was revered as a triumphant example of the national genius. Henri Duchêne set up his office in 1877 and his son, Achille, joined him at the age of 12. Their first great project, for a wealthy and patriotic industrialist, was the restoration of Le Nôtre's design at Vaux-le-Vicomte. It was very successful and the office prospered. In addition to restoring other Le Nôtre Parks (e.g. Champs-sur-Marne, Le Marais and Courances), they designed new parks somewhat in the style of le Nôtre. These included Voisins in France and the water parterre at Blenheim Palace in England.

Germany had several reasons for a nationalist approach to landscape. First, a love of German forests and soil had been present in the culture since ancient times. Second, the romantic love of nature, fanned by Goethe, had grown strong. Third, the study of ecology and native habitats had originated in Germany, under the influence of Humboldt and Haeckel. Fourth, the nation, unified in the 1870s, took a new pride in its history. In *Heimatschutz* (*Homeland Protection*), published in 1901, Ernst Rudorff protested at the destruction of nature and called for protected reserves. The architect Paul Schultze-Naumburg used these ideas in his books *Gärten* (*Gardens*; 1902) and *Die Entstellung unseres Landes* (*The Disfigurement of Our Countryside*; 1905). Willy Lange, often referring to Rousseau, Goethe, Schiller and Humboldt, advocated nature gardens in his book, *Gartengestaltung der Neuzeit* (*Garden Design for Modern Times*; 1907). Such ideas were discredited after the Second World War because Hitler had supported them.

Holland developed an ecological approach to gardens under the influence of Jac P. Thijsse and others. The results can be seen at the Amsterdam Bos Park, the Jac P. Thijsse Park and the Thijsse Hof. Thijsse favoured the use of native plants in garden design.

England was influenced by nationalism in the late nineteenth century, for sentimental, patriotic and artistic reasons.[20] Writers and artists rebelled against High Victorian eclecticism and yearned for gardens to be as they had been in the merrie days of Bacon and Shakespeare. The restoration of Penshurst in the 1870s, based on an illustration from Kip, was an early product of this sentiment. Pre-Raphaelite painters dreamed of Olde England, and painted their visions. This contributed to the Arts and Crafts movement and, supported by William Morris, the dream led to the establishment of Britain's National Trust and its own style of garden management.

America was proud of its nationhood but always aware of its European roots. It was natural for designers to adopt an eclectic approach, based on paintings, drawings and plans from the Old World. Colonial gardens were often the work of immigrant designers and European influence remained strong in the work of Andrew Jackson Downing, Calvert Vaux, Frederick Law Olmsted, Charles Platt, Beatrix Farrand and others. Yet the twentieth century saw a growing demand for an American style.

Australia, largely peopled by British and Irish settlers, had a strong sense of 'the old country'. Colonists yearned for gardens and parks like those they had known in Victorian Britain. It was only towards the end of the twentieth century that Australian garden designers took an interest in the native flora and in the garden cultures of the other nations from which immigration was then allowed.

Landscape architecture

Repton, Price and Knight accepted the compositional principles of the great landscape paintings as an unimpeachable standard of good taste. Sir Walter Scott was of the same opinion and one of his friends took the idea further. Gilbert Laing Meason published 150 copies of a book on *The Landscape Architecture of the Great Painters of Italy* in 1828.[21] Meason advised designers to study relationships between buildings and their settings in the landscape paintings of Giotto, Titian, Poussin, Veronese, Claude, Tintoretto, Raphael, Domenichino, Michelangelo and others. Meason did not make a name for himself with this idea but the most prolific garden author of the day liked the title of his book. Loudon used the term 'landscape architecture' in his 1840 edition of Repton's works: *The Landscape Gardening and Landscape Architecture of the Late H. Repton Esq.* It was then taken up by the American author, Andrew Jackson Downing, who considered Loudon 'the most distinguished gardening author of the age'.[22]

9.26 The cover of Thijsse's book *De bloemen in onzen tuin door* (*The plants in our garden*) celebrates native plants

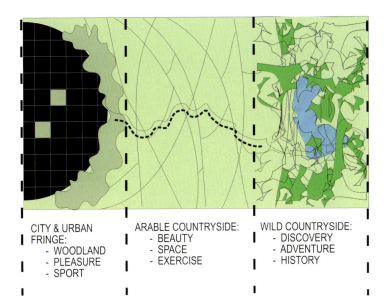

CITY & URBAN FRINGE:
- WOODLAND
- PLEASURE
- SPORT

ARABLE COUNTRYSIDE:
- BEAUTY
- SPACE
- EXERCISE

WILD COUNTRYSIDE:
- DISCOVERY
- ADVENTURE
- HISTORY

9.27 The landscape style led, in the twentieth century, to the idea of planning compact towns, greenways through an agricultural hinterland and national parks in distant hills and valleys

9.28 Meason's own house at Lindertis, Tayside, was an example of landscape architecture based on the great painters of Italy

Calvert Vaux, a young architect persuaded by Downing to move from London to New York, also liked the term. When he collaborated with Frederick Law Olmsted on an entry for the Central Park competition of 1858 they described themselves as 'landscape architects'. Since Olmsted spent most of his subsequent career on parks and park systems, his chosen professional title became associated with public projects, as distinct from private gardens, and this remains its predominant use. The strengths landscape architecture draws from its garden design heritage include:

- The Vitruvian design tradition of balancing utility, firmness and beauty
- Use of the word 'landscape' to mean 'a good place' – as the objective of the design process
- A comprehensive approach to open space planning involving city parks, greenways and nature parks outside towns
- A planning theory about the contextualisation of development projects
- The principle that development plans should be adapted to their landscape context.

Landscape architecture is now an internationally accepted professional title for exponents of these skills. Its adoption caused garden design and landscape architecture to split apart, with significant damage to both activities. Landscape architects, though well trained, were deprived of a history or theory for their profession. Garden design suffered the same fate for a different reason: it became a branch of horticulture, supported by a largely scientific and technical education. After the establishment of the world's first landscape architecture course, at Harvard University in 1900, most education courses adopted this title during the second half of the twentieth century. At the University of Greenwich, where I work, we have tried to heal the breach at an educational level by establishing parallel degrees in Landscape Architecture and Garden Design. The former emphasises open space and public projects; the latter emphasises enclosed space and private projects. Technical and theoretical courses are shared.

Landscape architecture was often concerned with creating areas of natural scenery and public gardens in towns. The Olmsted and Vaux design for Central Park had areas equivalent to the stages of a transition from art to nature. Olmsted and Eliot applied the same idea of transition to the entire Boston metropolitan region. The first European to use 'landscape architect' as a professional title, Patrick Geddes, designed a park in Dunfermline and went on to become one of the most inspirational planning theorists of the twentieth century. Some of the best examples of landscape planning at the scale of an urban region are in continental Europe, including the cities of Stockholm, Stuttgart and Barcelona. In America, the Greenways Movement has injected new energy into open space planning and new life into old cities.[23]

Styles and examples

Gardenesque style

Use: Picturesque gardens, of the type discussed in the previous chapter, came to be used for collections of exotic plants. Loudon, believing this should be a primary role of gardens, invented the term 'gardenesque' to describe a Picturesque design which was 'recognisable' as a work of art because it incorporated non-native (garden) plants. He also argued that such places would help working men to educate themselves and thus improve their economic status.

Form: To begin with, few aristocratic owners were willing to surround their dwellings with wholly 'irregular' gardens. But in the second half of the nineteenth century many woodland valleys were converted into 'natural compositions' of exotics. Himalayan plants (e.g. rhodo-dendrons and camellias) and North American plants proved particularly well suited to this idea. The diagram shows a Picturesque estate, converted to the gardenesque by planting exotics. Loudon favoured circular beds because they allow plantsmen to show their skill in combining plants in schemes that look good from all angles. Such beds can still be seen in the flower garden at Greenwich Park.

9.29
Gardenesque style

Kew Gardens 1841

The original garden was created for Augusta, Princess of Wales around Kew Palace. She was helped by Sir William Chambers, a sharp critic of Brown's vapidity and an admirer of Chinese gardens, who designed the Pagoda and other buildings for Kew. The estate was acquired by the nation in 1841, as a centre for horticulture, and now contains what is said to be the largest collection of plants in the world. The variety is overwhelming. Designers complain about the lack of aesthetic order but Loudon, one cannot doubt, would have seen it as a prime example of his gardenesque principles. He would also have admired splendid examples of the building type he did much to promote in his youth: the glasshouse, used for tropical and sub-tropical plants.

> At Kew, avenues of different species were planted in various parts of the grounds, taking their position from local features of ground and water without being aligned on one focus or in a mutually symmetrical pattern . . . when Nesfield proposed grading trees by height in the vistas at Kew, and abandoning rigorous botanical order, Glendinning accused him of sacrificing the object of an arboretum for the sake of appearance. [24]

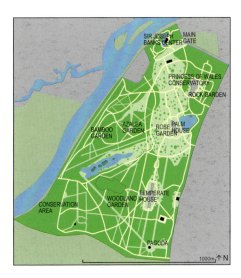

9.30 Kew Gardens, Surrey

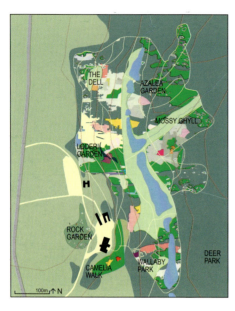

9.31 Leonardslee, Sussex

Leonardslee 1889

Leonardslee is a development of the planting ideas of Sir Uvedale Price, Richard Payne Knight and J. C. Loudon. It displays the Gardenesque principle of composing exotic plants in a picturesque manner, derived from landscape painting. Sir Edmund Loder bought the estate in 1888 and imported a herd of Wallabies, whose descendants still thrive on the site. The garden lies in a sheltered valley with a string of ponds, made a century earlier to provide waterpower for the local iron industry. Being damp and slightly acid, the soil is well suited to rhododendrons, camellias and magnolias. Like Sir Edmund, one can walk through the garden imagining oneself in a misty Himalayan valley. Before visiting the garden one might read Sir Joseph Hooker's *Himalayan Journals*. Hooker, who collected *Rhododendron griffithianum*, a parent of the 'Loderi' hybrids, tells of high adventure and intrepid plant collecting. Leonardslee exudes the romance of travel and adventure.

There must always have been forest here and so it is a perfect site for a woodland garden which is precisely what Sir Edmund Loder set out to create when he started planting in 1888. Within a few years he was raising new rhododendrons as well as buying existing ones. Many fine hybrids were produced by Sir Edmund and his successors, but none destined to have a greater impact on rhododendron breeding than *Rhododendron loderi*.[25]

Mixed style

9.32 Mixed style

Use: The gardenesque taste for plant collecting developed into a wider enthusiasm for collecting styles of garden design. The collection helped the owner envisage historically and geographically remote areas. As with the landscape style, the area near the dwelling was used for domestic pleasure. Owners would take tea, play summer games and admire their collections. Gardens slaked the nineteenth-century thirst for awe, landscape painting, travel, adventure and scientific knowledge.

Form: Towards the end of his career, Humphry Repton argued that there is no more absurdity in collecting styles in a garden than books in a library or pictures in a gallery. This led to a vogue for American, Chinese, Japanese, Italian and other eclectic gardens. Victorian gardens came to be characterised by their mixed collections of zones laid out in different styles, although, as the century progressed, the 'Italian' style became the most popular. The diagram shows the style as it was used in suburban gardens. In large parks, there was scope for larger collections of styles.

Alton Towers 1827

An early example of the Mixed style, Alton Towers became a popular theme park in the twentieth century. The garden was begun by the eccentric fifteenth Earl of Shrewsbury, who, Loudon relates, consulted every authority, only to avoid 'whatever an artist might recommend'. Loudon himself – and perhaps Repton also – was one of the artists, yet Alton Towers grew under the Reptonian principle that collecting design styles in a garden is no more absurd than collecting diverse pictures in a gallery or books in a library. There is a Swiss Cottage, a Stonehenge, a Dutch garden, a Pagoda Fountain, a Choragic Monument copied from Athens and much else. The rides and slides of the modern theme park merely add to the eccentricity of an early nineteenth-century earl's fancy.

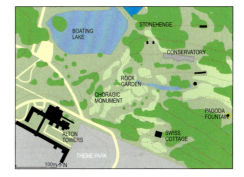

9.33 Alton Towers, Staffordshire

> This nobleman, abounding in wealth, always fond of architecture and gardening, but with much more fancy than sound judgement, seems to have wished to produce something different from everything else. Though he consulted almost every artist, ourselves among the rest, he seems only to have done so for the purpose of avoiding whatever an artist might recommend.[26]

Branitz 1846

This is the 'small' estate which Prince Pückler-Muskau bought when forced to leave Muskau (see p. 211). Still working with English precedents, he made a Serpentine Lake, a Pyramid Lake, a Blue Garden, a Smithy Garden, a Rose Mount, a Moon Mount and Island of Venus, a light iron Kiosk and a series of waterways. It is a good example of the Mixed style. The Prince and his wife lie at rest in a pyramid tomb, in a lake, with an inscription from the Koran: 'Graves are the mountain tops of a distant, lovely land'.

> For the prince, an indispensable component of the artistic effect of the garden was its separation from the park. The garden was related to the castle, and was seen by him as an 'extended dwelling place', whereas he interpreted the surrounding park area as 'concentrated idealized nature'.[27]

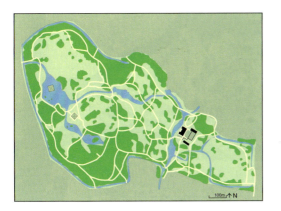

9.34 Branitz, Cottbus

Biddulph Grange 1860

Biddulph Grange epitomises the Mixed style as effectively as Vaux-le-Vicomte and Stourhead represent the styles of the two preceding centuries. The way in which funding was obtained for these representative projects is indicative of the way in which power moved: Vaux was made for a government minister, Stourhead for a banker, Biddulph for a manufacturer. If one does not admire eclecticism, one will not admire this garden.

> The garden at Biddulph Grange, by evoking vanished and alien civilisations, served as an affirmation that the millennium was coming . . . Bateman may well have overstretched his resources in his works at Biddulph . . . But by the time of Bateman's departure, the impact of Biddulph on the development of Victorian gardens had already been decisive.[28]

Linderhof 1874

This garden, made for the 'mad' King Ludwig II of Bavaria, is a choice German example of the Romantic enthusiasm for mixing styles. After a lonely youth, Ludwig turned to fantasy, dreams, historical epics and wild buildings. His castle at Neuschwanstein is justly famous. It parodies European castle-architecture, just as Linderhof parodies palace-architecture. Ludwig, wanting to be an absolute monarch, thought of naming the place 'Meicost Ettal', an anagram of Louis XIV's epigram, 'L' état c'est moi'. Schloss Linderhof has a neo-rococo style. The garden was designed by the Bavarian Royal Garden Director, Karl von Effner. The ancient lime tree, after which the estate is named, is near the southern terrace. Linderhof has a sunken parterre with a 'French' pond and fountain. Beside the Schloss, 'Italian' garden rooms and water steps lead to a gazebo. The adjoining park, in the 'English' style, makes imaginative use of a valley in the foothills of the, real, Alps. The Venus Grotto, inspired by Ludwig's love of Wagner, has a shell-throne, a coral table and a mural depicting a scene from Act I of

9.35 (left) Biddulph Grange, Staffordshire

9.36 (right) Linderhof, Bavaria

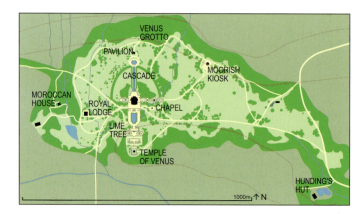

Tannhäuser. Hunding's Hut, twice destroyed and twice restored, was designed using the libretto from the Ring of the Nibelungen. Unquestionably, Linderhof is a product of the Romantic movement.

> In the midst of the solitude of the Graswang Valley, he sought while smoking a chibouk in the Moorish Kiosk and in the Moroccan House to revive the fairy-tale world of the Arabian Nights; in Hunding's Cabin lying on bearskins with his retainers and drinking mead, he wanted to re-experience the mythical content of the Valkyrie; in the golden skiff on the lake of the Venus Grotto he desired to feel the enchantment of Tannhäuser and on the morning of Good Friday to sense the consecrating effect of Parsifal in Gurnemanz's hermitage.[29]

Landscape style

Use: The plan comprised three zones with distinct functions:

- A zone near the house for the quiet enjoyments of polite society
- A park for farm animals and forest trees
- A scenic backdrop for the aesthetic pleasure of looking at nature.

Form: The form also comprised three zones:

- A rectilinear or terraced zone with beds of colourful plants near the house
- A serpentine park with undulating ground, woods and water
- An irregular 'natural' area of woodland, mountain, coast, river or wild vegetation.

The estate was thus 'composed, like a landscape painting with foreground, middleground and background'. Repton, Price and Knight supplied the principle behind the style *c.* 1794 and it was used throughout the nineteenth century. In England, there was generally a linear transition from foreground to background, while in Germany and other continental European countries, the transition was achieved by surrounding a baroque garden with a naturalistic park.

9.37
Landscape style

Crystal Palace 1852

The Crystal Palace was designed by Joseph Paxton for the Great Exhibition in 1851 and first erected on the exhibition site in Hyde Park. It was moved to Sydenham in 1852 and set in a large Italianate park, also designed by Paxton. Most of the park has

9.38 The Crystal Palace, Sydenham, in 1860

gone but one fine terrace survives, as do Paxton's extraordinary prehistoric monsters round the lake in the southern corner of the park. The central area of the site has been laid out as the National Sports Centre in a grim Soviet style.

> Aside from the central axis and the waterworks, the layout of the park lost its formality after descending from the terraces, and the winding paths and woods of Paxton's landscape style superseded the Italianate features above them, although there were two further circular motifs, the maze and the rosary.[30]

Nymphenburg 1820

Maximilian Emanuel's park, 2 km from the centre of Munich, has a baroque heart. Ludwig II lived here as a child and later remembered with distaste the formality of the surroundings, which was of a piece with the strictness of his upbringing. Like Schleissheim, it was designed by Zuccali and Girard with a central canal, on which a gondola service used to operate. Canaletto painted the garden in 1761. At the end of eighteenth century, the baroque garden was fringed with a landscape park. The classical and Romantic geometries work well together. The three elegant baroque pavilions once had geometrical gardens: the Pagodenburg (1716), the Badenburg (1719) and a hermitage known as the Magdalenenklause (1725). Today the temples stand in a landscape park designed (c. 1800) by Germany's leading exponent of the landscape style: Ludwig von Sckell. He has the credit of making an 'English garden' without destroying a baroque garden. A circular temple, the Monopetros, was added in 1865. The canals often freeze in winter and are used by skaters and curlers.

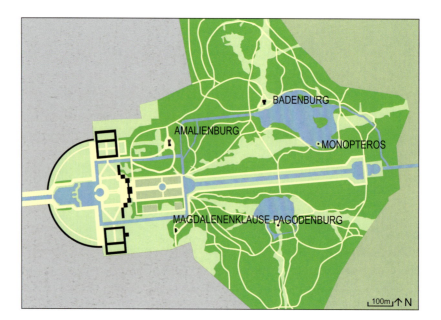

9.39 Nymphenburg, Munich

Although Friedrich Ludwig von Sckell turned most of the garden into a romantic park with natural-looking lakes in front of two pavilions in 1804-23, he incorporated some elements of the baroque layout in his wider scheme, including the *basin* surrounded by fountains and the *parterre de broderie* under the west front.[31]

Landscape architecture

Use: When landscape architecture became an organised profession, first in America, then in Europe and the rest of the world, it led to the planning of open spaces with distinct uses:

- City parks and squares for urban uses
- Greenways, using coasts, river valleys and other corridors, for recreation: hiking, cycling, riding, organised games, water conservation, nature conservation, scenic preservation, historic conservation, etc.
- Protective ordinances and reservations in country areas – variously described as metropolitan parks, country parks, nature parks and national parks – for the enjoyment of nature and natural scenery.

Form: Landscape architecture was founded on the idea of using the compositional principles of the great landscape paintings of Italy to establish relationships between buildings and contexts. This led to the planning of foregrounds, middle grounds and back-grounds. Land use planning, zoning and environmental regulations were used to encourage the formation of compact cities with good open spaces; green-ways and public open space corridors were used to provide natural areas within towns and links to the country-side, and conservation policies were used to provide public access and environmental protection for areas of farming, forestry and natural scenery.

9.40
Landscape
architecture

Boston landscape plan 1890

When asked to advise on the selection of land for open space development in Boston, in 1880, Olmsted proposed a chain of parks which became world famous as Boston's 'Emerald Necklace'. It linked the 'foreground' of Boston Common to the 'background' of Franklin Park. In 1890 Charles Eliot extended Olmsted's scheme into a proposal for the Boston Metropolitan region. Eliot pressed, successfully, for legislation to establish the Trustees for Reservations, which protects historic spaces by holding them in trust for the nation.

[Eliot] suggested that 'for a district such as ours' the system as a whole ought to include five types of area: spaces on the ocean front, shores and islands of the inner bay, the courses of the larger tidal estuaries, two or three large areas of wild forest on the outer rim, and small squares, playgrounds,

9.41 Boston, Massachusetts, with Olmsted's 'Emerald Necklace' in green and Charles Eliot's Metropolitan Open Space System in black

251

and parks in the densely populated sections, to be provided by the local communities.[32]

Stockholm 1938

Sweden's capital city developed one of the first modern park systems in Europe. Holger Blom took charge of the Parks Department in 1938, at the age of 31. He planned a park system which spread out from the old city centre, along the shore of Lake Mälaren and into the Stockholm region. Blom's designs for Norr Mälastrand and Fredhällsparken became famous outside Sweden. He used natural materials and was a great advocate of children's play areas. One can visit the most interesting section by taking the metro to Kristineberg and walking back to the *Stadhuset* (City Hall).

> Stockholm's parks are part of a very complete park system – not large segregated parks, but rather a system of linked strips – which is gradually being developed . . . In almost every other city this lake front [on Lake Mälaren] would have been an urban promenade: here a natural and varied landscape has been created in which one can walk or stroll or picnic, where mothers can rest and children play.[33]

Stuttgart 1950

A series of garden shows held over 50 years has established a chain of green spaces in the form of the letter 'U'. It proceeds north from the city centre, reaches the River Neckar and then turns back on itself. Garden shows were held in 1939, 1950, 1961, 1977 and 1993. The 1939 and 1950 designs for the Killesberg quarry used a traditional

9.42 Stuttgart

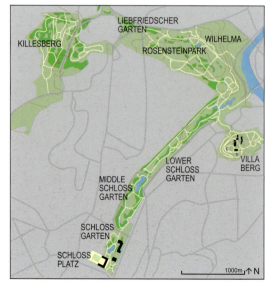

9.43 Stockholm

approach with drystone walls and steps. Hans Luz and Partners, as landscape architects, were involved in four of the garden shows. The 1961 scheme for the Upper Schlossgarten is a prime example of rectilinear abstract modernism – the outdoor equivalent of a cubist painting. The 1977 scheme can be categorised as curvilinear abstract expressionism. The 1993 design team, which included ecologists and social scientists, aimed at a more ecological approach for the Rosensteinpark, encouraging contact between people and nature. Walking from the city centre to the Rosenstein allows one to see textbook examples of design evolution from 1939 to 1993.

> On both a citywide and human scale, the parks and working landscapes within and surrounding Stuttgart are among the most climatically functional, socially useful and aesthetically pleasing of any modern city in the western world.[34]

Barcelona 1992

Two events occasioned the outpouring of design energy which led to the planning of Barcelona's open space system: the death of General Franco in 1975 and the preparations for the 1992 Olympic Games. The General oppressed the city because it had opposed him in the Spanish Civil War. After he died, power was devolved to the region of Catalonia and a programme of civic improvements was launched. The Rambla was extended from the city centre to the old port (Port Vell) and a waterfront greenway leads to an extensive beach park and to Montjuic. In 1987 the encircling hills came under a management plan, as the Parc de Collserola. A swimming park (Parc de la Creueta del Coll) was made near the Parc Güell, where the hills touch the city. The dense urban fabric was enlivened with a series of new parks and squares designed by teams of sculptors and architects. Public art became a symbol of the city's renewal. Over 70 public gardens were made, with many successes and failures.

> The great success of Barcelona is in the total acceptance of contemporary needs and values. For once the needs of the pedestrian and the inhabitant have been recognised . . . 'No other metropolis has so cleverly utilized public space as a foundation for re-thinking the concept of the city' (Domus 1992).'[35]

9.44 Barcelona

Notes

1   Gothein, M-L., *A History of Garden Art*, London: J. M. Dent, 1928, Vol. 2, p. 325.

2   ——, op. cit., Vol. 2, p. 318

3   Gombrich, E. H., *The Story of Art*, London: Phaidon, 1995, p. 503.

4   Quatremère de Quincy, A. C., *An Essay on the Nature, the End and the Means of Imitation in the Fine Arts*, transl. Kent, J. C., London, 1837.

5   Knight, R. P. *The landscape: a didactic poem*, London, 1795.

6   Turner, T., *English Garden Design*, Woodbridge: Antique Collectors Club, 1986, p. 115.

7   Pope, A., *Epistle to Lord Burlington*, London 1731.

8   Turner, T., op. cit., Chapter IV.

9   Pevsner, N., *The Englishness of English Art*, London: Architectural Press, 1956, p. 168.

10   Turner, T., *Landscape Planning and Environmental Impact Design*, London: Spon, 1998, p. 92.

11   Loudon, J. C. (ed.), *The Landscape Gardening and Landscape Architecture of the Late H. Repton Esq*, London, 1840, p, 536.

12   Turner, T., 'Loudon's stylistic development', *Journal of Garden History*, Vol. 2, No. 2, 1982, pp. 175–88.

13   Kemp, E., *How to Lay Out a Small Garden*, London: Bradbury Evans, 1864, p. 117.

14   Newton, N. T., *Design on the Land: The development of landscape architecture*, Harvard: Belknap Press, 1971, p. 337.

15   Loudon, J. C., op. cit., p. 331 ff.

16   Picturesque improvement is the subject of the second volume of J. C. Loudon's *Country Residences*, 1806.

17   Loudon, J. C., *The Suburban Gardener and Villa Gardener*, London, 1838, p. 137.

18   ——, *Gardener's Magazine*, Vol. XVI, 1840, p. 622.

19   Hirschfeld, C. C. L., *Theory of Garden Art*, (abridged and edited by Linda B. Parshall), Penn Studies in Landscape Architecture Philadelphia: University of Pennsylvania Press, 2001).

20   Elliot, B., *Victorian Gardens*, London: Batsford, 1986, p. 162.

21   My copy of the book contains a letter, dated 28 May 1828, which includes the following: 'Mr Laing Meason requests Lord Granville will do him the honour of accepting a copy of a work which he has printed privately, and given only a hundred for sale to a bookseller, "On the Landscape Architecture of the great painters of Italy". Had Mr Meason had the opportunity of visiting Italy, and of comparing the remains of ancient country residences with the specimens to be found in the Italian pictures, the work might have been made more interesting, and more decisive on the artistry of those buildings.'

22   Downing. A. J., *A Treatise on the Theory and Practice of Landscape Gardening Adapted to North America*, New York: Putnam, 1850.

23   Fabos, J. G. and Ahern, J. *Greenways: the beginning of an international movement*, Amsterdam: Elsevier, 1996.

24   Elliott, B., *Victorian Gardens*, London: B. T. Batsford, 1986, p. 118.

25   Hellyer, A., *The Shell Guide to Gardens*, London: Heinemann, 1977, p. 169.

26   Loudon, J. C., Gardener's Magazine, 1831, Vol VII, p. 390.

27   Kluckert, E., *European Garden Design*, Cologne: Konemann, 2000, p. 436.

28   Elliott, B., op. cit., p. 106.

29   Hojer, G., and Schmid, E. D., *Linderhof Palace, München*, Bayerische Vertwaltung Der Staatlichen Schlosser, 1999.

30   Chadwick, G. F., *The Park and the Town*, Architectural Press, 1966. p. 92.

31   Hobhouse, P. and Taylor, P., *The Gardens of Europe*, George Philip Ltd, 1990, p. 268.

32   Newton, N. T., op. cit., p. 326.

33   Shepherd, P., *Modern Gardens*, London: Architectural Press, 1953, p. 120.

34   Hough, M., *City Form and Natural Process*, London: Routledge, 1995, p. 279.

35   Lancaster, M., *The New European Landscape*, London: Butterworth Architecture, 1994, p. 93.

Chapter 10

Abstract and post-abstract gardens 1900–2000

History and philosophy

Visually, it is easy to identify the art, architecture and gardens of the twentieth century. But the adjective 'modern', used to describe this work, has an inherently limited shelf-life[1] and in my view the year 2000 was the expiry date. A replacement is due and in this chapter 'abstract' will be tried as an alternative. It pinpoints a key feature of twentieth-century gardens: the abstraction of universal principles from the everyday world. Artists and designers, admiring the way scientists abstracted the laws of nature and applied them as technology, sought an analogous design procedure. Painting, architecture, gardens, furniture and fashion design thus became characterised by analytically clean lines, freedom from ornament, simple colours and geometrical elegance.

The central phase of high modernism was followed by a period of diversity which is usually described as postmodern – using a term which cannot long outlive its parent. 'Post-abstract' is more explanatory, indicating a retreat from the clinical purity of abstraction and a return to the realm of stories, symbols and meanings. The designers of Hatshepsut's temple, Pompeii, the gardens of the Middle Ages, the Villa Lante, Versailles and Stowe used design to speak of other things: allegory was their preoccupation. The word derives from *allos* (other), and *-agoria* (speaking). Children, the Victorians said, should be seen and not heard. But why should gardens be silent? For two reasons: first, the deliberate rejection of symbols, allegory and literary themes in high modern design; second, the use of pesticides, as described in Rachel Carson's *Silent Spring*.[2]

The previous chapter began with Gothein's remark that the nineteenth century 'must complete its tale of sins before the foundations are shattered'. During the first half of the twentieth century the 'sin' of most concern to avant-garde designers was the very foundation of Victorian gardens: eclecticism. In 1938 Christopher Tunnard charged that:

10.1 Abstract garden design was characterised by clean lines and freedom from ornament: German Pavilion, Barcelona, by Mies van der Rohe

10.2 Post-abstract garden design saw a return to representation: Swarovski Crystal World, Austria (above) and *Head* by Sue and Peter Hill at Heligan, England

The unfortunate duality of temperament with which the Victorian garden was endowed was not an aid to its establishment as an artistic entity . . . And what a glorious, gaudy blotch it made . . . A cedar of Lebanon, a clump of plumous pampas grass and some pieces of rockwork were used to make a miniature landscape on the front lawn with a crescent moon and stars carved out of the turf for bedding at the back. The gross indecency of either act would not have been admitted then.[3]

Tunnard believed that selecting plants and styles from everywhere had made gardens spotty, haphazard and amateurish. Garden ornaments, often inferior copies, were collected like trinkets on a mantelshelf. Owners had boasted about the brightness of their plants and the sizes of their forced pineapples. Modernist critics and designers raised their hammers, dipped their pens, sharpened their pencils and screamed for reform. Order, they said, must be abstracted from chaos. Four approaches to abstraction are outlined below.

The first approach was nationalism (see Chapter 9). Reformists looked to heroic periods in their nations' histories and aimed to abstract the stylistic essence of each period. The problem was that every 'national' style had roots elsewhere. In their days of glory, Greece had drawn from West Asia, Italy from Greece, France from Italy and Spain from Italy and France. England, Germany and America drew from everywhere. Nationalism thus gave way to internationalism.

The second approach was to abstract design methods from the past – albeit a past that was viewed through rose-tinted spectacles. Designers hoped that an artistic approach wedded to honest, traditional craftsmanship would improve design standards. Arts and Crafts gardens were often excellent. One has to wonder how the principles behind them ever came to be neglected and why they still are.

The third approach was to abstract compositional principles from historic gardens. Edith Wharton explained the approach in 1904:

The cult of the Italian garden has spread from England to America, and there is a general feeling that, by placing a marble bench here and a sun-dial there, Italian 'effects' may be achieved . . . The first lesson is that, if they are to be a real inspiration, they must be copied, not in the letter but in the spirit. That is, a marble sarcophagus and a dozen twisted columns will not make an Italian garden; but a piece of ground laid out and planted on the principles of the old garden-craft will be, not indeed an Italian garden in the literal sense, but, what is far better, a garden as well adapted to its surroundings as were the models which inspired it. This is the secret to be learned from the villas of Italy.[4]

Geoffrey Jellicoe agreed that 'the bases of abstract design, running through history like a silver thread, are independent of race and age'.[5]

10.3 Victorian gardens were criticised in the early twentieth century for their gaudiness and spottiness

10.4 (top left and right and lower left) Though conceived nationally, England's Arts and Crafts gardens looked abroad and to the principles of composition. Hidcote Manor garden, Gloucestershire, was designed by Lawrence Johnston, an American

10.5 (lower right) Ditchley Park, Oxfordshire, designed by Geoffrey Jellicoe, drew upon the compositional principles of Italian gardens, but not their iconography

The fourth approach was to abstract concepts from history and from elsewhere. In the last quarter of the twentieth century, this led to the notion of double coding, characterised as postmodern. Gardens can, for example, have a primary code legible to all observers and a historic, symbolic or literary or scientific code intelligible only to the erudite. Every visitor can see the mound, trees and water in Jencks' design for the Scottish National Gallery of Modern Art. Only the well-informed understand their relationship with the nature of the cosmos. Postmodern designers have interests in ontology, epistemology, semiology, quantum mechanics, cosmogenesis and recondite branches of knowledge.

10.6 (above) Ueda Landform, Scottish National Gallery of Modern Art, Edinburgh, by Charles Jencks

10.7 (below) Ragnar Ostberg's design for the *Stadshuset* (City Hall), Stockholm, abstracts the Swedish character, the principles of design and the principles of craftsmanship

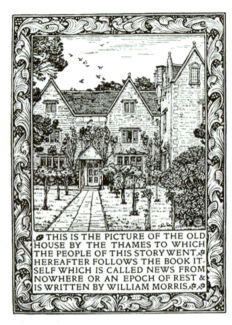

10.8 The frontispiece to William Morris' *News from nowhere or an epoch of rest* (1891) featured Kelmscott Manor and contributed to the enthusicasm for artisitc gardens made by craftsmen and craftswomen

Arts and Crafts design

Edith Wharton and Geoffrey Jellicoe both attempted Italian gardens and their attempts illustrate the difficulties involved. Wharton's garden at The Mount in Lenox, Massachusetts, despite her good intentions, showed little skill with 'the principles' of Italian gardens.[6] A harsh critic might compare it to a novel with a weak plot, poor characterisation and inelegant style. In later years Jellicoe used to chuckle that when younger 'I could do a *pretty good* classical garden'. So he could, but his Italian design for Ditchley Park lacked the excellence of its Italian precursors.

Forward-looking critics and designers argued that work of the first quality could be produced only when artists were also craftsmen. John Ruskin was one of the first to advance this view, and William Morris developed and implemented Ruskin's ideas. Morris was a craftsman, a poet, a painter and much else. He made gardens for himself and referred to them in his book, *Hopes and Fears for Art*, published in 1882.[7] Loving the 'pure' work of medieval craftsmen, Morris despised the products of nineteenth-century eclecticism. His gardens at Red House, Bexleyheath, and Kelmscott Manor (Figure 10.8), Oxfordshire, were products of these tastes. They had neat enclosures, flowers and clipped hedges. Morris was a founder of the Art Workers Guild, which young architects and other designers rushed to join. They reconsidered the art of design, the craft of making things, and the convenience of users. First cousins of the classical Vitruvian virtues of *venustas, firmitas* and *utilitas* (see p. 4), these principles reshaped design theory and produced what became known as the Arts and Crafts style. It did not originate in gardens but it had a profound influence on them, re-shaping garden art. Marie-Luise Gothein, in 1914, felt able to look to the future with a new confidence: 'All garden lovers and artists may rejoice in the consciousness that in our own time a new development has come about, and one that is full of promise.'[8]

In England, the leading practitioners of Arts and Crafts gardens were Gertrude Jekyll, Edwin Lutyens, Reginald Blomfield and Thomas Mawson. The men were members of the Art Workers Guild, from which Jekyll was excluded on account of her sex. They produced some of the best and most popular gardens which have ever been made in England: most so popular that one can visit them only by special arrangement. Excellent examples of the style can, however, be seen at Sissinghurst and Hidcote.

Jekyll was the most successful garden designer in the group. She practised many arts and crafts herself, and had excellent judgement as to what types of place it is good to have in gardens. On joint projects with Lutyens, I believe she was responsible for the design and he worked up the details of the hard landscape following her outline plan – although her 'plan' was a concept rather than a drawing on paper.

The Arts and Crafts approach was particularly suited to small gardens designed, built and maintained by their owners. Even large gardens, like Sissinghurst were treated as compartments.

In France garden designers sensed that the flow of private commissions for great estates was drying up and hoped that new work would come from the public sector. Duchêne wrote that:

10.9 (top left) Red House, Bexleyheath, outside London, was William Morris' first garden design project

10.10 (top right) Axel Munthe, a Swedish author, made a very popular Italian Arts and Crafts garden on Capri, making extensive use of collected antiquities

10.11 (left) Harold Peto, the architect son of a builder, used fragments collected in Italy to make his own garden at Iford Manor, Sussex

Looking at the art of gardens from the social angle, we will create a new formula which will give birth to an art of great power put in the service of the community. Here luxury will cease to have an end in itself . . . it must satisfy the aesthetic aspirations of the masses.[9]

He was right to the extent that public commissions were to provide a source of new work and there was wide agreement that professional designers should satisfy 'the

10.12 An Arts and Crafts garden in London, designed by Margaret Turner (left)

10.13 Sissinghurst, Kent, made by Vita Sackville-West and Harold Nicolson, is perhaps the most famous garden of the twentieth century. It demonstrates the popularity of the Arts and Crafts approach and the use of compartments

aesthetic aspirations of the masses'. Most designers did not, however, see Duchêne's approach, an Arts and Crafts interpretation of the French baroque, as being an appropriate style for the social circumstances of a new age. In most countries, they adopted the name 'landscape architecture' for public projects.

In Germany, a revolt against garden eclecticism was led by the architectural profession. Hermann Muthesius delivered a series of lectures in 1904 in which 'he attacked landscape gardening on similar and often identical grounds with Blomfield, finding it still the leading fashion in Germany'.[10] Gothein emphasises that Muthesius' aim was not to adopt a Renaissance approach to geometry and ornament, as Blomfield and Peto had done. He wished to make outdoor living rooms in which 'the garden, the seats, the borders of hedge or pergola, the paths – all should show some likeness to the inside arrangements of a house'. She sees this as more akin to Greek and Roman courtyard gardens than to their Renaissance successors. Paul Schultze-Naumburg's book *Gärten* (*Gardens*),[11] showed how to design garden rooms in conformity with the principles of aesthetic art.

In America, Beatrix Farrand (Edith Wharton's niece) became a leading practitioner of the Arts and Crafts style in garden design. She admired Jekyll and purchased her planting plans, sold to raise funds for Britain's war effort. Farrand was a founder member of the American Society of Landscape Architects, and her approach was more professional than Jekyll's. Whereas Jekyll only drew planting plans, Farrand drew all the plans and elevations for building work as well as planting work. This requires a higher level of technical and professional skill (but may be accompanied by less design judgement or imagination).

In many parts of Europe, admiration for natural forms and flowing lines led to the development of a new style. It was known as art nouveau in England, *Jugendstil* in Germany and *Style Liberty* in France. In Catalonia, which, in Gaudí's design for the Parque Güell, has the only major outdoor design in the style, it was known as *Modernista*. Elsewhere, the word 'modern' was used for the abstract art and architecture of the twentieth century.

Modern design

Modern architecture had become a recognised phenomenon by 1930. But modern gardens, even today, are not so easy to interpret. Did they really exist? If so, when and where did they originate? Who were the practitioners? Were modern gardens as bare as Bauhaus architecture? Are they still being made? Despite writing a book entitled *Modern Gardens* in 1953, Peter Shepheard believed that it was almost impossible for modern architecture to have a stable companion, because such modern materials as glass, steel and concrete were inherently unsuited to garden design.[12] The otherwise reliable American historian, Norman T. Newton, in *Design on the Land*[13] (1971) had a blind spot concerning modern gardens. Ignoring Fletcher Steele, a fellow Harvard man and America's pioneer modernist, Newton contented himself with the remark that Church, Eckbo, Royston and Halprin, were 'inventive designers' – and failed to say what they invented.

10.14 (above) Parc Güell, Barcelona, Spain, is the only major example of Art Nouveau garden design

10.15 (below) Dumbarton Oaks, Washington, DC, designed by Beatrix Farrand, is an excellent American example of the Arts and Crafts style

10.16 The front cover of *De Stijl* magazine reads: 'The Style: Magazine for the modern visual arts Editor Theo van Doesburg with assistance from well-known national and international artists', Issue 10, 1917

10.17 The cover of *De Stijl* could – and deserves to – be used as a garden plan

Jane Brown introduced the subject as follows in her book, *The Modern Garden*, published in 2000:

> The modern garden achieved stature in America, so much so that it tended to become an interpretation of the modern landscape, and it was re-exported to a rather mystified Europe in the 1950s. Within a decade it was dead, mainly through misunderstanding, and a smothering in historical revivals and rampantly eclectic postmodernism.[14]

Nevertheless, her book is replete with examples of modern gardens made after 1960 and their inclusion is surely correct. Modern art in general and abstract art in particular continue to have a deep influence on gardens, which is best understood by looking beyond garden walls.

The evolution of modernist ideas was traced by Pevsner. He found the impetus to have come from William Morris, through the Arts and Crafts ideas outlined above.[15] They led to the principle that form should follow function. As framed by the American architect Louis Sullivan, this became the mantra of modernist design. Sullivan's pupil, Frank Lloyd Wright, believed design should also draw on a scientific and aesthetic appreciation of nature, which he called 'organic'. The quotations below reveal his sensitivity to places, functions and organic form:

> I chose Taliesin for a name – it means 'shining brow', and this place now called Taliesin is built like a brow on the edge of the hill – not on top of the hill – because I believe you should never build on top of anything directly. If you build on top of the hill, you lose the hill.[16]

> We see an airplane clean and light-winged – the lines expressing power and purpose; we see the ocean liner, streamlined, clean and swift – expressing power and purpose . . . Why are not buildings, too, indicative of their special purpose? The forms of things that that are perfectly adapted to their function, we now observe, seem to have a superior beauty of their own. We like to look at them. Then, as it begins to dawn on us that form follows function – why not so in architecture especially? . . . Buildings are made of materials too. Materials have a life of their own that may enter into the building to give it more life. Here certain principles show countenance. It is the countenance of organic simplicity.[17]

Had anyone asked him, Frank Lloyd Wright might have invented the modern garden in a morning: he was an astonishingly inventive designer. Most of his work was residential and he had an instinctive sense for relationships between indoor and outdoor space. At the Robie house (1908–1909), the abstract geometry of the building was projected into the garden plan. At Falling Water (1936–1937), a relationship between architecture and landscape is the leading idea: the house grows out of the land. But the America which had spurned Sullivan was not ready for Wright. Instead, it chose a Beaux Arts Renaissance revival. Wright therefore had little influence on American architecture in the first half of the twentieth century and even less influence on its gardens. He was, however, admired in Europe, which became the trial ground for modernist design.

The *de Stijl* movement in Holland, was excited by Wright's work and the cover of *De Stijl* magazine could be mistaken for – or used as – a garden plan. The *Exposition des Arts Décoratives Modernes* (which became known as the 'Art Deco Exposition'), held in Paris in 1925, showed work by Tony Garnier, Gabriel Guevrekian and André Vera. Guevrekian exhibited a Garden of Water and Light that inspired Charles de Noailles to commission a triangular, abstract garden for his villa at Hyères in the South of France. Le Corbusier was also a creative influence on modern gardens. A sculptor at heart, he cared about the relationship of buildings to sites and had that love of scenery one would expect in a child of the Swiss Alps. The Villa Savoie (1928–1931) has a garden terrace on the roof. A similar principle was used for the *Unité d'Habitation* (1946) in Marseilles, where the roof terrace is as much a garden as a modern sculpture. Abstract designers looked back to the classical principles of composition, often using primary colours and the primary geometrical forms.

Another strand of influence on modernism came from Germany. The Bauhaus was founded in Weimar 1919 by combining the Art Academy with the Arts and Crafts School of design. Under its first director, Walter Gropius, the school aimed to integrate art, economics and engineering into a unified design process. 'Let us', Gropius wrote, 'create a new guild of craftsmen, without the class distinctions which raise an arrogant barrier between craftsmen and artist. Together, let us conceive and create the new building of the future, which will embrace architecture "and" sculpture "and"

10.18 The Bauhaus and the Meisterhauser in Dessau influenced the design of space around buildings: blocks of grass, paving and planting were treated as components in an abstract composition

10.19 The House of World Cultures in Berlin (1957) was designed by Hugh Stubbins, Walter Gropius's assistant in Harvard. The Butterfly sculpture is by Henry Moore

10.20 Guevrekian designed one of the earliest Abstract modern gardens for a villa at Hyères in the south of France

painting in one unity and which will one day rise toward heaven from the hands of a million workers, like the crystal symbol of a new faith.' The Bauhaus moved to Dessau in 1924 and to America in 1933. Gardens were not an interest of the school but the emphasis on design unity thrust Bauhaus principles into the landscape. Tall blocks were composed with rectangles of grass to create unitary abstract compositions.

In England, clients were slow to become interested in modern gardens, probably because of their nostalgia for the Imperial Age then passing. Design schools, more open to the future, looked across the Atlantic and the Channel for inspiration. London's Architectural Association became a test bed for new ideas. Geoffrey Jellicoe, a student there in the 1920s, designed a strikingly modern garden in 1933 (see p. 258). Christopher Tunnard, also associated with the AA, wrote a book, *Gardens in the Modern Landscape* which, in the event, had more influence in America than England.[18] He looked to Japan, and sought to understand the compositional principles used in Japanese gardens, in a way that compares with Jellicoe's interest in Italy.

Fletcher Steele was the most important American designer to take an early interest in modern gardens. During the 1920s his practice was sufficiently profitable to fund his regular European tours. These included a visit to the Art Deco Exposition in Paris in 1925. He met Guevrekian and visited the garden at Hyères. Steele admired Le Corbusier for his 'strikingly original ideas' and 'odd patterns of concrete walks' but criticised him for becoming 'banal'. Steele had good design judgement but his work was more Art Deco than abstract. Writing in *Landscape Architecture* (October 1930) Steele gave his opinion that 'What a modernistic garden may be is everybody's guess. The reason is that it does not yet exist as a type'.[19]

'The International Style: Architecture since 1922', an exhibition organised by Henry-Russell Hitchcock and Philip Johnson and held in New York in 1932, showed the work of Walter Gropius, Mies van der Rohe and Le Corbusier. In 1937, the Dean of the Graduate School of Design at Harvard invited Gropius, a refugee from Hitler's Germany, to America. Though not personally interested in the design of outdoor

space, Gropius influenced garden designers through his advocacy of Bauhaus principles. Garrett Eckbo, James Rose and Dan Kiley were in the same Harvard class. They read *Gardens in the Modern Landscape* and two of the youngsters went to work for Thomas Church on the West Coast. Kiley remained on the East Coast and developed a practice with famous modern movement architects: Eero Saarinen, Kevin Roche and John Dinkeloo.

Design slogans from the period provide a useful summary of International style principles. Designers were urged to:

- develop form by following function
- express structure
- be true to materials
- use modern materials for modern construction
- avoid stories and sentimentality
- remember that the styles are dead
- avoid decoration, because less is more.

In parks and gardens, these principles had the following consequences: nationalistic styles, stories and allegories were spurned; functional spaces for outdoor living were created; native plants were used to create natural habitats and wild-flower meadows; a new geometry inspired by abstract art was employed. Often, the paving was rectilinear and the planting areas curvilinear. Concrete, glass and steel made an appearance. Apart from private and domestic gardens, the Amsterdam Bos was the first major example of how these principles could be used to design space on a scale comparable to that of the great estates which are the main subject of this book. (See Abstract style, page 278)

The Brazilian designer Roberto Burle Marx is perhaps the most representative designer of modernist gardens. Born in 1909, his father (Marx) was German-Jewish and his mother (Burle) was French-Brazilian. The son developed a love for the native

10.21 The meadows at Great Dixter (left) and Iford Manor (right), both in Sussex, were a twentieth-century approach to the imitation of nature. The long grass represents wild nature and the semi-circles represent ideal nature

10.22 Burle Marx was a cubist painter and garden designer

flora of Brazil. He studied fine art in Berlin and on returning home made friends with a group of Brazilian architects, all influenced by Corbusier: Oscar Niemeyer, Alfonso Reidy and Locio Costa. Burle Marx's cubist paintings translated easily into garden designs for flat surfaces, especially near buildings. His use of native plants in gardens complies with modernist principles: it is functional; it represents truth to materials; it relates to the structure of natural plant communities. Burle Marx's work with natural landform was less happy. As Marc Treib notes 'More often that not, he appears to blanket the contours in forms derived from his own flat artworks rather than from the lay of the land. Rarely is there any perceivable attempt to, say, derive a shape from the profile of the topography.'[20]

In the 1940s, the progress of European garden design was interrupted by war, except in neutral Sweden. The country's relatively short summers had not favoured the development of a strong a garden design profession but architects, imbued with Bauhaus principles, took a serious interest in outdoor design. The projects which became best known outside Sweden were Stockholm's park system and the Woodland Cemetery designed by Gunnar Asplund. Finland and Denmark adopted a similar approach, which came to be known by the catch-all description 'Scandinavian'.

Germany emerged from the Second World War with a strong desire to look forward, not back. West Germany became the richest country in Europe and East Germany the richest part of the Soviet Empire. Both Germanys adopted the modernist approach that Hitler had discouraged.

America became the world's richest country in the 1950s and the abstract approach to garden and landscape design was widely adopted. Dan Kiley was born in Boston in 1912 and studied landscape architecture at Harvard. In 1953 he worked with Saarinen on the Miller garden in Columbus, Indiana. Inspired by Mies van der Rohe's German Pavilion in Barcelona, and the *de Stijl* movement, it had a grid plan and full integration of indoor with outdoor space. There was also a picturesque transition from garden to meadow to wood. The design was widely acclaimed and became a key American example of the abstract style, at once splendidly modern and rooted in the landscape tradition. Kiley's subsequent projects include the United States Air Force Academy, the Oakland Museum, Independence Mall in Philadelphia, the Dallas Museum of Art, and Fountain Place in Texas. Jane Brown rightly described Kiley as 'the supreme master of the modern garden'.[21]

Peter Walker belongs to a later generation than Kiley. The title of his book, *Minimalist Gardens*,[22] implies respect for those minimalist painters who remained true to the principles of abstract art, basing their work on the primary geometrical forms. The best of Walker's design work has this quality.

There were good and bad aspects to the International style as applied to garden design. One can understand why the nationalism over which nations fought lost its appeal to those who, like Gothein, had seen friends and family die in the First World War. But the modernist thirst for internationalism resulted in the loss of local identity now associated with the word globalisation. After the Second World War, Hitler's

10.23 (top left) The lakeside park, Stockholm, by Holger Blom

10.24 (top left and centre left) The woodland cemetery, Stockholm, by Gunnar Asplund

10.25 (centre right and bottom left) The Louisiana Art Gallery, Humlebaek, Denmark, used the principles of abstract design to integrate architecture and landscape

10.26 (right) Marx-Engels Platz in the former East Berlin. The figures, now objects of curiosity, were ideological patrons of functionalist design. The Palace of the Republic is in the background

10.26 (centre left and right) The Munich Olympia Park is perhaps the best example of curvilinear functionalism, integrating architecture and landscape in a manner bearing comparison with Ancient Greek sanctuaries

10.28 (right) Peter Walker's design for the Sony Centre Plaza in Berlin, demonstrates his belief in the principles of abstract composition using minimalist shapes

10.29 (far right) A sustainable 'form follows function' approach to water management is the central aspect of Herbert Dreisitl's design for the for the Marlene Dietrich Plaza in Berlin

fondness for vernacular design and native plant species was seen as dangerously close to racism, leading to a continued distrust of localism in design. Postmodern design philosophy therefore appeared to offer the desirable solution of keeping what was good about internationalism while bringing back localism and some of the other good things which had been jettisoned.

Post-abstract design

The closing decades of the twentieth century saw many artists turn away from abstraction. Poets and painters renewed their interest in figurative themes; musicians recovered an interest in melody; architects resumed their flirtation with the classical orders; garden designers drew inspiration from meanings, iconography and allusion; wild animals and plants returned to garden design.[23] Since all these developments came after the vacant period of abstract modernism, it makes sense to classify them as post-abstract or postmodern. Modernists believed in purity, simplicity and abstraction from context; postmodernists believed in complexity, pluralism, conceptualism, layering and recontextualisation.

Sir Geoffrey Jellicoe's career highlights the relationship between abstract and post-abstract design. He began his book *Italian Gardens* with the remark that 'Pandora never loosed a livelier spirit than the one for ever parting Fancy from Design' and stated that the best gardens were made when 'Fancy and Design roam undivided'.[24] His 1933 design for Ditchley Park was allegory-free but his design for the Caveman Restaurant, in the same year, combined an allegorical theme with a modernist composition in white concrete. Looking up through the glass roof and fish pond, visitors to the restaurant were challenged to speculate on man's evolution from the miasmal mire. In 1956 Jellicoe designed a magical roof garden for a department store in Guildford. Again, the composition appeared abstract, but the design had meaning: the circular stepping stones and plant pots that orbited the rooftop pool were inspired by the launch of the first Russian satellite in that year.

10.30 Jellicoe saw the design for the Kennedy Memorial in Runnymede, Surrey, as his first allegorical project. The granite setts are an allegory for 'a multitude of pilgrims on their way upwards'

10.31 The Time Garden at the London home of Charles Jencks: a 'four-square window on the world'

In 1964 Jellicoe designed a memorial garden for President Kennedy. There was a classical aspect to the Kennedy story – of a bronzed young hero, slain in his prime. As this was before the subsequent revelations about Kennedy, Jellicoe was also reminded of *The Pilgrim's Progress* by Bunyan and of Bellini's *Allegory of the Progress of the Soul*. These works provided the theme for an exercise in allegory. Granite setts ascend the hill, an allegory for 'a multitude of pilgrims on their way upwards'. The difficulty of the journey is a preparation for the tranquillity of the sculptured stone memorial. The lettering reads as texture, as though 'the stone itself were speaking'.[25]

The Sutton Place project of 1980 was an opportunity to develop a Bunyan-Bellini allegory of Creation, Life and Aspiration. Creation was represented by the lake. Life was represented by the gardens, which, as in the landscape style, adjoin the house. Aspiration was represented by the Nicholson Wall. When asked about the meaning of the Wall, Ben Nicholson replied, 'How should *I* know?'[26] He asked because he was an abstract artist. Jellicoe, who was not, began to take an interest in Jung's theory of symbols as representations of the collective unconscious.

Charles Jencks, author of *The Language of Postmodern Architecture*,[27] borrowed the term 'postmodern' from literary criticism and used it with brilliance in architectural criticism. He then designed three postmodern gardens. The first was a Time Garden for his London home.[28] It is divided into four quadrants, representing the four seasons, and making play with a four-square window-on-the-world motif. Both house and garden have explicit iconographic programmes. Each detail contributes to the symbolic meaning of the whole. Belief, not eclecticism, guided their composition. After writing *The Architecture of the Jumping Universe*,[29] Jencks designed two gardens which draw upon a scientific understanding of nature: for his house in Dumfriesshire and for the Scottish National Gallery of Modern Art in Edinburgh. These projects can be seen as a return of garden design theory to its ancient theme: the imitation of nature, with nature used to mean the laws which govern the universe. Having lost its way in the 1790s, garden design theory returned to a historic path in the 1990s.

Speaking about his design for the Gallery of Modern Art in Edinburgh, Jencks explained:

I am trying to create a new language of landscape. If you look at the way nature organises itself, it has inherent principles of movement. I wanted to design something that reflected these natural forces but heightened them. The shapes have been partly inspired by two so-called 'strange attractors', one of them called the Ueda Attractor, named after the Japanese scientist that discovered it. These 'attractors' (weather systems, for example) create a series of self-similar curves that overlap but never repeat, and are attracted to a certain point or 'basin'. I think the landform will create a gateway to the area and identify the gallery from the road as a special place – the locus of contemporary art in Scotland.[30]

Jencks' design was inspired by patterns of nature, from meteorological effects to chaos theory. 'I am trying to create a new language of landscape,' he stated. 'If you look at the way nature organises itself, it has inherent principles of movement. I wanted to design something which reflected these natural forces but heightened them.'[31]

One of the most intriguing postmodern gardens in Britain lies about 20 km south of Edinburgh. It is the work of 'Scotland's leading concrete poet', Ian Hamilton Finlay. Concrete poetry is a genre that uses graphic effects to enhance the meaning of a poem. Originally, the effects were typographical, carrying echoes of the pattern poems of the Babylonians, Islamic calligraphy and the quotations which eighteenth-century landscape designers inscribed on temples and urns. A modern revival of the idea began with the work of a Bolivian-born Swiss poet, Eugen Gomringer, in 1951. A 1970 anthology of *Concrete Poetry* contained a quotation from Finlay:

> My point about poems in glass, actual concrete, stone or whatever is – simply – that new means of constructing a poem aesthetically, ought to lead to consideration of new materials. If these poems are for 'contemplating', let them be sited where they can be contemplated.[32]

From concrete poetry, it was a natural progression to think of gardens as places of where words could be inscribed on stones, sculptures, posts and other objects. Concrete poetry works as code, leading the reader from surface structures to deep structures.

Peter Latz's design for Duisburg-Nord Landschaftspark represents another approach to meaning in outdoor design. Turning its back on mythological and poetic

10.32 Little Sparta, the garden of Ian Hamilton Finlay, near Edinburgh, has a postmodern garden, rich in allusion

10.33 Hundertwasser's approach is as much postmodern as anti-modern

10.34 Duisburg-Nord seeks meaning in the site's industrial history

allusion, it refers instead to the site's industrial history: chemicals, steel, fire, blood and toil produced the site's character. A similar approach was taken at Sudgelande Nature Park in Berlin. These projects look forward to a more sustainable future and back, nostalgically, to the pre-post-industrial age. They are postmodern and anti-modern. Friedensreich Hundertwasser's radical integration of gardens with architecture is overtly anti-modern.

The Jewish Museum in Berlin could serve as the mausoleum of abstract modernism, a place to wail forever against functionalism, master planning and racial purity. The design abjures cubism, truth to materials, expression of structure, curtain walls, doors, windows and every aspect of functional modernism. Whether or not the architect, Daniel Libeskind, had them in mind, this project clearly has a relationship with the use of allegory at the Kennedy Memorial by Jellicoe, and the Vietnam War Memorial in Washington D.C. by Maya Lin.

It is pleasing that the design of memorials allows this book to finish by returning to the subject with which it began: the design of outdoor space for memorials which explain the past and look to the future. The Jewish Museum reminds us, in George Santayana's words, that 'Those who cannot remember the past are condemned to repeat it'.[33] Looking back is the necessary prelude to moving forwards. A garden 'is, or ought to be, cultivated'.

10.35 (right) Sudgelande Nature Park, Berlin, finds post-industrial meaning in pre-industrial fragments

10.36 (below) The Jewish Museum, Berlin, was deliberately postmodern and anti-modern

10.37 Arts and Crafts style

Styles and examples

Arts and Crafts style

Use: Using one's hands came to be seen as a physically and spiritually rewarding activity. This gave wealthy owners a significant involvement in the maintenance of their own gardens – for the first time in European history. The poor must always have worked their own land and the rich sometimes had a dilettante involvement. But the hard physical work had always been done by gardeners. Arts and Crafts admiration for the honesty of manual work led to a marriage of gardens with gardening.

Form: Led by Ruskin and Morris, designers sought a return to the principles of art and to the craft skills on which, it was held, true style must rest. Arts and Crafts gardens generally have a clear demarcation between an enclosed area, with geometrical beds, and a naturalistic 'wild garden'. Refined discernment was exercised in the choice of good plants, fine building materials and craft-based construction.

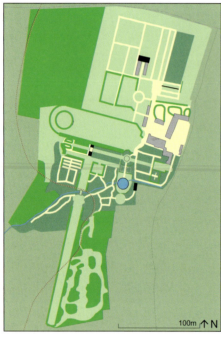

Hidcote 1905

Hidcote was made by an American owner-designer after 1905. Lawrence Johnston was a keen plantsman with a strong sense of artistic composition. He was reticent about his stylistic influences but his work sings of the Arts and Crafts movement. Yew, holly and beech hedges are used to define a series of garden rooms. A stream crosses the garden and one room is occupied only by a circular pool, perhaps the most beautiful bathing pool in England. Other garden rooms derive their character from the planting. The standard of craftsmanship is exceptional and the number of plants which have the varietal name 'Hidcote' point to Johnston's expertise with plants.

> It appeals alike to the advanced gardener in search of rare or interesting plants, and on the aesthetic side to the mere lover of beauty, content to wander down broad grass walks flanked with colour, turning continually aside as the glimpse of little separate gardens lures him.[34]

Stockholm Stadshuset (City Hall) 1911

The City Hall, on the north shore of Riddarfjarden, exemplifies a Swedish Arts and Crafts approach, known as the 'national romantic style'. Both the Hall and its south-facing garden were designed by Ragnar Ostberg. They are well proportioned and beautifully detailed. The garden has a central lawn framed by a grid of stone paths with grass-filled joints. Water steps fall south and east into the lake, as though it were a vast lily-pond. The statues which flank the southward steps, by Carl Eldh, are of a man and a woman, dancing above the waters in a celebration of life. A small parterre and pleached limes close the space to the west, with the lake beyond.

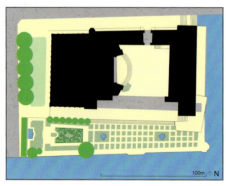

10.38 (upper) Hidcote Manor garden, Gloucestershire

10.39 (lower) *Stadshuset* (City Hall), Stockholm

The waters of Lake Mälar surround the Garden on three sides, washing, on the west, against the Wallenberg Wall. This wall . . . surrounds a parterre which is embellished with fountains, greenery, ponds and sculptures. This sequestered spot enables the general public to enjoy in peace the beauties of the waterside, and has attractions for the little folks.[35]

Sissinghurst 1930

Sissinghurst was made around the remains of a fortified manor dating from the sixteenth century, a period admired by the Arts and Crafts movement. The garden was designed by its owners, who knew Jekyll and Lutyens. Harold Nicolson, a diplomat and author, laid down the main lines of the plan in the 1930s. Vita Sackville-West, a poet, a garden writer and Harold's wife, took responsibility for the planting. She worked as an 'artist-gardener'. Her planting design was brilliant and, though the garden is well maintained, those who knew it in the 1950s believe she achieved a quality which has not been equalled since her death. The historical importance of Sissinghurst comes from its role in transmitting the Arts and Crafts design philosophy to a host of visitors.

Sissinghurst seems to stand out for one particular quality; shades of its design and all its planting ideas might be found elsewhere, but where else was such a comforting, intimate garden? Even in this company of the great and good, Sissinghurst shone out for its quality of love.[36]

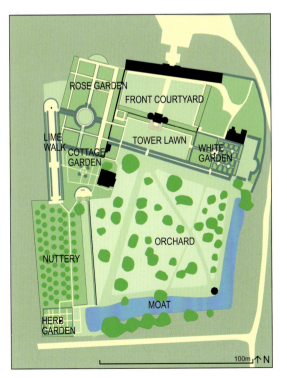

10.40 Sissinghurst Castle garden, Kent

10.41
Abstract
style

Abstract style

Use: The abstract style of garden design, like the modern movement in architecture, grew by degrees out of the Arts and Crafts Movement. Corbusier said that a house should be a machine for living. Gardens were designed as space for outdoor living and exercise grounds for machines: mowers, pumps, cultivators, sprays and other gadgetry. This enabled owners to undertake as much of the maintenance work as they pleased, even in large gardens.

Form: Twentieth-century designs were inspired by the startling shapes and patterns of abstract art. Mondrian, Nicholson and the rectilinear geometry of the *de Stijl* movement, influenced |the design of paving and walls; the curvilinear geometry of landform and planting has been influenced by Moore, Miro, Brancusi and Arp. New materials appeared in gardens: concrete, steel and glass. There was often a transition from rectilinear to curvilinear.

Mies van der Rohe Pavilion 1929

Mies van der Rohe's German Pavilion for the 1929 Barcelona Exhibition 'became the true archetype of modernist spatial composition'.[37] The building and garden were designed for the Barcelona International Exposition of 1929, dismantled after the show and rebuilt in 1983, on the same site and using the same materials. They are a prime example of how the principles of abstract, cubist design can be applied to the integration of outdoor and indoor space. The materials are sheet glass, polished steel, marble, travertine and onyx. Partly because of stone's wonderful colour and texture, partly because of the beautiful composition and partly because of the water and vegetation, the pavilion is vastly more appealing than most modernist-brutalist concrete structures which use related principles.

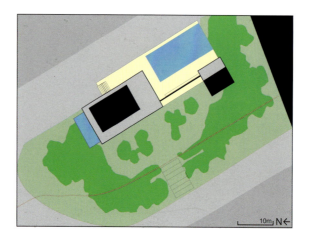

10.42 The German Pavilion, Barcelona

The German Pavilion – the Palace of Reflections – is the most authentic expression of Cubism, the chief manifestation of that dead, quartered aesthetic which Picasso invented one gloomy day.[38]

Miller Garden 1957

Dan Kiley traced the genesis of his design to the European gardens he had seen in 1945 'From that point onward, I experimented with the translation of various classic elements into a modern spatial sensibility'.[39] The result is widely regarded as a classic: structures, planting, paving and pool are treated as compositional elements in a neoplastic composition.

The Miller garden, Kiley's masterpiece, was designed for a client rare in modern times, a real patron, Irwin Miller . . . [It] does not shock or even amuse the eye. Rather it leads one gently from space to space through a witty and ambiguous game of discovery . . . The spaces one moves through are clearly defined yet fluid, ever expanding outward from the house to the street and the river.[40]

Louisiana 1958

Louise was the name of the owner's three wives. His nineteenth-century seaside house became a museum of painting, sculpture, graphics, architecture and landscape design. The building and its landscape are a work of modern art in their own right. Glass corridors join pavilions, creating an abstract composition with an unusually successful fusion of indoors and outdoors. Louisiana has been greatly admired since its opening in 1958 and was particularly influential in the 1960s. The original landscape designers, Ole and Edith Norgaard, were followed by Lea Norgaard and Vibeke Holscher.

10.43 (left) The Miller garden, Columbus, Indiana

10.44 (right) Louisiana, Denmark

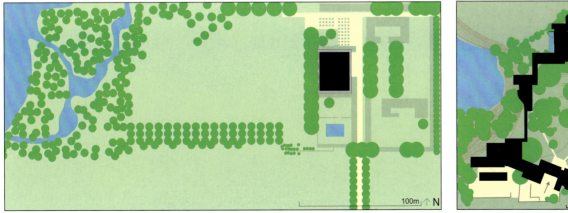

The new building is situated across the existing park where the view opens up to the sea but is connected with the old house by long twisting walkways. Sometimes these are closed in on both sides, with walls displaying works of art, sometimes one or both sides are glass from ceiling to floor. Thus a wonderful succession of glimpses of art and nature alternating has been achieved, and the landscape floats through the walkways.[41]

Munich Olympiapark 1972

Munich has a remarkable modern landscape, made for the 1972 Olympics. Previously, the site was dull and flat, surrounded with ugly buildings and strewn with heaps of rubble cleared from the 1945 bombing. It was transformed into a sinuous web of tented structures, lakes and hills. The roof flows with the land and the landform sweeps into the water. Geometrically, there were two varieties of abstract modernism: rectilinear and curvilinear. The Olympiapark is the purest example of curvilinear international modernism. Behnisch were the architects, Frei Otto designed the tented structures, Günter Grizmek was the landscape architect – and they worked together. Of all the Olympic parks built in the twentieth century, this is the only one which has a landscape quality matching that of the ancient Olympia.

It was not to be a copy of nature; rather an imitation of nature in an architectonically conceived composition combining landform, buildings, water and plants.[42]

10.45 The Olympiapark, Munich

Post-abstract

Use: Postmodern ideas encourage garden owners to deconstruct their preconceptions, allowing experimentation with new materials, new geometries, concrete poetry, hot tubs, glass rooms, non-traditional plants and the transformation of pavements into water features. Above all, it can be used to overlay uses and ideas in a multifaceted postmodern structural composition. Towards the end of the twentieth century, the style was used to win design competitions.

Form: Geometrically, postmodernism is associated with layered, fractured and deconstructive geometries. Relationships are overturned. Rectangles clash with circles and are intersected by hapazard diagonals, as in Russian constructivist art. Steel and concrete structures are painted in bright colours. Glass and other reflective surfaces help create illusions.

10.46
Post-abstract
style

Parc de la Villette 1982

Parc de la Villette, in Paris, was the first major landscape design to draw upon deconstructionist philosophy. It was the result of a competition won by Bernard Tschumi. Rejecting the old idea of a 'park', Tschumi sought to create 'the largest discontinuous building in the world'. Jacques Derrida, the philosopher, encouraged him to fix form *before* function: an anti-modernist reversal of the traditional design procedure. Tschumi laid down three geometries: of points, lines and curves. Clashes were encouraged. The points took the form of a collection of steel pavilions, inspired by Russian constructivist art and painted red. The lines were not unlike traditional French avenues. The most dramatic curved feature was the Cinematic Promenade. Alongside the Promenade are a number of themed areas. Alexandre Chemetoff's Bamboo Garden is an exotic oasis. There is a Fog Garden (by Alain Pélisier), a Dragon Garden, a Mirror Garden (by Tschumi), and a Wind and Dune Garden. The public and the professions were puzzled by the original drawings but have come to admire the result.

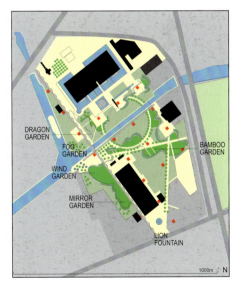

10.47 Parc de la Villette, Paris

'If this is a landscape design', one could hear the landscape designers thinking, 'then pink atoms will learn to yodel'. Now that Parc de la Villette is substantially complete, one can see that it was a landscape design, and that alternative readings of the scheme are possible ... Whether or not they appertain to the designer's intentions is, of course, strictly irrelevant in deconstructionist theory.[43]

10.48 Landschaftspark, Duisberg-Nord

Landschaftspark Duisberg-Nord 1991

The Landschaftspark in Duisberg-Nord is part of the 300 sq km Emscher Park system. It returns to an ancient principle: 'consult the genius of the place'. Since the local genius was a steel works, the policy produced, for a park design, a wholly new range of features, shapes, forms and textures. Appearing in the guise of constructivist painting, the forms result from deconstructing the industrial facility: ugly becomes beautiful; wastes become productive; weeds become habitat; contaminated water becomes pure. The design is postmodern, post-horticultural, post-machine-age – and popular.

> The aesthetic ambition calls for a revolution in one's thinking of what a park can be ... The design is based on an appreciation of the industrial inheritance: lines of old railway embankment are seen as a form of land art and will be managed as grassland. Visitors can wander through the site and from the embankments view the land around with a sense of liberation.[44]

> At Emscher Park, the idea of nature is not confused with that of landscape. For Latz, nature is usually something divorced from landscape: landscape exists as a cultural phenomenon, while nature is a self-determining force ... The Piazza (Metallica) also draws attention to two aspects of the nature of metal. The industrial infrastructure reminds the visitor of the creation, over many generations, of the solid, hardened product, a process that demands temperatures of some 1300 degrees centigrade. Metal is also present in the eroded form, deprived by time of its molten, energizing force.[45]

Jewish Museum, Berlin 1998

The design of the museum is based on a burst Star of David, abjuring right angles, doors, windows and other architectural conventions. The notice beside the Garden of Exile states (2002) 'Here architect Daniel Libeskind asks us to think about the disorientation that exile brings. The 49 columns are filled with earth in which willow oaks grow. Forty-eight of the columns contain the earth of Berlin and stand for 1948 and the formation of the state of Israel. The central and 49th pillar is filled with earth from Jerusalem and stands for Berlin itself.'

10.49 Jewish Museum, Berlin

> References to the history of Berlin's Jews are implicit in the site's design – references which can be found, for example, in the composition of the paving, or the lines on the building, in the engraved stones and in the use of gravel to emphasize the 'voids' created by the forms of the building.[46]

What next?

There is much to learn about what could happen in the gardens of the future, should designers wish to learn from the past.

From the ancient world they could relearn the twin arts of making outdoor rooms and using roof space as living space: the ground in modern towns lacks seclusion and is dominated by motor vehicles; roof space is delightful and would be more so if adorned with rush awnings and pot plants.

From the classical world, they could learn the outstanding merit of peristyle courts and of treating whole landscapes as sacred, in the sense of 'safeguarded or required by religion or reverence, or tradition, indefeasible, inviolable, sacrosanct'. To a degree, we do this in natural and national parks, but they are too often violated by tourist facilities, motor vehicles, folksy signage, litter and wardens in mock-military costume.

From the medieval world of Christianity and Islam, designers could learn to make gardens with an other-worldly perfection: sweet, quiet, calm, geometrically perfect and as carefully designed as illuminated manuscripts. The love of labour is the labour of love.

From the Renaissance, baroque and Romantic periods, designers could learn first to integrate architecture with gardens, so that these arts compliment and complement one another. Second, they could learn to weld great and small building projects into the wider landscape. Third, they could relearn the skill of coordinating the arts (building, planting, painting, music, sculpture etc.).

From the nineteenth century, designers could learn that, on occasion, it is good to be bold, brash and colourful. Gardens can be different. There is much to be learned from other climes and other countries.

From the twentieth century, designers could learn to employ the principles of abstract design – and the pure fun of overthrowing them.

Having lasted for 4,000 years, the use of nature's materials to express ideas about nature may be expected to continue. The best garden designs are produced with an awareness of the art, science, history, geography, philosophy, social habits and construction techniques of their period. Furthermore, and especially on mass housing projects, it is necessary to plan gardens before dwellings.

10.50
What next?

Notes

1   The 'modern gardens' Horace Walpole wrote of *c.* 1770 were looking dated by the time his essay was published. To us they are 'classical'.

2   Carson, R., *Silent Spring*, London: Penguin, 1965.

3   Tunnard, C., *Gardens in the Modern Landscape*, London: Architectural Press, 1938, p. 49.

4   Wharton, E., *Italian villas and their gardens*, New York: Century Co., 1904, p. 12.

5   Jellicoe, G. A. and Shepherd, J. C., *Italian Gardens of the Renaissance*, London: Ernest Benn, 1925, p. 18.

6   For more information, visit: http://www.edithwharton.org/

7   Morris, W., *Hopes and Fears for Art*, London: Ellis & White, 1882.

8   Gothein, M-L., *A History of Garden Art*, London: J. M. Dent, 1928, Vol. 2.

9   Woodbridge, K., *Princely Gardens: The origins and development of the French formal style*, London: Thames & Hudson, 1986, p. 291.

10 Gothein, M-L., op. cit., Vol. 2, p. 358.

11 Schultze-Naumburg, P., 'Kulturarbeiten Band 2', in *Garten*, Munchen, 1902.

12 Shepheard, P. F., *Modern Gardens*, London: Architectural Press, 1953.

13 Newton, N. T., *Design on the Land: The development of landscape architecture*, Harvard: Belknap Press, 1971.

14 Brown, J., *The Modern Garden*, London: Thames & Hudson, 2000, p. 8.

15 Pevsner, N., *The Sources of Modern Architecture and Design*, London: Thames & Hudson, 1968, p. 18.

16 Wright, F. L., *The Future of Architecture*, New York: Mentor, 1963, p. 21.

17 ——, op. cit., pp. 142–3.

18 Tunnard, op. cit.

19 Steele, F., in *Landscape Architecture*, October 1930.

20 Treib, M., *Modern Landscape Architecture: A critical review*, Cambridge, Mass: MIT Press, 1993, p. 53.

21 Brown, J., op. cit., p. 98.

22 Walker, P., *Minimalist Gardens*, Washington, DC and Cambridge, Mass: Watson-Guptil Publications and Hearst Books, 1997.

23 Baines, C., *How to Make a Wildlife Garden,* London: Elm Tree, 1985.

24 See discussion in Turner, T., 'Jellicoe and the subconscious', in Harvey, S. (ed.), *Geoffrey Jellicoe*, Reigate: LDT Monographs, 1998.

25 Jellicoe, G. A., *The Guelph Lectures on Landscape Design*, Guelph: University of Guelph, 1983, p. 94.

26 ——, op. cit., p. 194.

27 Jencks, C., *The Language of Post-Modern Architecture*, New York: Rizzoli, 1977.

28 ——, *Towards a Symbolic Architecture*, London: Academy Editions, 1985.

29 ——, *The Architecture of the Jumping Universe*, London: Academy Editions, 1997.

30 Scottish National Gallery of Modern Art, Press Release 26 July 2002.

31 *National Galleries of Scotland Bulletin*, July and August 2002, p. 14.

32 Solt, M. E., *Concrete Poetry: A world view*, London: Indiana University Press, 1968.

33 Santayana, G., *The Life of Reason, or, The Phases of Human Progress*, New York: Charles Schribner's Sons, 1924, p. 284.

34 Sackville-West, V., *Journal of the Royal Horticultural Society*, Vol. LXXIV, Part II, November 1949.

35 Ostberg, R., *Stockholm City Hall*, Stockholm, 1929, p. 35.

36 Brown, J., *Vita's Other World*, London: Penguin, 1987, p. 173.

37 Treib, M., op. cit., p. 43.

38 Marsa, A. and Marsillach, L, 'La montana iluminada' quoted (1929) in Quetglas, J., *Fear of Glass*, Barcelona: Actar, 2001, p. 15.

39 Kiley, D., *Dan Kiley: in his own words: America's master landscape architect*, London: Thames and Hudson, 1999, p. 21.

40 Walker, P. and Simo, M., *Invisible Gardens*, Cambridge, Mass: MIT Press, 1994, p. 191.

41 Hutton, T., *Journal of the Institute of Landscape Architects*, February 1961.

42 Lancaster, M., *New European Landscapes*, Oxford: Butterworth Architecture, 1994, p. 23.

43 Turner, T., *City as Landscape*, London: Spon, 1996, p. 208.

44 Holden, R., *International Landscape Design,* London: Laurence King, 1996, p. 13.

45 Spens, M., *Modern Landscape*, London: Phaidon Press, 2003, p. 40.

46 Holden, R., *New Landscape Design*, London, Laurence King, 2003, p. 114.

Maps of garden locations

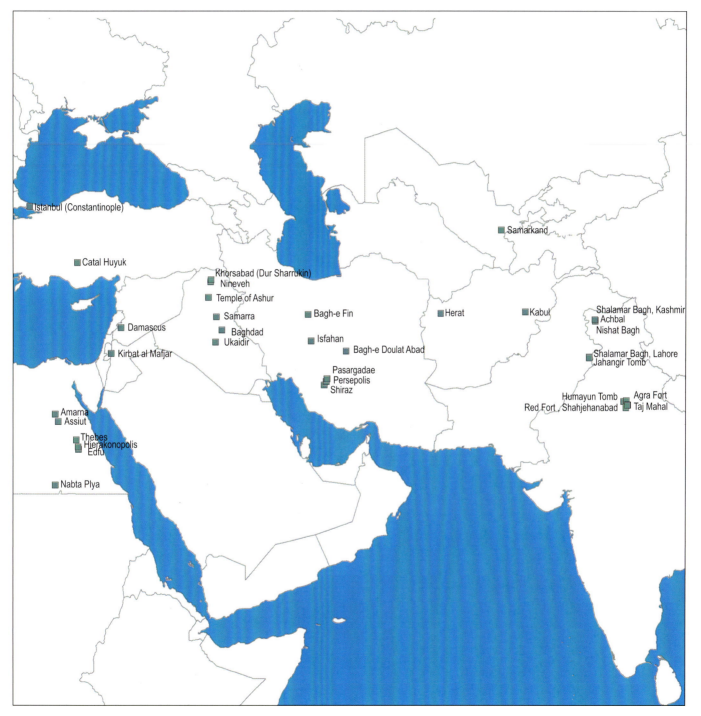

Istanbul (Constantinople)

Samarkand

Catal Huyuk

Khorsabad (Dur Sharrukin)
Nineveh
Temple of Ashur

Damascus

Samarra
Baghdad
Ukaidir

Kirbat al Mafjar

Bagh-e Fin

Isfahan

Bagh-e Doulat Abad

Herat

Kabul

Shalamar Bagh, Kashmir
Achbal
Nishat Bagh

Shalamar Bagh, Lahore
Jahangir Tomb

Pasargadae
Persepolis
Shiraz

Humayun Tomb
Red Fort   Shahjehanabad

Agra Fort
Taj Mahal

Amarna
Assiut
Thebes
Hierakonopolis
Edfu

Nabta Plya

Asia

Maps of garden locations

Pitmidden

Edzell Castle

Stirling Dunfermline
Edinburgh
Little Sparta
Howick Hall
Cragside Alnwick Castle

Rievaulx Terrace
Levens Hall Duncombe Park
Studley Royal Castle Howard
Harewood Bramham Park

Biddulph Grange Chatsworth
Alton Towers
Hawkstone Melbourne Hall
Leasowes Hidcote
Downton
Cirencester Park Stowe
Kelmscott Manor Rousham
Bowood Blenheim
Prior Park Iford
Stourhead

LONDON
REGION

Lost Gardens of Heligan Eden Project
Trebah Caerhays

Haga Royal Park
Drottningholm Peterhof
Stockholm City Hall (Stadshuset) Tsarskoe Selo
Woodland Crematorium (Skogskyrkogarden) Pavlosk

Fredensborg
Frederiksborg Castle Louisiana
Tivoli Garden

Amsterdam Bos Park Herrenhausen
Het Loo BERLIN
REGION
Duisburg Nord

Wilhelmshohe Bergpark
Agustusburg Ilm Park, Weimar
Bruges Charlemagne Palace, Aachen
Prague Castle
Ermitage Wallenstein Garden
Hortus Palatinus Veitshochheim
Schwetzingen
Karlsruhe
Stuttart Green U Kosterneuberg
Schleissheim Olympiapark Belvedere, Vienna
Nymphenburg Englisher Garten Schonbrunn
Munich Hofgarten Satzburg Esterhazy
Montargis St Gall Linderhof Mirabelle
Amboise Blois Clairvaux Ambras Castle Hellbrunn
Saumur Chenonceaux Swarovski Crystal Worlds
Villandry

PARIS
REGION

Isola Bella
Monza Orto Botanico, Padua

Villa Garzoni Pratolino
Villa Castello Villa Gamberaia
Boboli
Hyeres

Barcelona ROME
Parc Guell REGION
Monasterio dos Pedralbes
Sevovia La Granja Herculaneum Caserta
Escorial Buen Retiro Oplontis
Pompeii Capri
Aranjuez

Quelez, Palacio
Frontiera, Palacio
Monasterio dos Jeronimos Delphi Eleusis (Elefsina)
Bacalhoa, Palacio Cordoba Athens
Alcazar, Seville Olympia
Alhambra and Generalife Mycenae Delos

Europe

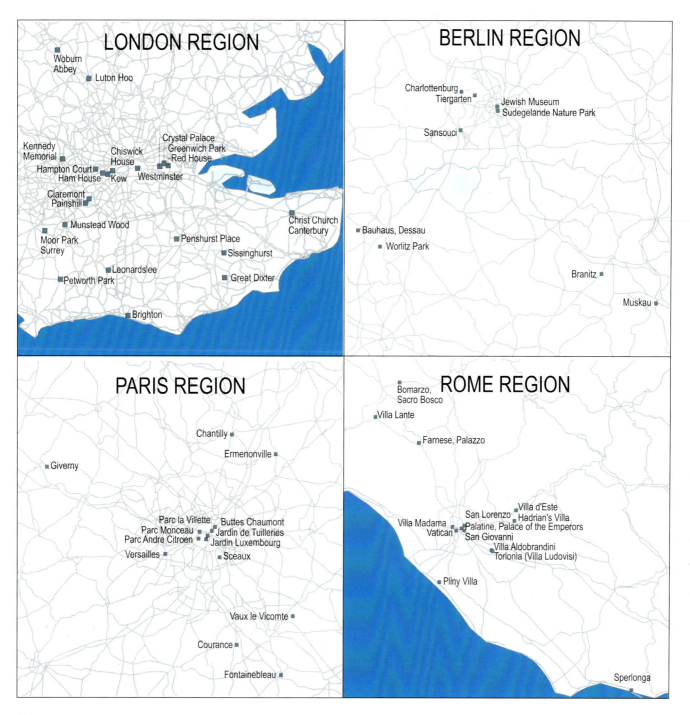

LONDON REGION

Woburn Abbey
Luton Hoo
Kennedy Memorial
Chiswick House
Crystal Palace
Greenwich Park
Red House
Hampton Court
Ham House
Kew
Westminster
Claremont
Painshill
Munstead Wood
Moor Park Surrey
Penshurst Place
Christ Church Canterbury
Sissinghurst
Leonardslee
Petworth Park
Great Dixter
Brighton

BERLIN REGION

Charlottenburg
Tiergarten
Jewish Museum
Sudegelande Nature Park
Sansouci
Bauhaus, Dessau
Worlitz Park
Branitz
Muskau

PARIS REGION

Chantilly
Ermenonville
Giverny
Parc la Villette
Buttes Chaumont
Parc Monceau
Jardin de Tuilleries
Parc Andre Citroen
Jardin Luxembourg
Versailles
Sceaux
Vaux le Vicomte
Courance
Fontainebleau

ROME REGION

Bomarzo, Sacro Bosco
Villa Lante
Farnese, Palazzo
Villa d'Este
San Lorenzo
Hadrian's Villa
Villa Madama
Palatine, Palace of the Emperors
Vatican
San Giovanni
Villa Aldobrandini
Torlonia (Villa Ludovisi)
Pliny Villa
Sperlonga

Cities

Maps of garden locations

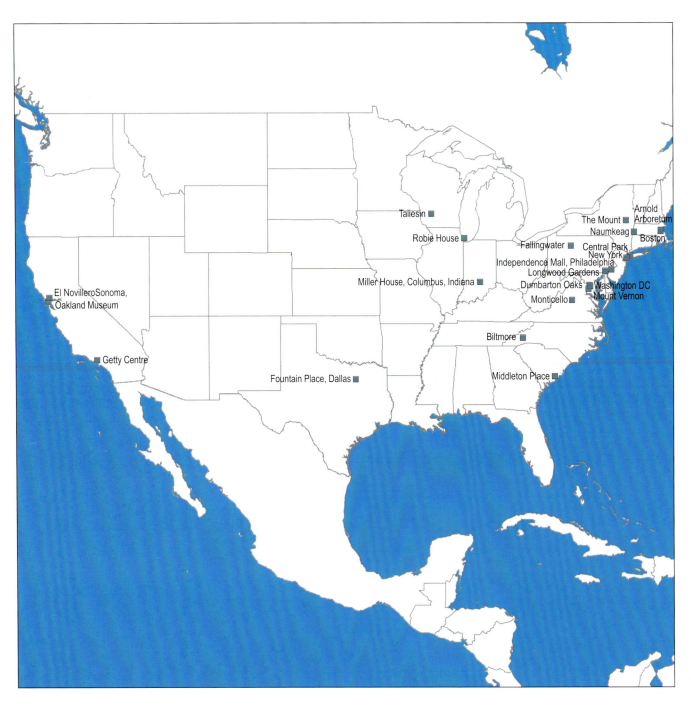

Taliesin

Arnold
Arboretum
The Mount
Naumkeag
Boston
Robie House
Fallingwater
Central Park
New York
Independence Mall, Philadelphia
Longwood Gardens
Miller House, Columbus, Indiana
Dumbarton Oaks
Washington DC
Mount Vernon
El NovilleroSonoma,
Oakland Museum
Monticello

Biltmore

Getty Centre

Fountain Place, Dallas

Middleton Place

America

Illustration credits

The author and publisher would like to thank these individuals and organizations for permission to reproduce material. Every effort has been made to contact and acknowledge copyright holders, but if any errors or omissions have been made we would be happy to correct them at a later printing.

Index